Transportation 12

Editorial Advisory Board

The Career Information Center includes:

- Agribusiness, Environment, and Natural Resources / 1
- Communications and the Arts / 2
- Computers, Business, and Office / 3
- Construction / 4
- Consumer, Homemaking, and Personal Services / 5
- Engineering, Science, Technology, and Social Science / 6
- Health / 7
- Hospitality and Recreation / 8
- Manufacturing / 9
- Marketing and Distribution / 10
- Public and Community Services / 11
- Transportation / 12
- Employment Trends and Master Index / 13

Transportation 12

Career Information Center

Ninth Edition

MACMILLAN REFERENCE USA
An imprint of Thomson Gale, a part of The Thomson Corporation

THOMSON
GALE

Detroit • New York • San Francisco • New Haven, Conn. • Waterville, Maine • London

Career Information Center, Ninth Edition

Paula Kepos, Series Editor

Project Editor
Mary Rose Bonk

Editorial
Jennifer Greve

Imaging
Lezlie Light, Daniel Newell, Christine O'Bryan

Permissions
Kelly A. Quin, Tim Sisler, Andrew Specht

Manufacturing
Rhonda Dover

For permission to use material from this product, submit your request via Web at http://www.gale-edit.com/permissions, or you may download our Permissions Request form and submit your request by fax or mail to:

Permissions
Thomson Gale
27500 Drake Rd.
Farmington Hills, MI 48331-3535
Permissions Hotline:
248-699-8006 or 800-877-4253 ext. 8006
Fax: 248-699-8074 or 800-762-4058

Since this page cannot legibly accommodate all copyright notices, the acknowledgments constitute an extension of the copyright notice.

While every effort has been made to ensure the reliability of the information presented in this publication, Thomson Gale does not guarantee the accuracy of the data contained herein. Thomson Gale accepts no payment for listing; and inclusion in the publication of any organization, agency, institution, publication, service, or individual does not imply endorsement of the editors or publisher. Errors brought to the attention of the publisher and verified to the satisfaction of the publisher will be corrected in future editions.

ISBN 0-02-866047-1 (set)
ISBN 0-02-866048-X (v.1)
ISBN 0-02-866049-8 (v.2)
ISBN 0-02-866050-1 (v.3)
ISBN 0-02-866051-X (v.4)
ISBN 0-02-866052-8 (v.5)
ISBN 0-02-866053-6 (v.6)
ISBN 0-02-866054-4 (v.7)
ISBN 0-02-866055-2 (v.8)
ISBN 0-02-866056-0 (v.9)
ISBN 0-02-866057-9 (v.10)
ISBN 0-02-866058-7 (v.11)
ISBN 0-02-866059-5 (v.12)
ISBN 0-02-866060-9 (v.13)
ISSN 1082-703X

This title is also available as an e-book.
ISBN 0-02-866099-4
Contact your Thomson Gale representative for ordering information.

Printed in the United States of America
10 9 8 7 6 5 4 3 2

Contents

Job Summary Chart vii

Foreword x

Using the Career Information Center xi

Comprehensive Job Profile List xiii

Looking Into Transportation 1

Getting Into Transportation 11

Job Profiles—No Specialized Training 27

Job Profiles—Some Specialized Training/Experience 84

Job Profiles—Advanced Training/Experience 113

Resources—General Career Information 139

    Books 139

    Internet Sites 146

    Audiovisual Materials 148

    Computer Software 150

Resources—Transportation 153

Directory—Institutions Offering Career Training 157

Index 173

Job Summary Chart

Job	Salary	Education/ Training	Employment Outlook	Page
Job Profiles—No Specialized Training				
Airline Baggage and Freight Handler	Median—$21,570 per year	High school	Good	27
Airline Reservations Agent	Median—$27,750 per year	High school	Poor	28
Airline Ticket Agent	Median—$28,420 per year	High school	Poor	30
Airport Utility Worker	Median—$21,570 per year	High school	Fair	31
⭐ **Auto Body Repairer**	Median—$16.68 per hour	High school	Good	32
Bicycle Mechanic	Median—$9.76 per hour	None	Good	34
Bridge and Lock Tender	Median—$37,050 per year	High school plus training	Poor	35
Car Wash Worker	Median—$8.41 per hour	None	Good	37
Dockworker	Median—$9.67 per hour	None	Poor	38
Gas Station Cashier	Median—$7.54 per hour	None	Good	40
Industrial Truck Operator	Median—$12.78 per hour	None	Poor	41
⭐ **Intercity Bus Driver**	Median—$14.30 per hour	Training; license	Good	43
Local Transit Operator	Varies—see profile	Training; license	Good	45
⭐ **Local Truck Driver**	Median—$11.80 per hour	License	Good	47
⭐ **Long-Haul Truck Driver**	Median—$16.11 per hour	License	Good	48
Marine Technician	Average—$32,000 to $40,000 per year	None	Good	51
Motorboat Mechanic	Median—$14.74 per hour	High school plus training	Fair	52
Motorcycle Mechanic	Median—$13.70 per hour	Training	Good	54
Mover	Median—$9.67 per hour	None	Good	56
Parking Attendant	Median—$16,820 per year	License	Poor	57
Parking Cashier	Median—$7.81 per hour	None	Poor	59
Railroad Clerk	Median—$22,770 per year	High school	Poor	60
Railroad Maintenance Worker	Varies—see profile	High school	Poor	62
Railroad Signal or Switch Operator	Median—$21.46 per hour	High school plus training	Poor	63
Railroad Track Worker	Median—$19.03 per hour	None	Poor	65
⭐ **Route Delivery Driver**	Median—$9.96 per hour	High school; license	Good	67
Sailor	Median—$14 per hour	None	Poor	68
⭐ **School Bus Driver**	Median—$11.18 per hour	License	Good	70
Service Station Attendant	Median—$8.33 per hour	None	Poor	71

⭐ **High-growth job**

Job	Salary	Education/ Training	Employment Outlook	Page
Special Service Bus Driver	Median—$10.81 per hour	High school; license	Good	73
Taxi Dispatcher	Median—$30,920 per year	High school plus training	Good	75
⭐ Taxi Driver	Median—$10.68 per hour	Licenses	Good	76
Tire Changer and Repairer	Median—$9.99 per hour	None	Poor	78
Tow Truck Dispatcher	Median—$30,920 per year	High school	Good	79
Tow Truck Operator	Average—$18,000 to $25,000 per year	High school plus training	Good	80
⭐ Truck and Bus Dispatcher	Median—$30,920 per year	High school plus training	Good	82

Job Profiles—Some Specialized Training/Experience

Job	Salary	Education/ Training	Employment Outlook	Page
Aircraft Dispatcher	Varies—see profile	Some college; certification	Fair	84
⭐ Aircraft Mechanic	Median—$21.77 per hour	High school plus training	Good	86
⭐ Airline Flight Attendant	Median—$43,440 per year	High school plus training	Good	88
Automobile Driving Instructor	Varies—see profile	Varies—see profile	Good	90
Automotive Exhaust Emissions Technician	Median—$15.68 per hour	High school plus training	Fair	92
⭐ Automotive Mechanic	Median—$15.60 per hour	Varies—see profile	Good	93
Avionics Technician	Median—$21.30 per hour	High school plus training; license	Fair	95
⭐ Car Rental or Leasing Agent	Varies—see profile	Varies—see profile	Very good	96
⭐ Diesel Mechanic	Median—$17.20 per hour	Varies—see profile	Good	98
Merchant Marine Steward and Cook	Varies—see profile	Varies—see profile	Poor	101
Parking Analyst	Median—$38,480 per year	Some college plus training	Varies—see profile	102
Railroad Conductor	Median—$22.28 per hour	High school plus training	Poor	104
Railroad Engineer	Median—$24.30 per hour	High school plus training; license	Poor	106
Traffic Technician	Median—$38,480 per year	College plus training	Good	108
⭐ Transportation Inspector	Median—$47,920 per year	Varies—see profile	Good	109
⭐ Truck Terminal Manager	Median—$32.36 per hour	Some college	Good	111

Job Profiles—Advanced Training/Experience

Job	Salary	Education/ Training	Employment Outlook	Page
Air Traffic Controller	Median—$102,030 per year	Varies—see profile	Fair	113
⭐ Airplane Pilot	Varies—see profile	Varies—see profile	Good	115
⭐ Airport Manager	Median—$47,450 per year	College	Good	118
⭐ Fleet Manager	Varies—see profile	College	Good	120
Flight Engineer	Median—$129,250 per year	College plus training; license	Fair	121

⭐ High-growth job

Job	Salary	Education/Training	Employment Outlook	Page
Flight Instructor	Median—$31,530 per year	Varies—see profile	Good	123
Industrial Traffic Manager	Median—$71,932 per year	College	Good	125
Merchant Marine Captain	Median—$24.20 per hour	Advanced degree	Poor	127
Merchant Marine Engineer	Median—$26.42 per hour	Academy	Poor	129
Merchant Marine Purser	Average—$30,514 per year	Varies—see profile	Poor	130
Merchant Marine Radio Officer	Median—$14 per hour	Varies—see profile	Fair	132
Traffic Engineer	Median—$64,230 per year	College	Good	133
Transportation Engineer	Median—$64,230 per year	College	Good	135

⭐ **High-growth job**

Foreword

The ninth edition of the *Career Information Center* mirrors the ongoing changes in the job market caused by new technological and economic developments. These developments continue to change what Americans do in the workplace and how they do it. People have a critical need for up-to-date information to help them make career decisions.

The *Career Information Center* is an individualized resource for people of all ages and at all stages of career development. It has been recognized as an excellent reference for librarians, counselors, educators, and other providers of job information. It is ideally suited for use in libraries, career resource centers, and guidance offices, as well as in adult education centers and other facilities where people seek information about job opportunities, careers, and their own potential in the workforce.

This ninth edition updates many of the features that made the earlier editions so useful.

- A Job Summary Chart, a quick reference guide, appears in the front section of each volume to help readers get the basic facts and compare the jobs described in the volume. High-growth jobs are highlighted and identified with a star.

- Each volume of the *Career Information Center* begins with an overview of the job market in that field. These "Looking Into..." sections have been completely revised and updated. They also include new graphs, charts, and boxes providing information such as industry snapshots and the fastest-growing and top-dollar jobs in the field. The "Global View" feature tells how the new global economy is affecting jobs in the field.

- Each volume has a section called "Getting Into...," which contains useful information on entering the particular field. It offers self-evaluation tips and decision-making help, and it relates possible job choices to individual interests, abilities, and work characteristics. There is also practical information on job hunting, using the Internet and classified ads, preparing resumes, and handling interviews. "Getting Into..." also includes a section on employee rights.

- Each volume has a listing of all job profiles in the series and the volumes in which they appear, making access to profiles in other volumes easy.

- *Career Information Center* contains 694 job profiles. Each profile describes work characteristics, education and training requirements, getting the job, advancement and employment outlook, working conditions, and earnings and benefits.

- Job summaries, provided for each job profile, highlight the education or training required, salary range, and employment outlook.

- Volume 13 has been revised to reflect career concerns of the new century and employment trends through the year 2014. This volume includes updated articles on benefits, employment law, health in the workplace, job search strategies, job training, job opportunities at home, and identifying opportunities for retraining.

- More than 530 photographs provide a visual glimpse of life on the job. Photos have been selected to give the reader a sense of what it feels like to be in a specific field or job.

- Updated bibliographies in each volume include recommended readings and Web sites in specific job areas. Additional titles for the vocational counselor are included in Volume 13.

- Each volume also contains a comprehensive directory of accredited occupational education and vocational training facilities listed by occupational area and grouped by state. Directory materials are generated from the IPEDS (Integrated Postsecondary Education Data System) database of the U.S. Department of Education.

The *Career Information Center* recognizes the importance not only of job selection, but also of job holding, coping, and applying life skills. No other career information publication deals with work attitudes so comprehensively.

Using the Career Information Center

The *Career Information Center* is designed to meet the needs of many people—students, people just entering or reentering the job market, those dissatisfied with present jobs, those without jobs—anyone of any age who is not sure what to do for a living. The *Career Information Center* is for people who want help in making career choices. It combines the comprehensiveness of an encyclopedia with the format and readability of a magazine. Many professionals, including counselors, librarians, and teachers, will find it a useful guidance and reference tool.

The *Career Information Center* is organized by occupational interest area rather than in alphabetical order. Jobs that have something in common are grouped together. In that way people who do not know exactly what job they want can read about a number of related jobs. The *Career Information Center* classifies jobs that have something in common into clusters. The classification system is adapted from the cluster organization used by the U.S. Department of Labor. Each of the first twelve volumes of the *Career Information Center* explores one of twelve occupational clusters.

To use the *Career Information Center*, first select the volume that treats the occupational area that interests you most. Because there are many ways to group occupations, you may not find a particular job in the volume in which you look for it. In that case, check the central listing of all the profiles, which is located in the front of Volumes 1 through 12. This listing provides the names of all profiles and the volume number in which they appear. Volume 13 also includes a comprehensive index of all the jobs covered in the first twelve volumes.

After selecting a volume or volumes, investigate the sections that you feel would be most helpful. It isn't necessary to read these volumes from cover to cover. They are arranged so that you can go directly to the specific information you want. Here is a description of the sections included in each volume.

- **Job Summary Chart**—This chart presents in tabular form the basic data from all profiles in the volume: salary, education and training, employment outlook, and the page on which you can find the job profile. Jobs with a high growth potential are highlighted and starred.

- **Looking Into...**—This overview of the occupational cluster describes the opportunities, characteristics, and trends in that particular field.

- **Getting Into...**—This how-to guide can help you decide what jobs may be most satisfying to you and what strategies you can use to get the right job. You will learn, for example, how to write an effective resume, how to complete an application form, what to expect in an interview, how to use networking, and what to do if someone has discriminated against you.

- **Job Summary**—These summaries, located at the beginning of each profile, highlight the most important facts about the job: education and training, salary, and employment outlook.

Education and Training indicates whether the job requires no education, high school, college, advanced degree, vocational/technical school, license, or training.

Salary provides median or average salaries that may vary significantly from region to region.

Employment Outlook is based on several factors, including the Bureau of Labor Statistics' projections through the year 2014. The ratings are defined as follows: *poor* means there is a projected employment decrease of any amount; *fair* means there is a projected employment increase of 0 to 8 percent; *good* means there is a projected employment increase of 9 to 17 percent; *very good* means there is a projected employment increase of 18 to 26 percent; and *excellent* means there is a projected employment increase of 27 percent or more. The outlook is then determined by looking at the ratings and other employment factors. For example, a job with excellent projected employment growth in which many more people are entering the field than there are jobs available will have an outlook that is good rather than excellent.

For all categories, the phrase *Varies—see profile* means the reader must consult the profile for the information, which is too extensive to include in the Job Summary.

- **Job Profiles**—The job profiles are divided into three categories based on the level of training required to get the job. Each profile explores the following topics: description of the job being profiled, the education and training requirements, ways to get the job, advancement possibilities and employment outlook, the working conditions, the earnings and benefits, and places to go for more information.

Job Profiles—No Specialized Training includes jobs that require no education or previous work experience beyond high school.

Job Profiles—Some Specialized Training/Experience includes jobs that require one, two, or three years of vocational training or college, or work experience beyond high school.

Job Profiles—Advanced Training/Experience includes jobs that require a bachelor's degree or advanced degree from a college or university and/or equivalent work experience in that field.

- **Resources—General Career Information** includes a selected bibliography of the most recent books and Web sites on general career information, including how-to books on such topics as resume writing and preparing for tests. In addition, there is a special guide to readings for the career counselor in Volume 13.

- **Resources—**Each volume also contains a bibliography of books and Web sites for specific fields covered in that volume.

- **Directory of Institutions Offering Career Training—**This listing, organized first by career area, then by state, includes the schools that offer occupational training beyond high school. For jobs requiring a bachelor's degree or an advanced degree, check a library for college catalogs and appropriate directories.

- **Index—**This index, which is located at the end of each volume, lists every job mentioned in that volume. It serves not only to cross-reference all the jobs in the volume but also to show related jobs in the field. For example, under the entry OCEANOG-

RAPHER, you will find chemical oceanographer, marine biologist, and marine geophysicist.

- **Volume 13, Employment Trends and Master Index—**This volume includes several features that will help both the job seeker and the career counselor. A useful guide provides the *DOT (Dictionary of Occupational Titles)* number of most of the job profiles in the *Career Information Center*. There is also a special section on career information for Canada. The updated and revised "Employment Trends" section contains articles on health in the workplace; search strategies for finding your first job; employment trends for women, minorities, immigrants, older workers, and the physically challenged; employment demographics; benefit programs; training; employment opportunities at home; employment law; and identifying opportunities for retraining. The articles provide job seekers and career professionals with an overview of current employment issues, career opportunities, and outlooks. Finally, there is a master index to all the jobs included in all 13 volumes.

The *Career Information Center* is exactly what it says it is—a center of the most useful and pertinent information you need to explore and choose from the wide range of job and career possibilities. The *Career Information Center* provides you with a solid foundation of information for getting a satisfying job or rewarding career.

Comprehensive Job Profile List

The following list includes job profiles and corresponding volume numbers.

Accountant, Management, 3
Accountant, Public, 3
Actor, 2
Actuary, 3
Acupuncturist, 7
Administrative Assistant, 3
Admitting Interviewer, 7
Adult Education Worker, 11
Advertising Account Executive, 10
Advertising Copywriter, 2
Advertising Manager, 10
Aerospace Engineer, 6
Aerospace Engineering and Operations
    Technician, 6
Aerospace Industry, 9
Agricultural Engineer, 1
Agricultural Inspector, 1
Agricultural Technician, 1
Agronomist, 1
AIDS Counselor, 7
Air Pollution Control Technician, 1
Air Traffic Controller, 12
Air-Conditioning Engineer, 6
Air-Conditioning, Heating, and
    Refrigeration Mechanic and
    Installer, 4
Aircraft Dispatcher, 12
Aircraft Mechanic, 12
Airline Baggage and Freight Handler, 12
Airline Flight Attendant, 12
Airline Reservations Agent, 12
Airline Ticket Agent, 12
Airplane Pilot, 12
Airport Manager, 12
Airport Utility Worker, 12
Alternative Fuels Vehicle Technician, 6
Aluminum and Copper Industries, 9
Ambulance Driver, 7
Amusement and Recreation Attendant, 8
Anatomist, 6
Anesthesiologist, 7
Animal Caretaker, 8
Animal Scientist, 1
Animal Trainer, 1
Announcer, 2
Anthropologist, 6
Apparel Industry, 9
Apparel Workers, 9
Appliance Service Worker, 5
Appraiser, 5
Architect, 4
Architectural Drafter, 4
Architectural Model Maker, 4
Armed Services Career, 11
Art Director, 2
Artificial Intelligence Specialist, 6
Artist, 2
Assembler and Fabricator, 9

Astronomer, 6
Athletic Coach, 8
Athletic Trainer, 8
Auctioneer, 10
Audiologist, 7
Auditor, 3
Auto Body Repairer, 12
Auto Parts Counter Worker, 10
Auto Sales Worker, 10
Automobile Driving Instructor, 12
Automotive Exhaust Emissions
    Technician, 12
Automotive Industry, 9
Automotive Mechanic, 12
Avionics Technician, 12

Baker, 1
Bank Clerk, 3
Bank Officer and Manager, 3
Bank Teller, 3
Barber and Hairstylist, 5
Bartender, 8
Bicycle Mechanic, 12
Billing Clerk, 3
Biochemist, 6
Biological Technician, 6
Biologist, 6
Biomedical Engineer, 6
Biomedical Equipment Technician, 7
Boilermaker, 9
Bookbinder, 2
Bookkeeper, 3
Border Patrol Agent, 11
Botanist, 6
Bricklayer, 4
Bridge and Lock Tender, 12
Broadcast News Analyst, 2
Broadcast Technician, 2
Brokerage Clerk, 3
Building Custodian, 11
Building Inspector, 4
Bulldozer, Grader, or Paving Machine
    Operator, 4
Business Family and Consumer
    Scientist, 5
Business Machine Operator, 3

Cable Television and
    Telecommunications Technician, 6
Cable Television Engineer, 6
Cafeteria Attendant, 8
Camera Operator, 2
Candy Manufacturing Worker, 1
Car Rental or Leasing Agent, 12
Car Wash Worker, 12
Cardiac Monitor Technician, 7
Cardiac Perfusionist, 7
Cardiology Technologist, 7

Carpenter, 4
Cartographer, 1
Cartoonist and Animator, 2
Cashier, 10
Caterer, 8
Ceiling Tile Installer, 4
Cement Mason, 4
Ceramic Engineer, 6
Ceramics Industry, 9
Chauffeur, 5
Cheese Industry Worker, 1
Chemical Engineer, 6
Chemical Technician, 6
Chemist, 6
Child Care Worker, Private, 5
Chiropractor, 7
Choreographer, 2
City Manager, 11
Civil Engineer, 4
Civil Engineering Technician, 4
Claims Adjuster, 3
Claims Examiner, 3
Clinical Laboratory Technician, 7
Clinical Laboratory Technologist, 7
College Student Personnel Worker, 11
College/University Administrator, 3
Companion, 5
Comparison Shopper, 10
Compensation and Benefits Analyst, 3
Composer, 2
Computer and Information Systems
    Manager, 3
Computer and Office Machine
    Repairer, 3
Computer Consultant, 3
Computer Control Operator, 9
Computer Control Programmer, 9
Computer Database Administrator, 3
Computer Network Technician, 3
Computer Operator, 3
Computer Programmer, 3
Computer Security Specialist, 3
Computer Software Documentation
    Writer, 3
Computer Software Engineer, 3
Computer Support Specialist, 3
Computer Systems Analyst, 3
Conservation Scientist, 1
Construction Electrician, 4
Construction Equipment Dealer, 4
Construction Equipment Mechanic, 4
Construction Laborer, 4
Construction Millwright, 4
Construction Supervisor, 4
Consumer Advocate, 5
Consumer Credit Counselor, 5
Controller, 3
Cook and Chef, 8

Corporate Travel Manager, 8
Correctional Officer, 11
Correspondence Clerk, 3
Cosmetologist, 5
Cost Estimator, 4
Costume Attendant, 2
Court Clerk, 11
Court Reporter, 11
Craftsperson, 2
Crane Operator, 4
Credit Authorizer, Checker, and Clerk, 3
Credit Collector, 3
Credit Manager, 3
Crime Laboratory Technician, 11
Criminologist, 11
Crop Scientist, 1
Custom Tailor and Dressmaker, 5
Custom Upholsterer, 5
Customer Service Representative, 3
Customs Worker, 11

Dairy Industry Worker, 1
Dancer, 2
Data Entry Keyer, 3
Day Care Worker, 11
Demographer, 6
Demolition Worker, 4
Dental and Medical Secretary, 7
Dental Assistant, 7
Dental Hygienist, 7
Dental Laboratory Technician, 7
Dentist, 7
Dermatologist, 7
Desktop Publisher, 2
Detective, 11
Dialysis Technician, 7
Diesel Mechanic, 12
Dietetic Technician, 5
Dietitian and Nutritionist, 5
Dining Room Attendant, 8
Direct Sales Worker, 10
Director, 2
Dishwasher, 8
Dispensing Optician, 7
Distribution Manager, 10
Diver, 1
Divorce Mediator, 5
Dockworker, 12
Doorkeeper, 8
Drafter, 9
Dry Cleaning Worker, 5
Drywall Installer and Taper, 4

E-Commerce Marketing Manager, 10
Economist, 6
Editor, Book, 2
Editor, Copy, 2
Editor, Magazine, 2
Editor, Newspaper, 2
Electric Power Service Worker, 11
Electric Power Transmission and
    Distribution Worker, 11
Electrical and Electronics Engineer, 6
Electrical and Electronics Engineering
    Technician, 6

Electrical and Electronics Installer and
    Repairer, 6
Electrologist, 5
Electromechanical Engineering
    Technician, 6
Electroneurodiagnostic Technologist, 7
Electronic Home Entertainment
    Equipment Installer and Repairer, 6
Electronics Industry, 9
Elevator Installer and Repair Worker, 4
Embalmer, 5
Emergency Medical
    Technician/Paramedic, 7
Employee Benefits Manager, 3
Employment Counselor, 3
Employment Interviewer, 3
Entomologist, 6
Environmental Engineer, 1
Environmental Engineering
    Technician, 1
Environmental Health Specialist, 7
Environmental Science and Protection
    Technician, 1
Environmental Scientist, 1
Epidemiologist, 7
Ergonomist, 6
Executive Search Recruiter, 3
Expediter, 4

Family and Consumer Science
    Researcher, 5
Family and Consumer Science Teacher, 5
Farm Equipment Mechanic, 1
Farm Laborer, 1
Farm Manager, 1
Farmer, Cotton, Tobacco, and Peanut, 1
Farmer, Dairy, 1
Farmer, Fruit, 1
Farmer, Grain, 1
Farmer, Livestock, 1
Farmer, Poultry, 1
Farmer, Vegetable, 1
Fashion Designer, 2
Fast Food Franchise Worker, 8
FBI Special Agent, 11
Federal Government Worker, 11
Fiction Writer, 2
File Clerk, 3
Film and Video Editor, 2
Financial Analyst, 3
Financial Planner, 3
Fire Protection Engineer, 6
Firefighter, 11
First-Line Supervisor, 9
Fish Hatchery Manager, 1
Fisher, 1
Fitness Trainer and Aerobics Instructor, 8
Fleet Manager, 12
Flight Engineer, 12
Flight Instructor, 12
Floor Covering Installer, 4
Floor Sander and Finisher, 4
Floral Designer, 5
Food Broker, 10
Food Canning and Freezing Worker, 1

Food Processing Technician, 1
Food Science Technician, 1
Food Scientist, 1
Foreign Service Worker, 11
Forensic Scientist, 6
Forester, 1
Forestry Technician, 1
Foundry Industry, 9
Fund-Raiser, 11
Funeral Director, 5
Furniture Industry, 9

Gaming Cage Worker, 8
Gaming Dealer, 8
Gaming Surveillance Officer, 8
Garage Door Mechanic, 4
Gardener and Groundskeeper, 5
Gas Station Cashier, 12
General Contractor, 4
General Manager, 3
Genetic Engineering Research
    Assistant, 6
Genetic Engineering Research
    Scientist, 6
Geographer, 1
Geological and Petroleum Technician, 1
Geophysicist, 1
Geriatric Aide, 11
Geriatric Social Worker, 7
Geriatrician, 7
Glass Industry, 9
Glazier, 4
Government Inspector and Examiner, 11
Gunsmith, 9

Hazardous Waste Management
    Technician, 1
Health and Safety Engineer, 1
Health Educator, 7
Highway Engineer, 4
Highway Inspector, 4
Highway Maintenance Worker, 11
Historian, 6
Home Caterer, 5
Home Health Aide, 7
Home Security Consultant, 5
Homemaker, 5
Hospitality Cashier, 8
Hotel Bellhop and Porter, 8
Hotel Housekeeper, 8
Hotel, Casino, and Resort Concierge, 8
Hotel, Motel, and Resort Desk Clerk, 8
Housekeeper, Domestic, 5
Human Resources Assistant, 3
Human Resources Manager, 3
Hydraulic and Pneumatic Technician, 6
Hydrologist, 1

Illustrator and Graphic Designer, 2
Import and Export Worker, 10
Industrial Chemical Industry, 9
Industrial Designer, 9
Industrial Engineer, 9
Industrial Hygienist, 6

Industrial Machinery Maintenance Worker, 9
Industrial Production Manager, 9
Industrial Traffic Manager, 12
Industrial Truck Operator, 12
Inspector and Tester, 9
Institutional Child Care Worker, 11
Institutional Housekeeper, 11
Instructional Designer, 2
Insulation Worker, 4
Insurance Agent and Broker, 10
Insurance Underwriter, 3
Intercity Bus Driver, 12
Interior Designer, 5
Internal Revenue Service Worker, 11
Internet Entrepreneur, 3
Interviewer, 3
Investment Banker, 3

Jeweler, 5
Judge, 11

Labor Relations Specialist, 9
Laboratory Animal Care Worker, 7
Landscape Architect, 4
Lather, 4
Laundry Worker, 5
Lawyer, 11
Lawyer, Corporate, 11
Lawyer, Public Service, 11
Leather and Shoe Industries, 9
Legal Assistant, Corporate, 11
Librarian, Public, 11
Librarian, School, 11
Librarian, Special, 11
Licensed Practical Nurse, 7
Lifeguard, 8
Lighting Technician, 2
Linguist, 6
Literary or Theatrical Agent, 2
Lithographic Worker, 2
Local Transit Operator, 12
Local Truck Driver, 12
Locksmith, 5
Lodging Manager, 8
Logger, 1
Long-Haul Truck Driver, 12
Lumber Mill Worker, 1

Machine Operator and Tender, 9
Machine Setter, 9
Machinist, 9
Mail Clerk, 3
Mail Service Worker, 3
Maintenance Electrician, 4
Makeup Artist, 2
Manufactured Home Assembler, 4
Manufacturers' Sales Worker, 10
Marble, Tile, and Terrazzo Worker, 4
Marine Engineer, 1
Marine Technician, 12
Marketing Director, 10
Marketing Research Worker, 10
Marriage and Family Counselor, 11
Massage Therapist, 5

Mathematician, 6
Meat Packing Worker, 1
Mechanical Engineer, 6
Mechanical Engineering Technician, 6
Media Buyer, 10
Medical and Health Services Manager, 7
Medical Assistant, 7
Medical Illustrator, 7
Medical Physicist, 7
Medical Records and Health Information Technician, 7
Meeting and Convention Planner, 8
Meeting Planner, 3
Merchandise Displayer and Window Trimmer, 2
Merchant Marine Captain, 12
Merchant Marine Engineer, 12
Merchant Marine Purser, 12
Merchant Marine Radio Officer, 12
Merchant Marine Steward and Cook, 12
Messenger Service Worker, 3
Metallurgical Engineer, 6
Metallurgical Technician, 6
Meteorologist, 1
Microbiologist, 6
Microwave Engineer, 6
Miner, Coal, 1
Miner, Metal, 1
Mining Engineer, 1
Mining Technician, 1
Model, 2
Motion Picture Projectionist, 8
Motorboat Mechanic, 12
Motorcycle Mechanic, 12
Mover, 12
Multimedia Developer, 2
Museum Conservator, 8
Museum Curator, 8
Music Teacher, 2
Music Video Producer, 2
Musician, 2

Nanny, 5
Natural Science Manager, 1
Naval Architect, 1
Network Administrator, 3
News Reporter and Correspondent, 2
Nuclear Engineer, 6
Nuclear Medicine Technologist, 7
Nuclear Technician, 6
Nursery Worker, 1
Nursery/Greenhouse Manager, 1
Nursing Aide and Orderly, 7

Occupational Health and Safety Specialist, 1
Occupational Therapist Assistant, 7
Occupational Therapist, 7
Oceanographer, 1
Office Clerk, 3
Office Machine and Computer Industry, 9
Office Manager, 3
Office Planner, 3
Operations Research Analyst, 3
Ophthalmic Laboratory Technician, 7

Ophthalmologist, 7
Optometric Assistant, 7
Optometrist, 7
Organizational Developer, 3
Orthoptist, 7
Osteopathic Physician, 7
Outdoor Guide, 8
Outplacement Consultant, 3

Paint, Varnish, and Lacquer Industry, 9
Painter and Paperhanger, 4
Painting and Coating Worker, 9
Paper Industry, 9
Paralegal Aide, 11
Park Naturalist, 1
Park Ranger, 8
Parking Analyst, 12
Parking Attendant, 12
Parking Cashier, 12
Parole Officer, 11
Party Planner, 8
Pastry Chef and Baker, 8
Pathologist, 6
Payroll Clerk, 3
Personal Exercise Trainer, 5
Personal Service Worker, 5
Personal Shopper, 5
Pest Control Worker, 5
Pesticide Handler, Sprayer, and Applicator, Vegetation, 1
Pet Care Worker, 5
Petroleum and Natural Gas Exploration and Production Worker, 1
Petroleum Engineer, 1
Petroleum Refining Industry, 9
Pharmaceutical Industry, 9
Pharmaceutical Sales Representative, 7
Pharmaceutical Technician, 6
Pharmacist, 7
Pharmacologist, 7
Photo Researcher, 2
Photographer, 2
Photographic Processing Machine Operator, 2
Photonics Engineer, 6
Photonics Technician, 6
Physical Therapist Assistant, 7
Physical Therapist, 7
Physician Assistant, 7
Physician, 7
Physicist, 6
Piano and Organ Tuner and Technician, 5
Pile-Driver Operator, 4
Plasterer and Stucco Mason, 4
Plastics Industry, 9
Plumber and Pipe Fitter, 4
Podiatrist, 7
Police Officer, 11
Political Consultant, 11
Political Scientist, 6
Postal Service Worker, 11
Power Plant Worker, 11
Power Tool Repairer, 4
Prepress Worker, 2

Printing Machine Operator, 2
Probation Officer, 11
Producer, 2
Product Manager, 10
Professional Athlete, 8
Professional Organizer, 5
Proofreader, 2
Property, Real Estate, and Community
    Association Manager, 8
Prosthetist and Orthotist, 7
Psychiatric Aide, 7
Psychiatrist, 7
Psychologist, 7
Public Relations Manager, 2
Public Relations Specialist, 2
Purchasing Agent, 10

Quality Control Manager, 9

Radiologic Technologist, 7
Railroad Clerk, 12
Railroad Conductor, 12
Railroad Engineer, 12
Railroad Maintenance Worker, 12
Railroad Signal or Switch Operator, 12
Railroad Track Worker, 12
Real Estate Appraiser, 10
Real Estate Developer, 4
Real Estate Sales Agent and Broker, 10
Receiving, Shipping, and Traffic Clerk, 10
Receptionist, 3
Recreation Worker, 8
Recreational Therapist, 7
Recruiter, 3
Recycling and Reclamation Worker, 1
Refuse Worker, 11
Registered Nurse, 7
Rehabilitation Counselor, 11
Reinforcing Ironworker, 4
Religious Vocation, 11
Rental Clerk, 10
Respiratory Therapist, 7
Restaurant Host or Hostess, 8
Restaurant Manager, 8
Resume Writer, 3
Retail Butcher, 10
Retail Buyer, 10
Retail Store Sales Worker Supervisor, 10
Retail Store Sales Worker, 10
Rigger, 4
Robotics Engineer, 6
Robotics Technician, 6
Roofer, 4
Route Delivery Driver, 12
Rubber Industry, 9
Rug and Carpet Cleaner, 5

Safety Engineer, 6
Sailor, 12
Sales Demonstrator and Product
    Promoter, 10
Sales Engineer, 10
Sales Manager, 10
School Administrator, 11

School Bus Driver, 12
School Counselor, 11
School Media Specialist, 11
Scriptwriter, 2
Secretary, 3
Securities Broker, 3
Security Guard, 11
Semiconductor Processor, 6
Septic Tank Installer and Servicer, 4
Service Station Attendant, 12
Set and Exhibit Designer, 2
Sheet Metal Worker, 4
Shipbuilding Industry, 9
Shoe Repairer, 5
Short-Order Cook, 8
Sign Language and Oral Interpreter, 2
Singer, 2
Small Animal Breeder, 1
Small Business Owner, 10
Social Worker, 11
Sociologist, 6
Software Quality Assurance Technician
    and Analyst, 3
Software Trainer, 3
Soil Scientist, 1
Solar Energy Technician, 4
Sound Engineering Technician, 2
Special Service Bus Driver, 12
Specification Writer, 4
Speech-Language Pathologist, 7
Sports Instructor, 8
Sports Management Professional, 10
Stagehand, 2
State Police Officer, 11
Stationary Engineer and Boiler
    Operator, 9
Statistical Assistant, 3
Statistician, 3
Steel Industry, 9
Stock Clerk, 10
Stonemason, 4
Store Manager, 10
Structural Clay Products Industry, 9
Structural Steelworker, 4
Substance Abuse Counselor, 7
Supermarket Worker, 10
Surgeon, 7
Surgical Technologist, 7
Surveying Technician, 4
Surveyor, 4
Swimming Instructor and Coach, 8
Swimming Pool Servicer, 5
Systems Engineer, 6

Tax Preparer, 3
Taxi Dispatcher, 12
Taxi Driver, 12
Teacher Assistant, 11
Teacher, College, 11
Teacher, Preschool, Kindergarten, and
    Elementary, 11
Teacher, Secondary School, 11
Teacher, Vocational Education, 11
Technical Writer, 2

Telecommunications Central Office
    Technician, 6
Telecommunications Consultant, 6
Telecommunications Design Engineer, 6
Telemarketer, 10
Telephone Operator, 3
Telephone Service Representative, 3
Telephone Service Technician, 6
Textile Industry, 9
Ticket Taker, 8
Tire Changer and Repairer, 12
Title Examiner, 10
Tobacco Industry Worker, 1
Tool and Die Maker, 9
Tour Escort, 8
Tow Truck Dispatcher, 12
Tow Truck Operator, 12
Trade Show Manager, 10
Traffic Engineer, 12
Traffic Technician, 12
Training and Development Specialist, 3
Translator or Interpreter, 2
Transportation Engineer, 12
Transportation Inspector, 12
Travel Agent, Retail and Wholesale, 8
Truck and Bus Dispatcher, 12
Truck Terminal Manager, 12

Umpire and Referee, 8
Union Business Agent, 3
Urban and Regional Planner, 11
Usability Researcher, 2
Usher, 8

Vending Machine Servicer and
    Repairer, 10
Veterinarian, 1
Veterinary Technician, 1
Vocational Counselor, 11

Waiter, 8
Ward Clerk, 7
Warehouse Worker, 10
Wastewater Treatment Plant Operator, 1
Watch Repairer, 5
Water Treatment Plant and System
    Operator, 1
Water Well Driller, 4
Web Designer, 2
Webmaster, 2
Wedding Consultant, 5
Welder, 4
Wholesale Sales Worker, 10
Window Cleaner, 5
Wireless Communications Technician, 6
Word Processor, 3

Youth Organization Worker, 11

Zookeeper, 8
Zoologist, 6

Looking Into Transportation

Throughout history, transportation has played a fundamental role in the development of civilization. Ancient peoples used animals and rudimentary carts to transport people and cargo over long distances. Around the fourth millennium B.C. the Egyptians developed the first crude waterborne vessels, which they used to navigate the Nile River. By 600 B.C. the Phoenicians traveled on ships as far as what is now Great Britain, engaging in trade and colonizing areas along the way. A few hundred years later, the Roman Empire expanded across the Western world, spreading trade and technology to its neighbors. It created a road system so extensive that it was often said, "All roads lead to Rome."

Over the following two thousand years, ships provided the primary means of engaging in commerce and exploration across vast oceans. On land, camels, horses, and other animals transported people and goods across large distances. Without the ability to travel and transport goods, civilizations would not have been able to trade with one another or to share technological and cultural advances.

Today the transportation industry continues to drive economic, cultural, and technological progress. New methods of travel have emerged to replace ancient ones. The industry is made up of a number of subindustries: the automotive, shipping, trucking, airline, mass transit, passenger railroad, and rail freight industries.

FROM CLIPPER SHIPS TO CABOOSES

The history of the United States illustrates the impact of the transportation system on every facet of economic, political, and social development. In the

The transportation industry is complex and turbulent. More than any other industry, shipping will continue to be influenced by the world market. (Copyright © 2005, Kelly A. Quin. Reproduced by permission.)

Global View: Transportation

The transportation industry is one of the driving forces behind globalization, helping markets and cultures around the world become more interconnected. The smooth operation of the global economy depends on the efficient movement of goods, services, and people across borders.

One example of globalization is the impact the North American Free Trade Agreement (NAFTA) has had on transportation systems. NAFTA has led to a significant increase in the shipment of goods between the United States, Canada, and Mexico, much of it by rail and road. New highways and bridges have been built and scanning equipment has been installed at crossing points to move goods faster. NAFTA has also led to international partnerships between transportation companies. For example, a Mexican ocean carrier and a U.S. railroad company have joined together to upgrade equipment on Mexico's north-south rail line. They are also investing in new technology and equipment to speed rail traffic between the two countries.

The development of the Internet has made it easier to ship goods globally as well. Some companies now have Web sites that provide customs forms for their clients to fill out and relay to border crossing points. This shortens the amount of time cargo spends in customs, saving time and money.

Because of the growth in international trade, shipping lines have ordered more vessels to carry cargo. The increased capacity has reduced shipping costs, particularly for goods crossing the Atlantic. Many countries are also signing "open skies" agreements that give air carriers from those countries virtually unrestricted access to each other's markets. Such agreements create a "borderless" environment that forces all transportation industries to be more responsive and flexible in providing competitive pricing, routing, and services.

While the threats of terrorism and biological warfare have led to more stringent regulations on goods being imported into and exported from the United States, they have not stopped the surge of globalization. Transportation is—and will remain—a vital connection between peoples, their cultures, and the goods they make and buy.

---

fifteenth century, European explorers landed on the shores of North America. Their ships had carried them thousands of miles in search of spices, precious metals, and other exotic goods. Settlers soon followed, establishing communities along the eastern coast that, by the eighteenth century, had been joined into colonies. They were connected by bumpy paths and primitive roads, which the colonists traveled on horseback or by foot.

As the United States achieved independence and its population grew, many settlers loaded their families into covered wagons and traveled west in search of opportunity. The wagon trails that rutted the prairies soon became vital lifelines, enabling merchants to transport goods to markets and ports. As it carried the mail, the Pony Express became an important medium for communicating across a country that was growing ever larger.

As people moved inland, the need for a national transportation system became acute. In the early 1800s the federal government built the Cumberland Road, which stretched from Cumberland, Maryland, to Vandalia, Illinois—a distance of 592 miles. At about the same time, Robert Fulton built the first steamboat, launching an era of canal transportation highlighted by the opening of the Erie Canal in New York. In 1830 the railroad—a wondrous new form of transportation—was imported from Great Britain. By the middle of the century, railroad tracks crisscrossed a good portion of the North American landscape.

The railroad had a profound effect on the development of industry in the United States. For the first time in the nation's history, large quantities of goods could be transported across long distances. Factories sprang up throughout the country, creating urban centers filled with new homes for many people. The railroad even lured politicians, who traveled the country's rails on "whistle-stop" tours, visiting small towns and communities to garner votes—and often promising more jobs to get those votes.

At the end of the nineteenth century, the invention of the automobile paved the way for yet another transportation-based social revolution. Henry Ford developed the first assembly-line production method, and by 1913 his company was churning out automobiles that most Americans could afford: The Ford company sold 15 million units of its Model T between 1908 and 1913. During the next two decades automobile manufacturing became the country's largest industry.

The automobile made it easier and more convenient for people to undertake both short- and long-distance travel. This new mobility enabled many Americans to move out of the cities into suburban areas. Federal, state, and local governments scrambled to pave roads that connected cities, small towns, and rural areas, as well as highways that went from one part of the country to another.

In 1903 Wilbur and Orville Wright launched the age of air travel in Kitty Hawk, North Carolina, by successfully flying a small powered aircraft. In 1914 the first airline passenger service was started in Florida. With the first international passenger service from London to Paris in 1919, long-distance air travel began to spread throughout the world. With the introduction of the jet engine in the 1950s, international travel became big business. At the start of the twenty-first century, air travel within the United States and around the world is fast, safe, and relatively inexpensive.

In recent years, the transportation industry has faced a number of new challenges. Terrorists have targeted airlines, railroads, and subways. Deregulation has led many companies to alter their operating practices, and technological advances have changed their methods. In some cases, technology has blurred the traditional distinctions between industries. As a result, the future of the U.S. transportation industry is hard to predict. New technology, new fuels, and changes in demographics and consumer taste may rewrite the transportation story in its next chapter.

THE AUTO INDUSTRY

Throughout the 1950s and 1960s the U.S. auto industry grew dramatically. Cars got ever bigger and flashier, and thousands of Americans got high-paying jobs in car and truck manufacturing. From the 1970s on, however, the industry experienced a painful cycle of recessions and recoveries, fueled partly by the national economy and partly by energy prices. Smaller auto companies disappeared, leaving the Big Three—Chrysler, Ford, and General Motors—to battle it out. But they felt another pressure: foreign competitors fiercely promoted their compact, fuel-efficient, cost-effective cars. By 1991 Japanese manufacturers had a firm grasp on a quarter of the American car and truck market. It seemed as if the glory days of the U.S. auto industry were skidding away.

On the Road Again

In the early 1990s, the Big Three made major changes in the way they operated. They streamlined manufacturing, developed new technologies, and designed more fuel-efficient vehicles. They also introduced light trucks and sport utility vehicles, which became highly popular.

The automobile industry has experienced financial difficulties since the 1980s. (Photograph by Kelly A. Quin. Thomson Gale. Reproduced by permission.)

Industry Snapshots

TRUCKING

During the 1990s the number of carriers on the road more than doubled. In the years ahead the trucking industry should continue to expand and dominate the freight industry. Intermodal transportation—truck trailers are loaded onto freight trains, which take them cross-country where other truckers are waiting to deliver the trailers—should become an even more important way of moving freight. However, rising labor costs and the price of new technology may limit trucking industry revenue. Some companies, especially long-distance providers, are having difficulty recruiting adequately skilled drivers.

AIR TRANSPORT

The air transport industry is expected to grow steadily over the next decade. Air carriers will continue to be affected by fuel prices, consumer income, and government regulations. Increased security measures may require the employment of many more law enforcement officials at airports.

RAILROAD

The rail freight industry will experience modest growth over the next decade. Employment decline is expected to continue, but at a slower pace than during the 1990s. The industry's health depends to a large degree on the industries it serves, including the automobile, steel, and construction industries.

MASS TRANSIT

Mass transit—the nation's system of trains, buses, and subways—is experiencing a turnaround that should continue into the next decade. The federal government is investing large amounts of money to improve mass transit systems and the rising price of gas is making more consumers choose to use them.

MOTOR VEHICLES

Over the past two decades the long-term outlook for the American motor vehicle industry has been pessimistic. However, the industry is expected to grow slightly throughout the next decade. As the lucrative light truck and sport-utility vehicle market fades through 2014, consumers should shift to more fuel-efficient vehicles, including hybrid cars, because of rising gas prices. U.S. automakers are anticipating continued pressure from imports.

SHIPPING

The economy continues to influence the international shipping market. Industry observers anticipate new opportunities for U.S. companies in trade with Southeast Asia. On the domestic front, the threat of terrorism has put more stringent guidelines on shipping; law enforcement has improved in the areas of customs and border controls. Shipping on the inland waterways may increase slightly (about ten percent) through 2014. Competition for all water transportation jobs should be strong—the number of jobs is expected to grow more slowly than the average over the next decade.

In 1997 the Big Three had about fifty-six auto-manufacturing plants in North America, providing jobs for more than 206,000 workers. Nearly 1 million workers were employed by industry suppliers, and 1.1 million others had jobs at dealerships.

But in 2002 sales at The Big Three dropped thirty percent. Unemployment, triggered by the loss of manufacturing jobs, was a major factor. Incentive packages such as "no money down" and "cash back" brought in some customers, but the industry was still hampered by sharply rising gas prices, sky-rocketing health-care costs for autoworkers, and increasing foreign competition. In April 2006, GM announced a first-quarter loss of $323 million.

Autoworkers are some of the nation's highest-paid employees, earning as much as $50 per hour (including benefits). The industry's efforts to re-duce costs have had a direct effect on their job security. Manufacturers have cut some eighty thousand jobs since 2001 in a bid to improve productivity and profitability.

Auto manufacturers are now looking to technology to change—and save—their industry. Increasingly, factory tasks are completed by robots and other machines. Many autos have parts made from plastic and composite materials that allow more flexibility in design and are much lighter than steel. Some are hybrids: cars that combine two or more sources of power—gasoline and a recharge-able battery, for example, or gasoline plus a nonpetroleum-based fuel such as ethanol. Almost all new cars and trucks have features developed for the aerospace industry. Devices that use the Global Positioning System, for example, which are standard on

Many trucking companies have trouble making profits because expenses, especially labor costs, continue to rise. (© F. Damm/zefa/Corbis.)

many U.S. cars, tell drivers exactly where they are and exactly how to get where they want to go. Some alarm systems already use radar technology to detect objects within a certain distance. Vehicles of the future may be equipped with night-vision capabilities.

Over the next decade about a quarter of a million automobile workers will be reaching retirement age. Many of their jobs should become available to young job seekers. Those who have technological skills and interests may find eager employers in the auto industry.

Automotive Parts and Dealerships

The U.S. automotive parts industry employs more than eight hundred forty thousand workers. They manufacture everything from shock absorbers to pistons to windshield wipers. Restructuring in the industry and foreign competition have put pressure on these companies: many small suppliers may go out of business during the next decade while larger companies expand and send much of their manufacturing overseas.

The forecast for automobile dealerships is similar. About 210 dealerships are expected to close by 2010, largely because of consolidation. To survive, dealers are maintaining staffs of highly skilled personnel to service cars' many technologically ad-

vanced parts. They are also extending technology to customer service: interactive equipment, such as CD ROM-based video, helps salespeople explain the features of their cars and trucks. Future innovations may include automobile simulators, which would enable customers to "test drive" cars without leaving the showroom.

THE TRUCKING INDUSTRY

In the early 1980s the federal government deregulated the massive trucking industry, allowing many trucking companies to set their own rates. This move set the stage for a period of fierce competition, in which thousands of small trucking companies went bankrupt or were absorbed by the industry's giants.

Although a streamlined industry has struggled through national cycles of growth and recession, it is now on firm ground. Trucking is the largest provider of total U.S. freight service in terms of revenue, accounting for almost ninety percent of the U.S. freight market.

The industry is made up of more than five hundred seventy thousand private and government fleets with more than 3.4 million drivers. Many long-distance trucking firms, which account for the majority of jobs in the industry, have trouble making a profit because of the expense of their opera-

Summer Jobs in Transportation

Jobs may be available in bus and railroad terminals for clerks and maintenance workers. Local businesses may need route delivery workers, as well as car wash workers, service station attendants, parking attendants, or parking cashiers. Contact:

- transit authorities
- service stations
- car wash businesses

SOURCES OF INFORMATION

American Public Transit Association
1666 K Street NW
Washington, DC 20006
http://www.apta.com

International Brotherhood of Teamsters
25 Louisiana Ave. NW
Washington, DC 20001
http://www.teamsters.org

SEA TRANSPORT

Workers who know boats can find jobs as motorboat mechanics. They can also prepare boats for the water by cleaning, scraping, and painting them. Marinas often need helpers to fill boats with gas and to run supply shops. Contact:

- marinas
- boating supply companies
- waterfront parks

SOURCES OF INFORMATION

Seafarers International Union of North America
5201 Auth Way
Camp Springs, MD 20746-4275
http://www.seafarers.org

Transport Workers Union of America
1700 Broadway
New York, NY 10019
http://www.twu.org

AIR TRANSPORT

Airline terminals have many jobs available, including positions for clerks, maintenance workers, and catering workers. Baggage handlers and other ground personnel are also needed during the busy summer travel season. Contact:

- public and private airports
- airlines
- concessions in airline terminals

SOURCES OF INFORMATION

Air Transportation Association
1301 Pennsylvania Ave. NW, Ste. 1100
Washington, DC 20004-1707
http://www.airlines.org

Airport Ground Transportation Association
8001 Natural Bridge Rd.
St. Louis, MO 63121-4499
http://www.agtaweb.org

---

tions—labor costs and fuel prices make up the largest parts of their budgets.

However, just as new methods and technology have shaped the automotive industry, trucking companies have also modified their operations. For example, advances in the rail freight segment of the transportation industry have made it less feasible to use trucks as a primary means of shipping goods over long distances. In 1980 it was common for trucks to haul goods more than one thousand miles; now most carriers haul goods fewer than five hundred miles. Many of them now fit into the intermodal transport system: they deliver trailers filled with goods to railroads, which haul the trailers across the country to depots where other truck drivers are waiting to pick them up and deliver the goods.

Many trucking companies use computers and satellites to track and direct the flow of goods transported on their carriers. Using a computerized database, workers can schedule pickups and deliveries, monitor truck locations, and record customer data. This information can then be relayed to computer terminals in the trucks.

The Future of Trucking

The trucking industry is expected to continue its dominance of freight transport. Profits may be slim because of rising expenses, especially the cost of labor: for some trucking companies, labor costs account for seventy percent of their *total* expenses. While the economy dictates the amount of freight moved by trucks, demand for truck drivers should remain strong through 2014, especially in the long-distance sector of the industry. Two factors (a shortage of drivers, including an estimated twenty thou-

New Jobs Projected in Transportation, 2004–2014*

OCCUPATION	NEW JOBS	PERCENT INCREASE
Heavy and Tractor-Trailer Truck Drivers	223,000	12.9
Automotive Mechanics	126,000	15.7
Transit and Intercity Bus Drivers	41,000	21.7
Aircraft Mechanic	16,000	13.4
Railroad Engineers	–1,000	–2.5

*Projected

SOURCE: Bureau of Labor Statistics, *Monthly Labor Review*, November 2005.

sand long-haul drivers) and the huge number of workers expected to retire in the next decade (some experts say more than two hundred nineteen thousand drivers) may determine the future of the industry.

THE AIRLINE INDUSTRY

During the twentieth century, the airline industry grew into a multibillion-dollar global network. For many years it was highly controlled by the government, which made it stable but, many owners and consumers said, lacking in real competition.

That all changed in 1978, when the industry was deregulated. The competition that followed bankrupted many companies. Some just faded into oblivion, while others were absorbed by their competitors. To lure customers, they engaged in "fare wars," offering dramatic discounts on ticket prices—a boon to consumers but not to the industry's profit margins. Many airlines downsized their operations by reducing new aircraft orders or buying smaller planes. Many negotiated new union contracts. Smaller airlines sprang up and became highly profitable by carving out small-market niches—and taking business away from the larger airlines.

The industry was still flying in uncertain skies when the events of September 11, 2001, dealt it a severe blow. After the attacks on the World Trade Center in New York and the Pentagon, the industry saw a significant decrease in business. Many people were afraid of hijackings in the sky or discouraged by the delays and inconvenience caused by the new security procedures at airports. Airlines responded with lower fares, vacation packages, and flying incentives.

Most observers expect modest long-term growth in domestic air travel and slightly better growth in international travel. Factors that may affect the industry include the health of the nation's economy, rising fuel prices, new technologies, and government regulations. The number of jobs in the industry is expected to increase by nine percent over the next decade. About seventy percent of air industry jobs are in ground occupations.

New Technology

Technological change can be felt in all parts of the airline industry, from security systems at airports to the materials used in airplane construction. Military planes are required by law to have sophisticated navigational equipment; governmental agencies want to make the same equipment mandatory for commercial aircraft. Traffic control technology is being improved to prevent mid-air and other types of aircraft collisions. New satellite communication systems make planes easier to track when they are flying over the world's oceans.

THE WATER TRANSPORTATION INDUSTRY

After years of decline, the U.S. deep-sea shipping industry appears to be stabilizing. Competition from foreign vessels has been reduced because the standards of operation have become more uniform for all vessels, making the costs of operating U.S. ships comparable to foreign-flagged ships. Moreover, federal support through a maritime security subsidy has aided the industry.

Top-Dollar Jobs in Transportation

These high-paying jobs are described in this volume. The figures represent typical salaries for experienced workers.

$92,000–$150,000	• Air Traffic Controller • Airplane Pilot • Flight Engineer
$60,000–$110,000	• Airport Manager • Fleet Manager • Transportation Engineer
$40,000–$60,000	• Railroad Conductor • Traffic Engineer • Transportation Inspector

The health of the rail freight industry depends to a large extent on strength of the industries it serves, such as the automobile, steel, and construction industries. *(AP Images.)*

The outlook for U.S. domestic shipping remains strong. American fleets that carry petroleum products, ore, steel, and other goods through the Great Lakes and other inland waterways should experience a period of slow but steady growth.

THE RAIL FREIGHT INDUSTRY

In 1980 Congress partially deregulated the railroads, which allowed carriers to control the scheduling of their own trains, set their own rates, and adjust service to meet customer needs. Since then, freight volume has almost doubled: trains now carry eight percent of all U.S. commercial freight, including motor vehicles, chemicals, grain, and coal. Meanwhile, freight rates have dropped about 1.5 percent each year.

However, deregulation had a profound effect on many railroad workers. Railroad employment plunged from nearly four hundred thousand in 1983 to one hundred twelve thousand in 2004 and is expected to decline through 2014. New technology allows railroads to reduce the sizes of their train crews. Only a few years ago standard freight trains would have had crews of four; most freight trains now have crews of only two or three workers. By reducing their labor costs, the largest part of their operating budgets, railroad companies that carry freight have increased their profits.

Intermodal Freight

Intermodal freight is revolutionizing the way freight trains operate. Traditionally, trains were made up of cars carrying freight slated for different destinations. The trains were brought to a yard where they were divided, by car, onto different tracks classified by destination. Then the cars on each track were reassembled into outbound trains. That method was time-consuming and costly.

Intermodal freight employs a different strategy. Truckers drive their trailers filled with freight to a train yard, where the trailers are loaded directly onto flatcars (a type of rail car), eliminating the need to couple and uncouple train cars. In the past twenty-five years, this type of traffic has grown by almost two hundred percent.

The Future of Rail Freight

Industry observers expect growth in the rail freight industry to be moderate through 2014. By improving delivery times and reducing shipping rates, railroads are able to compete with trucks, ships, and aircraft. Intermodal freight has also had a positive effect. However, the health of the industry may depend on the condition of the industries served by rail, including agriculture, automobiles, construction, paper, and steel.

MASS TRANSIT

The 1970s were lucrative years for mass transit. As an energy crisis gripped the nation, many consumers turned to buses, trolleys, railroads, and subways. Consequently, the federal government invested billions of dollars in the nation's transportation systems.

During the 1980s, however, when the national economy became stronger, the federal government sharply cut mass transit subsidies. Many cities were forced to abandon efforts to upgrade their systems. Some had to reduce operations, forgo repairs, and raise fares.

Two decades later the federal government again decided to help cities improve their transit systems. New subways are now running in Los Angeles, Miami, and Seattle. As gas prices continue to rise, more and more people are turning to public transportation.

Although long-distance buses continue to operate across the country at affordable prices, many riders prefer to travel by plane or passenger rail. Amtrak, the nation's largest passenger railroad, operates some 265 intercity passenger trains each day, carrying more than 25.4 million passengers each year.

Still, Amtrak has been losing money. According to a report by the U.S. Secretary of Transportation in February 2005, Amtrak cannot pay for innovative services because it is spending so much money "running trains that nobody rides between cities that nobody wants to travel between." Officials have proposed an end to federal subsidies for Amtrak. Instead, the federal government would help state and local agencies fund improvement and maintenance of tracks, bridges, and stations, thus freeing Amtrak to concentrate on running the trains. Some believe this would save Amtrak, while others fear it would bring an end to intercity passenger service.

TRANSPORTATION—AND YOU

This volume describes occupations available in the transportation field. As you read, keep in mind that technology is constantly shaping the industry and is playing a greater role in its future. Many industry employers value workers who have computer skills and technical training.

Good jobs do not magically appear. Anyone who has been in the job market knows that landing the right job takes planning, preparation, perseverance, and patience. This is true whether you are looking for your first job, reentering the job market, trying to get a new job, or planning a mid-career change. This essay is designed to guide you through the process of finding a job, from helping you define your career objectives to suggesting ways to prepare yourself for interviews. Use the advice and checklists below to help identify the kind of work that fits your personality, skills, and interests. Then learn how to locate job openings that match your criteria. Finally, use these tips to help you create a resume and prepare for the interview that helps you land the job that's right for you.

PLANNING YOUR CAREER

What are your unique skills? What kind of workplace appeals to you? What do you find most rewarding in your daily life? Answering these questions can help you identify a career path that will enrich your life, financially and otherwise. Most people enjoy doing a job well. There is an inner satisfaction that comes from taking on a challenge and accomplishing something worthwhile. Whether you are just starting out in the working world or you are at the midpoint of a career, it is worth taking some time to consider whether or not you are in the right kind of work—or looking for the right kind of job. If you are unhappy or dissatisfied in your daily work and are just trying to do enough to get by, you may not be in the right job or the right field. The following ideas can help you match your skills and interests with the kind of work you will find most rewarding.

Evaluate Yourself

Before you make any career decisions, think about subjects or topics that interest you and tasks you do well. This can help you pinpoint the kind of work you would be happy doing. One way to go about this is to compile a self-inventory chart. Such a chart will be helpful as you decide which jobs you want to consider. Including details about your work history and educational background will also make the chart useful to you as you compile your resume, write cover letters, complete job application forms, and prepare for job interviews.

Begin your self-inventory chart by listing all the jobs you have ever had, including summer employment, part-time jobs, volunteer work, and any freelance or short-term assignments you have done. Include the dates of employment, the names and addresses of supervisors, and the amount of money you earned. Then compile a similar list of your hobbies and other activities, including any special experiences you have had, such as travel. Next, do the same for your educational history, listing schools attended, major courses of study, grades, special honors or awards, courses you particularly enjoyed, and extracurricular activities.

At this point, you may see a career pattern emerging: perhaps your list is already suggesting a direction for your career search. If the picture still lacks detail or focus, expand your self-inventory chart by compiling a list of standard workplace aptitudes, and rate yourself *above average*, *average*, or *below average* for each one. Some skill categories to include in your list are administrative, analytic, athletic, clerical, language, leadership, managerial, manual, mathematical, mechanical, sales, and verbal abilities. Also rate your willingness to accept responsibility and your ability to get along with people. In combination with your educational background, work history, and list of personal interests, this information should help you understand why some kinds of work appeal to you and others do not.

Evaluate Workplace Characteristics

Another tool to help you find a rewarding job is the "Work Characteristics Checklist" below. Some of these characteristics will be attractive to you. Some will not. Perhaps you will discover that having a workplace with flexible hours, for example, is more important to you than being able to work outdoors. Or maybe you will find that these are both very significant issues in your quality of life.

This checklist can be useful as a guide as you compile your own list of what is important to you in a job or workplace. Do not expect a job to meet all your requirements, however. Focusing on the job characteristics that are most important to you will

Work Characteristics Checklist

Do you want a job in which you can

- work outdoors?
- be physically active?
- work with your hands?
- be challenged mentally?
- work with machines?
- work independently?
- work on a team?
- follow clear instructions?
- earn a lot of money?
- have a chance for rapid advancement?
- have good benefits?
- travel in your work?
- work close to home?
- work regular hours?
- have a flexible schedule?
- have a variety of tasks?
- have supervisory responsibilities?
- express your own ideas?
- be a decision maker?

help you identify the type of work you would find most rewarding. It will also be helpful when it is time to decide whether or not to apply for jobs you discover during the search process.

Evaluate Career Options

Now that you've evaluated your personal skills, aptitudes, interests, and experience, and you've identified the kinds of workplace characteristics that are important to you, do you feel confident that you know what kinds of jobs you'd be good at? If not, you may wish to consult an experienced career counselor or take advantage of online resources that can help you find a good career field match.

Most high schools, vocational schools, and colleges provide vocational testing and career counseling guidance for students and alumni. Some local offices of the state employment services affiliated with the federal employment service offer free counseling. Commercial career centers also offer guidance services.

There are many tools available to test your interests and aptitudes for the purpose of career counseling. The personal profile that emerges from a skills inventory can be matched with potential career fields to show you what kinds of jobs might be good matches for your interests. These assessment tools will also show you what kind of training is necessary to qualify for jobs in these career fields. You may find programs like this online that you can try for yourself. For a more comprehensive approach, you may prefer to look into aptitude tests that are administered and interpreted by a career counselor.

Most major cities have professional career consultants and career counseling firms. You should make sure to check their reputations before paying for their services. A list of counseling services in your area is available from the American Counseling Association in Alexandria, Virginia (http://www.counseling.org).

You can also search the Internet for many services that career counselors provide. Some sites have online counselors who can help you with a variety of tasks, such as obtaining information on jobs, careers, and training. They may be able to provide information on available services, including housing assistance, day care facilities, and transportation. A list of career planning resources, including Web sites, is available at the end of this volume.

EVALUATE SPECIFIC JOBS

After you have considered what you do well and what you enjoy doing, and identified some career options that provide a good match with your interests and abilities, you're ready to focus on the specific types of jobs that may be available to you. First, make a note of all the jobs in this volume that interest you. Then examine the education and training required for these jobs. Decide whether you qualify or would be able to gain the qualifications.

If possible, talk with people who have the kinds of jobs you are considering. Firsthand information can be invaluable. Also look through the appropriate trade and professional journals listed at the end of this essay and check the section at the end of the volume called "Resources" for books and Web sites that contain more detailed information about the jobs. In addition, counselors usually are helpful. For more detailed information, you can contact the trade and professional associations listed at the end of each occupational profile.

Once you have found out all you can about a particular type of job, compare the features of the job with your work characteristics checklist. See how many characteristics of the job match your work preferences. By completing these steps for all the jobs that appeal to you, you should be able to come up with a list of jobs that match your interests and abilities.

FINDING JOB OPPORTUNITIES

Once you've decided what kind of job suits you, the next step is to look for available positions. Obviously, the more openings you can find, the better your chance of landing a job. People usually apply

Job Finder's Checklist

The following list of job-hunting tips may seem obvious, but getting all the bits and pieces in order beforehand helps when you're looking for a job.

Resume Find out whether you will need a resume. If so, bring your resume up to date or prepare a new one. Assemble a supply of neatly printed copies and have an electronic version ready to e-mail to prospective employers.

References Line up your references. Ask permission of the people whose names you would like to use. Write down their addresses, phone numbers, and job titles.

Contacts Put the word out to everyone you know that you are looking for a job.

Job market Find out where the jobs are. Make a list of possible employers in your field of interest.

Research Do a little homework ahead of time—it can make a big difference in the long run. Find out as much as you can about a job, the field, and the company before you apply. A knowledgeable job applicant makes a good impression.

Organization Keep a file on your job-hunting campaign with names and dates of employers contacted, ads answered, results, and follow-up.

Appearance Make sure that the clothes you plan to wear to an interview are neat and clean. You may need to dress more formally than you would on the job, particularly if you are visiting a personnel office or meeting with a manager. Keep in mind that people will form an opinion of you based on their first impressions.

---

for many job openings before they find the right employment match.

There are many ways to find out about or apply for job openings. Some of these job-hunting techniques are explained on the pages that follow, along with information about how to follow up on job leads.

Applying in Person

For some jobs, especially part-time or entry-level jobs, you may be able to find employment by visiting the company or companies for which you would like to work. This works best when a company is expanding or jobs are plentiful for other reasons, or when a "help wanted" sign is posted at the company. Applying in person can sharpen your interviewing techniques and give you a chance to see a variety of workplaces. This direct approach is best for hourly labor or service jobs; when applying for other types of work, it is not the method to use unless you are directed to do so. Applicants for professional or supervisory jobs should always send a letter and resume to the company.

Phone and Letter Campaigns

To conduct a phone campaign, use the business listings of your telephone directory to build a list of companies for which you might like to work. Call their personnel departments and find out whether

they have any openings. This technique is not useful in all situations, and it has its drawbacks: you may not be able to make a strong impression by phone, and you will not have a written record of your contacts.

Letter writing campaigns can be very effective if the letters are well thought out and carefully prepared. Your letters should always be typed. Handwritten letters and photocopied letters convey a lack of interest or motivation.

You may be able to compile a good list of company addresses in your field of interest by reading the trade and professional publications listed at the end of this essay. Many of the periodicals publish directories or directory issues. Other sources you can use to compile lists of companies are the trade unions and professional organizations listed at the end of each job profile in this volume. The reference librarian at your local library can also help you find appropriate directories.

You can also e-mail letters to human resource departments of many companies. Be sure to follow all the same guidelines as you would for traditional letter correspondence.

Whether they are paper or electronic, your letters should be addressed to the personnel or human resources department of the organization. If possible, send the letter to a specific person. If you don't know who the correct person is, try to find the name of the personnel director through the directories in the library. You can also call on the phone and say, "I'm writing to ask about employment at your company. To whom should I address my letter?" If you can't find a name, use a standard salutation. It's a good idea to enclose a resume (described later in this essay) with the letter to give the employer a brief description of your educational and work experience.

Keep a list of all the people you write to, along with the date each letter was mailed, or keep a photocopy of each letter. Then you can follow up by writing a brief note or calling people who do not reply within about three weeks.

Job Databases Online

The World Wide Web can be an excellent resource for job hunters. The Internet currently has thousands of career-related sites where you can read about job openings or post your resume in a database for a possible match with available jobs. Some sites, such as The Monster Board (http://www.monster.com), help you build a resume and post it

online as well as allow you to search through a massive database of help-wanted listings. Others employ a search engine to find jobs that match your background, then post your resume online for employers. The Web site called CareerBuilder (http://www.careerbuilder.com) uses an interactive personal search program that lets you select job criteria such as location, title, and salary; you are then notified by e-mail when a matching position is posted in the database.

Many companies post job openings in their human resource Web pages. You can usually access these lists by visiting the Web site of a company and clicking on a link called "jobs," "careers," or "employment opportunities." If you find a job that interests you during your online search, whether it's posted at a company's own Web site or on a general listing of jobs, follow the directions given for applying for the position. Some online ads will provide the contact information you need to send your resume and cover letter directly to the employer, ei-

Many career-related Web sites can be found on the Internet. This hypothetical site (for illustration purposes only) allows job-seekers to search for a position by location and job category.

ther by e-mail or by traditional mail, but other ads direct job hunters to apply directly through a link at the job description.

Job hunters can often find job listings through the Web sites of the professional associations in their career fields. State government Web sites may also provide links to job listings—or to non-government sites that list available jobs.

Help-Wanted Ads

Many people find out about job openings by reading the "help-wanted" sections of newspapers, trade journals, and professional magazines. Employers and employment agencies often, though not always, use these classified ad sections to publicize available jobs.

Classified ads use unique terms to convey basic information. You will find some common abbreviations in the chart in this essay titled "Reading the Classifieds." You can usually decode the abbreviations by using common sense, but if something puzzles you, call the newspaper and ask for a translation. Classified ads usually list the qualifications that are required for a particular job and explain how to contact the employer.

As you find openings that interest you, answer each ad using the method requested. Record the date of your contact, and if you don't hear from the employer within two or three weeks, place another call or send a polite note asking whether the job is still open. Don't forget to include your phone number and address in your initial contact.

Some help-wanted ads are "blind ads." These ads give contact information for replying but provide no name, phone number, or address that would identify the company. Employers and employment agencies may place these ads to avoid having to reply to all of the job applicants or being contacted directly by job-seekers.

Situation-Wanted Ads

Another way to get the attention of potential employers is with a situation-wanted ad. You can place one of these in the classified section of your local newspaper or of a trade journal in your field of interest. Many personnel offices and employment agencies scan these columns when they're looking for new employees. The situation-wanted ad is usually most effective for people who have advanced ed-

Reading the Classifieds

HELP WANTED	CLASSIFIED ABBREVIATIONS		SITUATION WANTED
AIRLINE TICKET AGENCY $00,000. Fluent Spanish or French & exp. with international computerized system. XYZ Agency　　　　　Fifth Ave.	appt. bkgd. col. conslt. educ. engr. excel. exp., expd. fee neg. f/p., f/pd. f/t gd. bnfts. K M mech. mgr. nec. neg. oper. oppty. perm. pfd., prfr. p/t refs. sal. sta. subs. svce. trnee. w/ wk. yrs.	appointment background college consultant education engineer excellent experience, experienced fee negotiable (fee can be worked out with employer) fee paid (agency fee paid by employer) full time good benefits thousand thousand mechanic, mechanical manager necessary negotiable operator opportunity permanent preferred, prefer part time references salary station suburbs service trainee with week years	Hire an experienced **AIRCRAFT MECHANIC ELECTRICIAN** 4 years work on helicopters and teaching experience. Call (000) 000-0000
AUTO BODY SHOP MECHANIC—Allen Percy dealership has an immed. opening for an auto body shop mechanic. Excel. co. bnfts. To apply call: Mr. Jay Fisher　000-0000.			**AIRLINE CUSTOMER SERVICE Clerk** 8 yrs. airline airport svce. exp. Negotiable Call (000) 000-0000.
AUTO RENTAL AGENTS Attractive & Personable personnel are needed to staff our counters in City Airport, all shifts. Will provide fully paid trainee program. All benefits. Call 000-0000 between 11 a.m.–4 p.m. to arrange for an interview. Airline Rent-a-Car. Equal Opportunity Employer.			**AUTO MECHANIC** Desires position in Service Sta. Expd. in tune-ups, brakes & major repair of American engines. Call Len 000-0000
CAR WASH Machine oper. Full-time, must be 18 or over. 000-0000 between 10–3, Mon.–Fri.			**AUTO MECHANIC** Desires perm. position. Expd. w/tools, refs. 000-0000
Drivers, Bus—needed at once. Must be over 21 yrs. Full or part time. Excel. earning potential & liberal benefits program. Personnel Dept. 000-0000			**DRIVING INSTRUCTOR**—4 yrs. exp. county school system. 2 yrs. exp. private co. Will relocate. L3971 Herald.
DRIVERS TRACTOR TRAILER Local and long distance. Over 21. No points on driver's license. NO EXCEPTIONS. Call 000-0000 for appt.			**GO GETTER** Chauffer's license—Panel truck & retail exp. Call 000-0000.
Gas station attendants needed to work p/t evenings and weekends. Apply in person. Larry's Garage 65 Mountain St.			**PARKING ATTENDANT** expd. for p/t weekend work. Call Danny 000-0000
MECHANIC Diesel, experienced only, excellent benefits., top wages, gd. working conditions, call Mr. Grant, 000-0000			**TRAFFIC MANAGER** exp. & educ., resume available. K000 Courier.
			TRANSPORTATION ENGINEER WILL TRAVEL Desire full-time position. Offer graduate degree in engineering, experience as traffic consultant. Call (000) 000-0000
			TRUCK DRIVER—expd. knows city & subs. Desires full time. Refs. 000-0000

ucation, training, or experience, or who are in fields where their unique skills are in great demand.

A situation-wanted ad should be brief, clear, and to the point. Its main purpose is to interest the employer enough so you are contacted for an interview. It should tell exactly what kind of job you want, why you qualify, and whether you are available for full-time or part-time work. Use the same abbreviations that employers use in classified ads.

If you are already employed and do not want it known that you are looking for a new position, you can run a blind ad. A blind ad protects your privacy by listing a box number at the publication to which all replies can be sent. They are then forwarded to you. You do not need to give your name, address, or phone number in the ad.

Notes on Networking

Let people know you're looking. Tell friends, acquaintances, teachers, business associates, former employers—anyone who might know of job openings in your field.

Read newspapers and professional and trade journals. Look for news of developments in your field and for names of people and companies you might contact.

Use the World Wide Web. Make contacts through news groups, or find information on Web sites for professional organizations in your field.

Join professional or trade associations. Contacts you make at meetings could provide valuable job leads. Association newsletters generally carry useful information about people and developments in the field.

Attend classes or seminars. You will meet other people in your field at job-training classes and professional development seminars.

Participate in local support groups. You can gain information about people and places to contact through support groups such as those listed by *The Riley Guide*, available online at http://www.rileyguide.com/support.html, as well as through alumni associations.

Be on the lookout. Always be prepared to make the most of any opportunity that comes along. Talk with anyone who can provide useful information about your field.

Networking

A very important source of information about job openings is networking. This means talking with friends and acquaintances about your area of interest. If any of them have friends or relatives in the field, ask if they would be willing to speak with you. There's nothing wrong with telling anyone who will listen that you are looking for a job—family, friends, counselors, and former employers. This will multiply your sources of information many times over.

You can use the Internet to make contacts, too. You can meet people with similar interests in news groups, which are organized by topic. Then you can correspond individually via e-mail. Many fields have professional organizations that maintain Web sites. These can help you keep current on news affecting your field, including employment opportunities.

Sometimes a contact knows about a job vacancy before it is advertised. You may have an advantage, then, when you get in touch with the employer. Don't, however, use the contact's name without permission. Don't assume that a contact will go out on a limb by recommending you, either. Once you have received the inside information, rely on your own ability to get the job.

Placement Services

Most vocational schools, high schools, and colleges have a placement or career service that maintains a list of job openings and schedules visits from companies. If you are a student or recent graduate, you should check there for job leads. Many employers look first in technical or trade schools and colleges for qualified applicants for certain jobs. Recruiters often visit colleges to look for people to fill technical and scientific positions. These recruiters usually represent large companies. Visit your placement office regularly to check the job listings, and watch for scheduled visits by company recruiters.

State Employment Services

Another source of information about job openings is the local office of the state employment service. Many employers automatically list job openings at the local office. Whether you're looking for a job in private industry or with the state, these offices, which are affiliated with the federal employment service, are worth visiting, online or in person, if there are offices locally.

State employment service offices are public agencies that do not charge for their services. They can direct you to special programs run by the government in conjunction with private industry. These programs, such as the Work Incentive Program for families on welfare, are designed to meet special needs. Some, but not all, of these offices offer vocational aptitude and interest tests and can refer interested people to vocational training centers. The state employment service can be a valuable first stop in your search for work, especially if there are special circumstances in your background. For example, if you did not finish high school, if you have had any difficulties with the law, or if you are living in a difficult home environment, your state employment service office is equipped to help you.

Private Employment Agencies

State employment services, though free, are usually very busy. If you are looking for more personal service and want a qualified employment counselor to help you find a job, you might want to approach a private employment agency.

Private employment agencies will help you get a job if they think they can place you. Most of them get paid only if they're successful in finding you a job, so you need to show them that you are a good prospect. These agencies will help you prepare a resume if you need one, and they will contact employers they think might be interested in you.

Private employment agencies are in the business of bringing together people who are looking for jobs and companies that are looking for workers. For some positions, usually mid- and higher-level jobs, the employment agency's fee is paid by the employer. In such cases, the job seeker pays no fee. In other cases, you may be required to pay the fee, which is usually a percentage of your annual salary. Paying a fee can be a worthwhile investment if it leads to a rewarding career.

Some agencies may also ask for a small registration fee whether or not you get a job through them. Some agencies may demand that you pay even if you find one of the jobs they are trying to fill through your other contacts. Be sure to read and understand the fine print of any contract you're expected to sign, and ask for a copy to take home. Since the quality of these agencies varies, check to see if an agency is a certified member of a state or national association.

Some employment agencies, called staffing services, operate in a different way. They are usually paid by employers to screen and refer good candidates for job openings. They earn money when they refer a candidate who is hired by the employer. The employee pays no fee. Staffing firms, however, only spend time on candidates they think they may be able to place.

Private employment agencies are usually helping many people at one time. They may not have the time to contact you every time they find a job opening. Therefore, you may need to phone them at reasonable intervals after you have registered.

Civil Service

In your search for work, don't forget that the civil service—federal, state, and local—may have many jobs in your field. You may contact the state employment office or apply directly to the appropriate state or federal agency. The armed services also train and employ civilians in many fields. Don't neglect these avenues for finding jobs. Civil service positions usually require you to take a civil service examination. Books are available to help you prepare for these exams, and your local civil service office can also provide information.

Unions

In certain fields, unions can be useful sources of information. If you are a member of a union in your field of interest, you may be able to find out about jobs in the union periodical or through people at the union local. If you do not belong to a union, you may contact a union in the field you are interested in for information about available employment services. You will find addresses for some unions in the job profiles in this book.

Temporary Employment

A good way to get a feel for the job market—what's available and what certain jobs are like—is to work in a temporary job. There are both private and state agencies that can help place people in short-term jobs. Some jobs are seasonal, and extra workers may be needed in the summer or at another busy time.

Temporary employment can increase your job skills, your knowledge of a particular field, and your chances of hearing of permanent positions. In today's tight labor market, many companies are using the services of temporary workers in increasing numbers. In fact, temporary agencies may sign multimillion-dollar contracts to provide businesses with a range of temporary workers. In some cases, temporary workers are in such demand that they may receive benefits, bonuses, and the same hourly wages as equivalent permanent employees. Some temporary agencies are even joining with companies to create long-term career paths for their temporary workers.

MARKETING YOURSELF

An employer's first impression of you is likely to be based on the way you present yourself on print. Whether it is in an application form or on a re-

DO YOU KNOW YOUR RIGHTS?

JOB DISCRIMINATION—WHAT IT IS

Federal and State Law

An employer cannot discriminate against you for any reason other than your ability to do the job. By federal law, an employer cannot discriminate against you because of your race, color, religion, sex, or national origin. The law applies to decisions about hiring, promotion, working conditions, and firing. The law specifically protects workers who are over the age of forty from discrimination on the basis of age.

The law also protects workers with disabilities. Employers must make their workplaces accessible to individuals with disabilities—for example, by making them accessible to wheelchairs or by hiring readers or interpreters for blind or deaf employees.

Federal law offers additional protection to employees who work for the federal government or for employers who contract with the federal government. State law can also provide protection, for example by prohibiting discrimination on the basis of marital status, arrest record, political affiliations, or sexual orientation.

Affirmative Action

Affirmative action programs are set up by businesses that want to make a special effort to hire women and members of minority groups. Federal employers and many businesses that have contracts with the federal government are required by law to set up affirmative action programs. Employers with a history of discriminatory practices may also be required to establish affirmative action programs.

Discrimination against Job Applicants

A job application form or interviewer may ask for information that can be used to discriminate against you illegally. The law prohibits such questions. If you are asked such questions and are turned down for the job, you may be a victim of discrimination. However, under federal law, employers must require you to prove that you are an American citizen or that you have a valid work permit.

Discrimination on the Job

Discrimination on the job is illegal. Being denied a promotion for which you are qualified or being paid less than coworkers are paid for the same job may be forms of illegal discrimination.

Sexual, racial, and religious harassment are forms of discrimination and are prohibited in the workplace. On-the-job harassment includes sexual, racial, or religious jokes or comments. Sexual harassment includes not only requests or demands for sexual favors but also verbal or physical conduct of a sexual nature.

JOB DISCRIMINATION—WHAT YOU CAN DO

Contact Federal or State Commissions

If you believe that your employer practices discrimination, you can complain to the state civil rights commission or the federal Equal Employment Opportunity Commission (EEOC). If, after investigating your complaint, the commission finds that there has been discrimination, it will take action against the employer. You may be entitled to the job or promotion you were denied or to reinstatement if you were fired. You may also receive back pay or other financial compensation.

Contact a Private Organization

There are many private organizations that can help you fight job discrimination. For example, the American Civil Liberties Union (ACLU) works to protect all people from infringement on their civil rights. The National Association for the Advancement of Colored People (NAACP), National Organization

---

sume, you will want to make a good impression so that employers will be interested in giving you a personal interview. A potential employer is likely to equate a neat, well-written presentation with good work habits, and a sloppy, poorly written one with bad work habits.

Writing an Effective Resume

When you write to a company to follow up a lead or to ask about job openings, you should send information about yourself. The accepted way of doing this is to send a resume with a cover letter.

The work resume is derived from the French word résumer, meaning "to summarize." A resume does just that—it briefly outlines your education, work experience, and special abilities and skills. A resume may also be called a curriculum vitae, a personal profile, or a personal data sheet. This summary acts as your introduction by mail or e-mail, as your calling card if you apply in person, and as a convenient reference for you to use when

for Women (NOW), and Native American Rights Fund may negotiate with your employer, sue on your behalf, or start a class action suit—a lawsuit brought on behalf of all individuals in your situation.

WHAT TO DO IF YOU LOSE YOUR JOB

Being Fired and Being Laid Off

In most cases, an employer can fire you only if there is good cause, such as your inability to do the job, violation of safety rules, dishonesty, or chronic absenteeism.

Firing an employee because of that employee's race, color, religion, sex, national origin, or age (if the employee is over forty) is illegal. Firing an employee for joining a union or for reporting an employer's violation (called whistle-blowing) is also prohibited. If you believe you have been wrongfully discharged, you should contact the EEOC or the state civil rights commission.

At times, employers may need to let a number of employees go to reduce costs. This reduction in staff is called a layoff. Laying off an employee has nothing to do with the employee's job performance. Federal law requires employers who lay off large numbers of employees to give these employees at least two months' notice of the cutback.

Unemployment Compensation

Unemployment insurance is a state-run fund that provides payments to people who lose their jobs through no fault of their own. Not everyone is entitled to unemployment compensation. Those who quit their jobs or who worked only a few months before losing their jobs may not be eligible.

The amount of money you receive depends on how much you earned at your last job. You may receive unemployment payments for only a limited period of time and only so long as you can prove that you are actively looking for a new position.

Each claim for unemployment compensation is investigated before the state makes any payments. If the state unemployment agency decides to deny you compensation, you may ask the agency for instructions on how to appeal that decision.

OTHER PROTECTIONS FOR EMPLOYEES

Honesty and Drug Testing

Many employers ask job applicants or employees to submit to lie detector tests or drug tests. Lie detector tests are permitted in the hiring of people for high security positions, such as police officers. Some states prohibit or restrict the testing of applicants or employees for drug use. Aptitude and personality tests are generally permitted.

Other Federal Laws

The Fair Labor Standards Act prescribes certain minimum wages and rules about working hours and overtime payments. Workers' compensation laws provide payment for injuries that occur in the workplace and wages lost as a result of those injuries.

The Occupational Safety and Health Act sets minimum requirements for workplace safety. Any employee who discovers a workplace hazard should report it to the Occupational Safety and Health Administration (OSHA). The administration will investigate the claim and may require the employer to correct the problem or pay a fine.

Rights Guaranteed by Contract

Not every employee has a written contract. If you do, however, that contract may grant you additional rights, such as the right to severance pay in the event you are laid off. In addition, employees who are members of a union may have certain rights guaranteed through their union contract.

Before you sign any contract, make sure you understand every part of it. Read it thoroughly and ask the employer questions. Checking the details of a contract before signing it may prevent misunderstanding later.

filling out an application form or when being interviewed.

A resume is a useful tool in applying for almost any job, even if you use it only to keep a record of where you have worked, for whom, and the dates of employment. A resume is required if you are being considered for professional or executive jobs. Prepare it carefully. It's well worth the effort.

The goal of a resume is to capture the interest of potential employers so they will call you for a personal interview. Since employers are busy people, the resume should be as brief and as neat as possible. You should, however, include as much relevant information about yourself as you can. This is usually presented under at least two headings: "Education" and "Experience." The latter is sometimes called "Employment History." Some people add a third section titled "Related Skills," "Professional Qualifications," or "Related Qualifications."

If you prepare a self-inventory such as the one described earlier, it will be a useful tool in preparing a resume. Go through your inventory, and select

Danna Sandora

321 Birchwood Road

Arlington, VA 12345

(914) 277-4428

dsandora@email.com

EXPERIENCE

Delivery Van Driver, M. L. Pearlman Printing Company, Arlington, NY
Drove company vehicle to deliver printing work to clients throughout the county. Loaded and serviced vehicle. Maintained records, including signed receipts. Occasionally collected supplies from company suppliers. 2000–2004.

Gas Station Attendant, Bell's Service Station, Bedford, VA
Serviced customer's cars with gasoline, oil, and water. Filled and changed tires. Accepted cash and credit card payments. 1998–2000.

Counselor, Deepdale Camp for Exceptional Children, Clarksburg, VA
Responsible for 24-hour supervision of children with handicaps. Duties included organizing activities, monitoring attendance of children at therapy sessions, assisting with dressing and personal hygiene, and supervising meals. Prepared progress reports for camp records. Assisted in administration of medication prescribed by medical staff. Summer 1997.

Fund-Raiser, The United Way, Washington, DC
Collected funds for charitable causes and distributed educational materials to merchants with fund-raising information. Worked to coordinate community efforts with local office. Summe

EDUCATION

Diploma, George Washington Vocatio

1997–1999.

Program in automotive mechanics.

References Available upon request.

- State your name, address, telephone number, and email first.
- State job objective or general career goal in a few words.
- List education and work experience in reverse chronological order, with most recent item first.

KEVIN O'NEILL

15 ROBBINS LANE, CALIFON, NJ 07830

(908) 832-2761 • koneill@email.com

OBJECTIVE   Position in airport management.

EXPERIENCE

2000 to present   **Assistant Manager,** Westfield International Airport, Westfield, NJ
Responsible for maintenance of terminal buildings, runways, grounds, and parking areas. Supervise maintenance crews. Negotiate for services of contractors. Assist airport manager with financial planning, relations with airlines, and enforcement of safety regulations.

1999 to 2000   **Business Manager,** Westfield International Airport, Westfield, NJ
Responsible for management of commercial space in airport terminal. Negotiated leasing arrangements with retail shops, food and beverage suppliers, and other commercial clients. Supervised expansion of food arcade. Prepared annual financial plan for commercial space.

1996 to 1999   **Public Relations Manager,** Westfield Center City Bus Terminal, Westfield, NJ
Managed citywide publicity and advertising campaign. Worked with state tourism board on state and national promotion of bus support. Coordinated information services in terminal, including information booths, posters, maps, and signs. Worked with bus companies on discount fares and special travel options to promote bus services.

EDUCATION

1996   **Master of Business Administration,** Rutgers University, New Brunswick, NJ

1994   **Bachelor of Science,** New Jersey Institute of Technology, Newark, NJ
Major in Economics.

1993   **Private Pilot's License,** Standard Aviation Training School, Morristown, NJ

REFERENCES   Available upon request.

- List your work experience first if it is more important than your educational background.
- Keep descriptions of your education and work experience brief.
- List special skills and qualifications if they are relevant to the job.

the items that show your ability to do the job or jobs in which you are interested. Plan to highlight these items on your resume. Select only those facts that point out your relevant skills and experience.

Once you have chosen the special points to include, prepare the resume. At the top, put your name, address, and phone number. After that, decide which items will be most relevant to the employer you plan to contact.

State Your Objective Some employment counselors advise that you state a job objective or describe briefly the type of position for which you are applying. The job objective usually follows your name and address. Don't be too specific if you plan to use the same resume a number of times. It's better to give a general career goal. Then, in a cover letter, you can be more specific about the position in which you are interested.

Describe What You've Done Every interested employer will check your educational background and employment history carefully. It is best to present these sections in order of importance. For instance, if you've held many relevant jobs, you should list your work experience first, followed by your educational background. On the other hand, if you are just out of school with little or no work experience, it's probably best to list your educational background first and then, under employment history, to mention any part-time and summer jobs you've held or volunteer work you've done.

Under educational background, list the schools you have attended in reverse chronological order, starting with your most recent training and ending with the least recent. Employers want to know at a glance your highest qualifications. For each educational experience, include years attended, name and location of the school, and degree or certificate earned, if any. If you have advanced degrees (college and beyond), it isn't necessary to include high school and elementary school education. Don't forget to highlight any special courses you took or awards you won, if they are relevant to the kind of job you are seeking.

Chronological and Functional Resumes Information about your employment history can be presented in two ways. The most common format is the chronological resume. In a chronological resume, you summarize your work experience year by year. Begin with your current or most recent employment and then work backward. For each job, list the name and location of the company for which you worked, the years you were employed, and the position or positions you held. The order in which you present these facts will depend on what you are trying to emphasize. If you want to call attention to the type or level of job you held, for example, you should put the job title first. Regardless of the order you choose, be consistent. Summer employment or part-time work should be identified as such. If you held a job for less than a year, specify months in the dates of employment.

It is important to include a brief description of the responsibilities you had in each job. This often reveals more about your abilities than the job title. Remember, too, that you do not have to mention the names of former supervisors or how much you earned. You can discuss these points during the interview or explain them on an application form.

The functional resume, on the other hand, emphasizes what you can do rather than what you have done. It is useful for people who have large gaps in their work history or who have relevant skills that would not be properly highlighted in a chronological listing of jobs. The functional resume concentrates on qualifications—such as familiarity with particular equipment, organizational skills, or managerial experience. Specific jobs may be mentioned, but they are not the primary focus of this type of resume.

Explain Special Skills You may wish to include a third section called "Related Skills," "Professional Qualifications," or "Related Qualifications." This is useful if there are points you want to highlight that do not apply directly to educational background or work experience. Be sure these points are relevant to the kind of work you are seeking. This section is most effective if you can mention any special recognition, awards, or other evidence of excellence. It is also useful to mention if you are willing to relocate or can work unusual hours.

Have References Available Employers may also want to know whom they can contact to find out more about you. At the start of your job search, you should ask three or four people if you may use them as references. If you haven't seen these people for a while, you may want to send them a copy of your resume and let them know what kind of position you're seeking. Your references should be the kind of people your potential employer will respect, and they should be able to comment favorably on your abilities, personality, and work habits. You should indicate whether these people are personal references or former work supervisors. Avoid using any relatives. You can list the names and addresses of your references at the end of your resume or in a cover letter. Or, you can simply write, "References available upon request." Just be sure you have their names, addresses, and phone numbers ready if you are asked.

Present Yourself Concisely Tips for making your resume concise include using phrases instead of

Danna Sandora

321 Birchwood Road
Arlington, VA 12345
(914) 277-4428
dsandora@email.com

January 12, 2006

Ms. Amelia Harris
Director of Personnel
Department of Social Services
City Hall
Webster Avenue
Richmond, VA 12347

Dear Ms. Harris:

I am writing in response to your advertisement in the *City Ledger* for a bus driver for the Wheels for the Disabled program.

I have experience as a van driver and a background in mechanics. I have had a driver's license for six years with no accidents or violations. I am also interested in services for people who are disabled. I had the opportunity to work with children with both mental and physical disabilities in a camp environment and found the job very rewarding. I am familiar with some of the limitations experienced by people who have disabilities and am aware of methods of assisting them.

I enclose my resume. I would be pleased to visit you at City Hall

Very truly yours,

Dana Sandora

Dana Sandora

Enclosure

KEVIN O'NEILL
15 ROBBINS LANE, CALIFON, NJ 07830
(908) 832-2761   •   koneill@email.com

November 5, 2006

Ms. Lynn Newman
Director of Personnel Services
Palmer International Airport
Route 207
Peekskill, NJ 07832

Dear Ms. Newman:

I am writing with regard to your advertisement in the *Airport Administration Bulletin* for an airport manager. I would like to apply for the position.

I have been working in airport administration for several years. My background also includes experience in public relations for local and long-distance bus transit systems. I am familiar with management of terminal buildings, safety regulations, personnel supervision, and financial management. I have also worked with many of the major airlines in planning and managing their use of terminal space.

I am presently employed at Westfield Airport, and I would like a position of greater responsibility, such as airport manager. I enclose my resume for your reference.

I can arrange to be available for an interview at your convenience. You can leave messages for me at my home telephone number. I look forward to hearing from you.

Very truly yours,

Kevin O'Neill

Kevin O'Neill

Enclosure

sentences and omitting unnecessary words. When appropriate, start a phrase with a verb, such as "maintained" or "coordinated." There is no need to say "I"—that is obvious and repetitive.

Present Yourself Well Employment counselors often recommend that resumes be no longer than one page because employers won't take the time to read a second page. If you've held many positions related to your occupation, go on to the second page, but don't include beginning or irrelevant jobs. If you have a lot of work experience, limit the education section to just the essentials.

You should also concentrate on the appearance of your resume. A traditional resume should be printed on a good grade of 8½" x 11" white paper. Consult a resume preparation guide for specific information about the best ways to format a resume that will be processed by e-mail or other electronic means. If you don't have access to a computer and printer, you can pay someone to type your resume, but it is up to you to read it carefully and ensure that it is error-free. Be sure that it is neatly typed with adequate margins. The data should be spaced and indented so that each item stands out. This enables a busy executive or personnel director to see at a glance the facts of greatest interest.

These suggestions for writing a resume are not hard-and-fast rules. Resumes may be adapted to special situations. For example, people with a variety of work experience often prepare several versions of their resumes and use the experience that's most relevant when applying for a particular job.

If this is your first resume, show it to someone else, perhaps a guidance counselor, for constructive advice. Make sure there are no spelling or punctuation mistakes anywhere on the page. No matter what, be truthful while emphasizing your assets. You can do that by showing the abilities, skills, and specific interests that qualify you for a particular job. Don't mention any weaknesses or deficiencies in your training. Do mention job-related aptitudes that showed up in previous employment or in school. Don't make things up; everything that's in your resume can, and often will, be checked.

Writing Cover Letters

Whenever you send your resume to a prospective employer, whether it's on paper or in e-mail form, you should send a cover letter with it. This is true whether you are writing to apply for a specific job or just to find out if there are any openings.

A good cover letter should be neat, brief, and well written, with no more than three or four short paragraphs. Since you may use your resume for a variety of job openings, your cover letter should be very specific. Your goal is to get the person who reads it to think that you are an ideal candidate for a particular job. If at all possible, send the letter to a specific person—either the personnel director or the person for whom you would be working. If necessary, call the company and ask to whom you should address the letter.

Start your letter by explaining why you are writing. Say that you are inquiring about possible job openings at the company, that you are responding to an advertisement in a particular publication, or that someone recommended that you should write. (Use the person's name if you have received permission to do so.) Let your letter lead into your resume. Use it to call attention to your qualifications. Add information that shows why you are well suited for that specific job.

Completing the Application Form

Many employers ask job applicants to fill out an application form. This form usually duplicates much of the information on your resume, but it may ask some additional questions. Give complete answers to all questions except those that are discriminatory. If a question doesn't apply to you, put a dash next to it.

You may be given the application form when you arrive for an interview, or it may be sent to your home. When filling it out, print neatly in ink. Follow the instructions carefully. For instance, if the form asks you to put down your last name first, do so.

The most important sections of an application form are the education and work histories. As in your resume, many applications request that you write these in reverse chronological order, with the most recent experience first. Unlike your resume, however, the application form may request information about your earnings on previous jobs. It may also ask what rate of pay you are seeking on the job you are applying for.

Be prepared to answer these and other topics not addressed on your resume. Look at the sample application form, and make note of the kinds of questions that you are likely to be asked—for example, your Social Security number, the names of previous supervisors, your salary, and your reason for leaving. If necessary, carry notes on such topics with you to an interview. You have a responsibility to tell prospective employers what they need to know to make an informed decision.

Neatness Counts Think before you write on an application form so you avoid crossing things out. An employer's opinion of you may be influenced just by the general appearance of your application form. A neat, detailed form may indicate an orderly

1 Always print neatly in blue or black ink. When completing an application at home, type it, if possible.

2 Read the application carefully *before* you start to fill it out. Follow instructions precisely. Use standard abbreviations.

3 If you aren't applying for a specific job, indicate the kind of work you're willing to do.

4 You don't have to commit to a specific rate of pay. Write "open" or "negotiable" if you are uncertain.

5 Traffic violations and so on do not belong here. Nor do offenses for which you were charged but not convicted.

6 If a question doesn't apply to you, write "NA" (for not applicable) or put a dash through the space.

7 Take notes along to remind you of school names, addresses, and dates.

8 If you're short on "real" employment, mention jobs such as babysitting, lawn mowing, or any occasional work.

9 Your references should be people who can be objective about you, such as former employers, teachers, and community leaders.

10 Under the heading "Reason for Leaving," a simple answer will do. Avoid saying "better pay"—even if it's so.

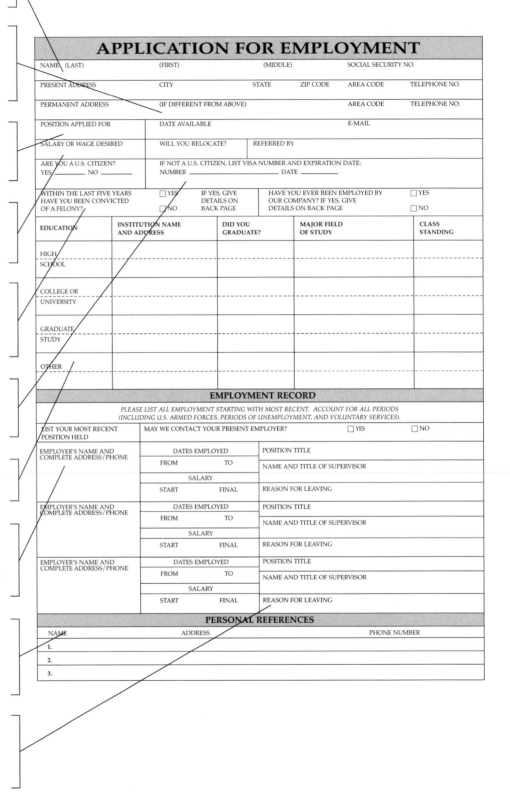

APPLICATION FOR EMPLOYMENT

| NAME (LAST) | (FIRST) | (MIDDLE) | SOCIAL SECURITY NO. |

| PRESENT ADDRESS | CITY | STATE | ZIP CODE | AREA CODE | TELEPHONE NO. |

| PERMANENT ADDRESS | (IF DIFFERENT FROM ABOVE) | AREA CODE | TELEPHONE NO. |

| POSITION APPLIED FOR | DATE AVAILABLE | E-MAIL |

| SALARY OR WAGE DESIRED | WILL YOU RELOCATE? | REFERRED BY |

| ARE YOU A U.S. CITIZEN? YES _____ NO _____ | IF NOT A U.S. CITIZEN, LIST VISA NUMBER AND EXPIRATION DATE: NUMBER _____ DATE _____ |

| WITHIN THE LAST FIVE YEARS HAVE YOU BEEN CONVICTED OF A FELONY? | ☐ YES ☐ NO | IF YES, GIVE DETAILS ON BACK PAGE | HAVE YOU EVER BEEN EMPLOYED BY OUR COMPANY? IF YES, GIVE DETAILS ON BACK PAGE | ☐ YES ☐ NO |

EDUCATION	INSTITUTION NAME AND ADDRESS	DID YOU GRADUATE?	MAJOR FIELD OF STUDY	CLASS STANDING
HIGH SCHOOL				
COLLEGE OR UNIVERSITY				
GRADUATE STUDY				
OTHER				

EMPLOYMENT RECORD

PLEASE LIST ALL EMPLOYMENT STARTING WITH MOST RECENT. ACCOUNT FOR ALL PERIODS (INCLUDING U.S. ARMED FORCES, PERIODS OF UNEMPLOYMENT, AND VOLUNTARY SERVICES).

| LIST YOUR MOST RECENT POSITION HELD | MAY WE CONTACT YOUR PRESENT EMPLOYER? ☐ YES ☐ NO |

EMPLOYER'S NAME AND COMPLETE ADDRESS / PHONE	DATES EMPLOYED		POSITION TITLE
	FROM	TO	NAME AND TITLE OF SUPERVISOR
	SALARY		
	START	FINAL	REASON FOR LEAVING
EMPLOYER'S NAME AND COMPLETE ADDRESS / PHONE	DATES EMPLOYED		POSITION TITLE
	FROM	TO	NAME AND TITLE OF SUPERVISOR
	SALARY		
	START	FINAL	REASON FOR LEAVING
EMPLOYER'S NAME AND COMPLETE ADDRESS / PHONE	DATES EMPLOYED		POSITION TITLE
	FROM	TO	NAME AND TITLE OF SUPERVISOR
	SALARY		
	START	FINAL	REASON FOR LEAVING

PERSONAL REFERENCES

NAME	ADDRESS	PHONE NUMBER
1.		
2.		
3.		

mind and the ability to think clearly, follow instructions, and organize information.

Know Your Rights Under federal and some state laws, an employer cannot demand that you answer any questions about race, color, creed, national origin, ancestry, sex, marital status, age (with certain exceptions), number of dependents, property, car ownership (unless needed for the job), or arrest record. Refer to the information on job discrimination in this essay for more information about your rights.

PRESENTING YOURSELF IN AN INTERVIEW

If your qualifications, as presented in your resume, cover letter, and application, are a strong match for the requirements of the job, you may be invited to a job interview. On the basis of this meeting, the prospective employer will decide whether or not to hire you, and you will decide whether or not you want the job.

Prepare in Advance

Before an interview, there are a number of things you can do to prepare. Begin by giving thought to why you want the job and what you have to offer. Then review your resume and any lists you made when you were evaluating yourself so that you can keep your qualifications firmly in mind.

Learn as much as you can about the organization. Check with friends who work there, read company brochures, search the Internet, or devise other information-gathering strategies. Showing that you know something about the company and what it does will indicate your interest and demonstrate that you are a well-informed job candidate.

Try to anticipate some of the questions an interviewer may ask and think about how you would answer. For example, you may be asked: Will you work overtime when necessary? Are you ready to go to night school to improve some of your skills? Preparing answers in advance will make the process easier for you. It is also wise to prepare any questions you may have about the company or the position for which you are applying. The more information you have, the better you can evaluate both the company and the job.

Employers may want you to demonstrate specific skills for some jobs. An applicant for a job in a lumber mill or a mine, for example, might be required to demonstrate mechanical ability. Prospective technicians might be expected to demonstrate mathematical skills.

On the appointed day, dress neatly and in a style appropriate for the job you're seeking. When in doubt, it's safer to dress on the conservative side, wearing a shirt and tie rather than a turtleneck or wearing a dress or sblouse and skirt rather than pants and a T-shirt. Be on time. Find out in advance exactly where the company is located and how to get there. Allow extra time in case you get lost, get caught in a traffic jam, can't find a parking spot, or encounter another type of delay.

Maintain a Balance

When your appointment begins, remember that a good interview is largely a matter of balance. Don't undersell yourself by sitting back silently, but don't oversell yourself by talking nonstop about how wonderful you are. Answer all questions directly and simply, and let the interviewer take the lead.

Instead of saying, "I'm reliable and hardworking," give the interviewer an example. Allow the interviewer to draw conclusions from your example.

It's natural to be nervous before and during a job interview. However, you need to try to relax and be yourself. You may even enjoy the conversation. Your chances of being hired and being happy if you get the job are better if the employer likes you as you are.

Avoid discussing money until the employer brings it up or until you are offered the job. Employers usually know in advance what they are willing to pay. If you are the one to begin a discussion about the salary you want, you may set an amount that's either too low or too high.

Be prepared to ask questions, but don't force them on your interviewer. Part of the purpose of the interview is for you to evaluate the company while you are being evaluated. For instance, you might want to ask about the company's training programs and its policy on promotions.

Don't stay too long. Most business people have busy schedules. It is likely that the interviewer will let you know when it's time for the interview to end.

Don't expect a definite answer at the first interview. Employers usually thank you for coming and say that you will be notified shortly. Most employers want to interview all the applicants before they make a hiring decision. If the position is offered at the time of the interview, you can ask for a little time to think about it. If the interviewer tells you that you are not suitable for the job, try to be polite. Say, "I'm sorry, but thank you for taking the time to meet with me." After all, the company may have the right job for you next week.

Follow Up after the Interview

If the job sounds interesting and you would like to be considered for it, say so as you leave. Follow up after the interview by writing a brief thank-you note to the employer. Express your continued interest in the position and thank the interviewer for taking the time to meet with you.

It's a good idea to make some notes and evaluations of the interview while it is still fresh in your mind. Write down the important facts about the job—the duties, salary, promotion prospects, and so on, which will help make a decision should you be offered the job. Also evaluate your own performance in the interview. List the things you wish you had said and things you wish you had not said, which will help you prepare for future interviews.

Finally, don't hesitate to contact your interviewer if you haven't heard from the company after a week or two (unless you were told it would be longer). Write a brief note or make a phone call in which you ask when a decision might be reached. Making such an effort will show the employer that you are genuinely interested in the job. Your call will remind the interviewer about you and could work to your advantage.

TAKE CHARGE

Job hunting is primarily a matter of organizing a well-planned campaign. Scan the classified ads, search through online job banks, watch for trends in local industry that might be reported in the news, and check with people you know in the field. Take the initiative. Send out carefully crafted resumes and letters. Respond to ads. Finally, in an interview, state your qualifications and experience in a straightforward and confident manner.

TRADE AND PROFESSIONAL JOURNALS

The following is a list of some of the major journals in the fields of transportation. These journals can keep you up to date with what is happening in your field of interest and can lead you to jobs through their classified advertising sections.

Automotive, Bus, and Truck Transportation

Automotive News, 1155 Gratiot Avenue, Detroit, MI 48207-2997.
   http://www.autonews.com
Car and Driver, 2002 Hogback Road, Ann Arbor, MI 48105.
   http://www.caranddriver.com

Heavy Duty Trucking, 38 Executive Park, Suite 300, Irvine, CA 92614.
   http://www.heavydutytrucking.com
Motor Trend, 260 Madison Avenue, 8th Floor, New York, NY 10016.
   http://www.motortrend.com
Truckin', 2400 E. Katella Boulevard, Suite 700, Anaheim, CA 92806.
   http://www.truckinweb.com

Aviation and Air Transportation

AOPA Pilot, 421 Aviation Way, Frederick, MD 21701.
   http://www.aopa.org/pilot
Aviation Mechanics Bulletin, 601 Madison Street, Suite 300, Alexandria, VA 22314-1756.
   http://www.flightsafety.org/amb_home.html
Aviation Week and Space Technology, 1200 G Street, Suite 922, Washington, DC 20005.
   http://www.aviationnow.com
Business and Commercial Aviation, 1200 G Street, Suite 922, Washington, DC 20005.
   http://www.aviationweek.com/bca
Flying, 1633 Broadway, 45th Floor, New York, NY 10019.
   http://www.flyingmag.com

Marine Transportation

American Shipper, 61 Broadway, Suite 1603, New York, NY 10006.
   http://www.americanshipper.com

Railroading

Railway Age, 345 Hudson Street, 12th Floor, New York, NY 10014.
   http://www.railwayage.com
Trains, 21027 Crossroads Circle, P.O. Box 1612, Waukesha, WI 53187-1612.
   http://www.trains.com

Transportation Engineering and Management

ITE Journal, 1099 14th Street NW, Suite 300 West, Washington, DC 20005-3438.
   http://www.ite.org/itejournal/index.asp
Mass Transit, 1233 Janeville Avenue, Fort Atkinson, WI 53538.
   http://www.masstransitmag.com
Sea Technology, 1501 Wilson Boulevard, Suite 1001, Arlington, VA 22209.
   http://www.sea-technology.com
Traffic World, 1270 National Press Building, Washington, DC 20045.
   http://www.trafficworld.com

Airline Baggage and Freight Handler

Definition and Nature of the Work

Airline baggage and freight handlers take care of the freight and luggage that passes through airports. Freight handlers must sometimes weigh the freight and prepare the shipping orders before the freight is put on the plane. Baggage handlers take luggage off planes that have landed and put baggage on planes that are about to take off.

To unload luggage, the handlers set up a conveyor belt that leads from the cargo hold of the plane to a baggage trailer. One of the handlers climbs into the plane and sorts out the baggage. Each piece of luggage has been tagged to show where it is going, so the handler can tell quickly which pieces of luggage should be sent down the conveyor to the trailer and which pieces should stay on the plane until it reaches the next airport.

The baggage trailers, which are attached to a jeep, are driven to the air terminal, where the baggage is placed on another conveyor belt that carries the luggage inside the terminal. In the meantime, handlers are busy putting new baggage onto the plane.

Luggage is not handled piece by piece on every plane, however. On larger planes both the baggage and the freight are loaded into huge containers. Each container holds baggage or freight that is going to the same destination. Handlers use machines to move the heavy containers.

Education and Training Requirements

Most employers prefer to hire applicants with high school diplomas or the equivalent. Very little training is necessary to become airline baggage and

Education and Training
High school

Salary
Median—$21,570 per year

Employment Outlook
Good

Airline baggage and freight handlers take luggage off planes and deliver it to the terminal using special jeeps that tow long strings of trailers. (© Robert Maass/Corbis.)

freight handlers. Beginning workers learn on the job from experienced workers and supervisors.

Getting the Job

Job seekers can apply directly to the employment offices of the airlines. Applications are usually accepted in person, online, or by mail. Airline Web sites and the Air Transport Association of America can provide information about application procedures.

Advancement Possibilities and Employment Outlook

Baggage and freight handlers may advance to some airline managerial jobs. Additional education may be needed to advance in this field.

Employment of baggage and freight handlers is expected to increase about as fast as the average for all occupations through 2014. Turnover in this field is relatively high. However, jobs in the airline industry are affected by the general state of the economy. Airlines may lay off workers during economic recessions.

Working Conditions

Because airplanes arrive and depart around the clock, baggage handlers work in shifts. Night, weekend, and holiday work may be necessary. Handlers must be agile and strong, because transfer of luggage must be made quickly and some bags are heavy. Handlers work outdoors in all kinds of weather.

Earnings and Benefits

Salaries vary depending on the level of experience. In 2004 the median salary for all baggage handlers was $21,570 per year. Supervisors earned an average salary of $27,880 per year.

Benefits include medical insurance and paid vacations and holidays. Some handlers earn retirement benefits as well. Many airline baggage and freight handlers belong to labor unions.

Where to Go for More Information

Air Transport Association of America
1301 Pennsylvania Ave. NW, Ste. 1100
Washington, DC 20004-1707
(202) 626-4000
http://www.air-transport.org

Transport Workers Union of America
1700 Broadway
New York, NY 10019
(212) 259-4900
http://www.twu.org

Airline Reservations Agent

Education and Training
High school

Salary
Median—$27,750 per year

Employment Outlook
Poor

Definition and Nature of the Work

Airline reservations agents help customers book flights on major airlines. When customers call to make reservations, agents enter the destination and desired date and time into the airline's computer system. It locates available flights and the best connections if more than one flight is necessary. It also determines the cost of the flights. Agents relay this information to customers and help them find the right itinerary for their needs. When the customers have chosen flights, the agents book the reservations. They take the customers' names, telephone numbers, and credit card information. Agents also apply any discounts or upgrades for which the customers may be eligible and help them choose seats and types of meals (if available). They also provide information about airport security and baggage requirements. Sometimes they provide information about hotels and rental cars.

Using the same technology, reservations agents can cancel or change reservations when customers request it. They also answer telephone inquiries about arrival and departure times and flight schedules.

Education and Training Requirements

Applicants for reservations positions must have high school diplomas or the equivalent. A growing number of employers prefer to hire applicants who have attended college. Prior office experience is helpful. Typing skills are necessary. Some airlines require knowledge of foreign languages.

Airlines provide four-week training courses that cover Federal Aviation Administration guidelines and regulations, customer service procedures, and technological issues.

Getting the Job

The Web sites of the major airlines list any job openings and provide information about application procedures. Usually, job seekers can apply directly to personnel departments. The Air Transport Association of America, school placement offices, Internet job sites, and newspaper classified ads can provide employment leads as well.

Advancement Possibilities and Employment Outlook

Airline reservations agents frequently become senior airline agents or traffic or sales representatives. Some become flight attendants. Additional education, including college degrees, may be necessary for advancement to some senior jobs.

Employment of reservations agents is expected to grow more slowly than the average for all occupations through 2014. The need for new agents is declining as more and more consumers make reservations, purchase tickets, and check in for their flights on the Internet. Most openings occur when experienced reservations agents retire or leave the field.

Working Conditions

Most of their work is limited to telephone conversations, so reservations agents have little personal contact with passengers. Agents usually work forty-hour weeks, which may include night and weekend shifts. They usually work in large offices.

Earnings and Benefits

In 2004 the median salary for all airline reservation agents was $27,750 per year. The most experienced agents earned $45,100 per year.

Benefits include two- to three-week paid vacations, paid holidays, sick leave, health insurance, and retirement plans. Agents and their immediate families may be eligible for reduced airline fares. Many reservations agents belong to labor unions.

Where to Go for More Information

Air Transport Association of America
1301 Pennsylvania Ave. NW, Ste. 1100
Washington, DC 20004-1704
(202) 626-4000
http://www.air-transport.org

Airline Ticket Agent

Definition and Nature of the Work

Airline ticket agents sell tickets at airports or downtown ticket offices. They also assign seats for passengers and rebook passengers who miss their flights. They often answer questions about airline schedules, fares, hotels, and taxis.

Agents also handle passengers' luggage. First they weigh it to make sure it falls within airline guidelines and then attach tags that indicate where the bags should be taken off the plane.

At airport gates they announce flight departures and board passengers. It is their job to ensure that flight attendants have the equipment they need.

Education and Training Requirements

Ticket agents generally must be high school graduates. Some college education is preferred. Previous experience dealing with the public is useful.

Most airlines provide some form of training program; in many cases it consists of a week of classroom instruction followed by a week of on-the-job training with an experienced ticket agent. Beginners usually start by tagging the luggage of ticketed passengers. They then gain experience reserving seats on flights, filling out ticket forms, and handling assignments at the gate.

Getting the Job

Job seekers can apply directly, in person or by mail, to the personnel office at any airline. The Air Transport Association of America provides a list of the addresses of major airlines on request. School placement offices, newspaper classified ads, and Internet job sites may provide employment leads.

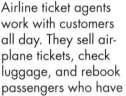

Airline ticket agents work with customers all day. They sell airplane tickets, check luggage, and rebook passengers who have missed their flights. (© Reuters/Corbis.)

Advancement Possibilities and Employment Outlook

With experience ticket agents may become supervisors. Some ticket agents advance into jobs as traffic or sales representatives for the airline. Others become flight attendants.

The employment of airline ticket agents is expected to increase more slowly than the average for all occupations through 2014. Despite anticipated growth in the number of airline passengers, automated ticketing and check-in procedures may reduce the demand for ticket agents. The airline industry is sensitive to fluctuations in the economy, so agents frequently are laid off during recessions.

Working Conditions

Ticket agents are in constant contact with people and often have to solve their travel problems quickly, which may result in stressful situations. Because they act as representatives of the airlines, they are required to be well groomed, friendly, and patient. Ticket agents work forty-hour weeks, usually in shifts that include nights, weekends, and holidays.

Earnings and Benefits

In 2004 the median salary of airline ticket agents was $28,420 per year.

Benefits include vacation, sick leave, health insurance, paid holidays, and retirement plans. Some airlines offer reduced air fares for agents and their families.

Where to Go for More Information

Air Transport Association of America
1301 Pennsylvania Ave. NW, Ste. 1100
Washington, DC 20004-1704
(202) 626-4000
http://www.air-transport.org

Airport Utility Worker

Definition and Nature of the Work

Airport utility workers are usually outdoors in all kinds of weather. They may direct incoming and outgoing aircraft near the terminal, using hand or light signals. When the aircraft is stationary, they operate the service vehicles that fill the fuel and water tanks. They add cooling-system and hydraulic fluids and check tires for specified air pressure. They also replace waste system chemicals and remove liquid waste. During the winter they remove ice and prevent ice buildup on the wings of aircraft by applying deicing chemicals.

In preparation for each flight, they clean the inside of the aircraft and make sure that lavatories and other equipment are functioning and stocked with supplies. They use portable platforms, ladders, and water brushes to clean the outside of the planes.

Some airlines have airport utility workers unload and load luggage and cargo from aircraft.

Education and Training
High school

Salary
Median—$21,570 per year

Employment Outlook
Fair

Education and Training Requirements

Applicants generally need high school diplomas or the equivalent. Workers receive on-the-job training, and most jobs can be learned quickly.

Getting the Job

Job seekers can apply directly to the personnel offices of the airlines. Their addresses can be obtained from the airlines' Web sites or from the Air Transport Association of America. Newspaper classified ads and Internet employment sites may list job openings.

Advancement Possibilities and Employment Outlook

With experience some airport utility workers move into supervisory positions. With additional training they can become mechanics or cargo service managers.

The employment outlook for airport utility workers is fair through 2014. The demand for air transportation is expected to grow, and additional planes may require more utility workers. Turnover is high. However, at most airlines more people apply for jobs as utility workers than there are positions to be filled.

Airport utility workers check an aircraft's tires for specified air pressure, fill the fuel and water tanks, and clean the aircraft. (© Reuters/Corbis.)

Working Conditions

Utility workers are scheduled in shifts, including night, weekend, and holiday hours. They generally work forty hours per week. They must take precautions against noise from jet engines and spills of aviation fuels and chemicals used in the deicing and cleaning of the airplanes.

Earnings and Benefits

In 2004 the median salary for airport utility workers was $21,570 per year.

Benefits include paid holidays and vacations, health insurance, and retirement plans. Airlines may allow employees and their families to fly free or at reduced fares. Some airport utility workers are members of unions.

Where to Go for More Information

Air Transport Association of America
1301 Pennsylvania Ave. NW, Ste. 1100
Washington, DC 20004-1704
(202) 626-4000
http://www.air-transport.org

Transport Workers Union of America
1700 Broadway
New York, NY 10019
(212) 259-4900
http://www.twu.org

Auto Body Repairer

Education and Training
High school

Salary
Median—$16.68 per hour

Employment Outlook
Good

Definition and Nature of the Work

Auto body repairers are skilled workers who fix cars and trucks that have been in collisions. Most of them work for auto body shops, car and truck dealers, and manufacturers. Others work for trucking companies or bus lines, where they repair trucks, truck trailers, or buses.

The repairers' supervisors decide which parts are to be replaced and which are to be repaired. They also estimate the cost of labor. When customers or insurance companies accept the estimates, the repairers begin their work.

Sections of the automobile that have been badly damaged are removed and replaced. If the frame has been bent, it is straightened with special machines.

Large dents are pushed out with prying bars. Repairers smooth small dents by holding a flat piece of iron, called an anvil, on one side of the damaged part while hammering on the other side. Small dents are sometimes filled with putty or solder, which is allowed to harden and then sanded smooth. In small shops, auto body repairers also paint repaired sections of cars and trucks. In large shops, this is done by auto body painters.

While the shop supplies the power tools and other large machines, repairers must buy their own hand tools, which can cost up to five hundred dollars. Trainees often purchase their tools gradually as they gain experience.

Education and Training Requirements

Employers prefer to hire auto body repairers who have completed high school, although this is not always a requirement. High school courses in auto body repair can be useful. Many vocational and trade schools also offer courses in auto body repair. Trainees must have driver's licenses.

Many auto body repairers learn their trade on the job, which takes three or four years. They begin as helpers, removing damaged parts and replacing them with new or repaired parts. They progress to more difficult jobs. The best way to learn the trade is in formal apprenticeship programs, although few of these are available.

Many auto body repairers learn their trade on the job. It usually takes three or four years to become an experienced repairer. (© G. Boutin/ zefa/Corbis.)

Repairers who work for auto manufacturers and dealers take formal training courses that last at least five days. During this training, experts demonstrate how to use tools; replace or repair damaged parts; and estimate the cost of repairs.

Voluntary certification is available through the National Institute for Automotive Service Excellence. To become certified, repairers must pass exams and have at least two years of experience in the field.

Getting the Job

The best way to enter this field is to apply for trainee jobs at auto body shops. Large auto dealers and auto manufacturers may have openings as well. Newspaper classified ads may offer job leads.

Advancement Possibilities and Employment Outlook

Auto body repairers can be promoted to supervisors of their shops. Many open their own shops if they can raise the capital. Nearly one out of four auto body repairers is self-employed.

Employment of auto body repairers is expected to grow as fast as the average for all occupations through 2014. While lightweight cars are both popular and vulnerable to more collision damage than older, heavier designs, technological innovations have reduced the likelihood of traffic accidents. In addition, improved equipment and specialization of labor have led to increased productivity in auto body shops, so fewer repairers may be needed in the future.

Working Conditions

Repairers must be able to work independently, without supervision. In some shops they have helpers. Repairers work between forty and forty-eight hours per week.

Auto body repair shops are often dirty and noisy. Repairers often have to work in cramped positions and lift heavy objects. They may get cuts from sharp metal edges, burns from torches, and injuries from power tools.

Earnings and Benefits

In 2004 the median wage, including incentives, for auto body repairers was $16.68 per hour. The most experienced workers earned more than $28.45 per hour. Helpers and trainees earned from thirty to sixty percent of the wage of experienced repairers.

Under incentive plans, which cover most workers in independent auto repair shops and car dealerships, repairers are paid a certain amount for each task. Their total earnings depend on how many tasks they are assigned and how quickly they complete the tasks. Repairers who work for trucking companies and other firms that have their own vehicles are usually paid by the hour. Wages of those who belong to unions are based on union scales.

Auto body repairers who are employed by companies get holiday and vacation pay and insurance benefits. Some are covered by retirement plans. Self-employed repairers have to arrange their own insurance and retirement plans.

Where to Go for More Information

Automotive Aftermarket Industry
  Association
7101 Wisconsin Ave., Ste. 1300
Bethesda, MD 20814-3415
(301) 654-6664
http://www.aftermarket.org

Automotive Service Association
PO Box 929
Bedford, TX 76095-0929
(800) 272-7467
http://www.asashop.org

National Institute for Automotive Service
  Excellence
101 Blue Seal Dr. SE, Ste. 101
Leesburg, VA 20175
(703) 669-6600
http://www.asecert.org

Bicycle Mechanic

Education and Training
None

Salary
Median—$9.76 per hour

Employment Outlook
Good

Definition and Nature of the Work

Because bicycling is popular as a form of exercise and recreation as well as a means of transportation, specialized mechanics are in demand. They usually work for bicycle shops or for the bicycle departments of large sporting goods or department stores.

After determining what repairs or services are needed, mechanics give estimates and order any parts that are not kept in stock. They may have to adjust the frames or replace or repair major parts such as wheels or brakes. They also upgrade bicycles by adding special tires or pedals or customize bikes to fit their riders.

Mechanics also provide basic maintenance, such as cleaning, lubricating, and adjusting chains and hub bearings. In some shops, mechanics teach bike owners to do basic maintenance themselves.

Some mechanics specialize in racing bicycles. They are usually employed by large bicycle shops or by racing teams.

Education and Training Requirements

No formal training is required, but good mechanical and communication skills are necessary. On-the-job training is usually provided, and some manufacturers offer free repair courses for employees of stores that carry their products. Some vocational schools and high school shop classes teach bicycle repair.

Getting the Job

Job seekers can apply directly to bicycle shops or to the bicycle departments of large stores. Many repairers contact the bike shops they patronize.

Advancement Possibilities and Employment Outlook

Bicycle mechanics may become sales representatives for manufacturers. They may also be promoted to shop or department managers, or they may open their own shops.

The demand for bicycle mechanics is expected to grow as fast as the average for all occupations through 2014.

Working Conditions

Mechanics generally work in rooms set aside at the back of bicycle shops. They use a variety of spare parts and tools such as air hoses and racks for mounting bicycles. They may use electronic monitoring equipment to make adjustments.

The demand for mechanics is often seasonal. Many mechanics work part time or only on weekends when their services are most in demand.

Earnings and Benefits

Earnings vary by location, but in 2004 the median wage for all bicycle mechanics was $9.76 per hour.

Benefits for mechanics who work for department stores and bicycle companies include paid holidays and vacations, medical insurance, and retirement plans.

Where to Go for More Information

National Bicycle Dealers Association
777 W. Nineteenth St., Ste. O
Costa Mesa, CA 92627-6130
(949) 722-6909
http://www.nbda.com

Bridge and Lock Tender

Definition and Nature of the Work

Bridge and lock tenders operate bridges and canal locks to permit vessels to pass through inland waterways and dangerous areas near shore. They also monitor and inspect canal and bridge equipment for defects, make minor repairs or adjustments, and report any factors that would inhibit the safety and efficiency of such equipment.

Stationed in small booths on bridges or near canal locks, a bridge and lock tender must vigilantly watch for approaching vessels that require passage. Once a whistle is blown to indicate a vessel needs to pass, the tender operates the machinery that opens and closes railroad or highway drawbridges; horizontally or vertically adjustable bridges; or canal locks and dams. Tenders can also receive

Education and Training
High school plus on-the-job training

Salary
Median—$37,050 per year

Employment Outlook
Poor

requests for clearance by radio. If necessary, they direct the movements of vessels using signals, telecommunication equipment, or loudspeakers.

As the vessel moves through the lock or across the bridge, the tender logs the name, type, and destination of the ship or train. In case of accident, the tender must fill out the necessary accident reports and make minor repairs if the equipment is damaged.

Tenders work for state or local governments or for private companies that are hired to operate and maintain bridges or canal locks.

Education and Training Requirements

Bridge and lock tenders must be at least eighteen years old, pass hearing tests, and must not be color-blind. They must also pass physical examinations, because some work may be strenuous. High school diplomas or the equivalent are usually required.

Some states have published guidelines on training, which include classroom instruction on safety procedures, Coast Guard regulations, state statutes related to bridges and railroads, and company or governmental policies. Applicants are required to pass written tests and participate in on-the-job training under the supervision of experienced supervisors.

Getting the Job

State or local employment offices should have information about job opportunities. Job seekers can also apply directly to private companies that are under contract to operate bridges and locks.

Advancement Possibilities and Employment Outlook

Bridge and lock tenders may advance to supervisory positions. Tenders can also move from one structure to another.

Employment growth for bridge and lock tenders is expected to be slower than the average for all occupations through 2014. Some of the work is now automated, so fewer workers are needed.

Where to Go for More Information

American Association of State Highway
and Transportation Officials
444 N. Capitol St. NW, Ste. 249
Washington, DC 20001
(202) 624-5800
http://www.aashto.org

International Bridge, Tunnel, and Turnpike
Association
1146 Nineteenth St. NW, Ste. 800
Washington, DC 20036-3725
(202) 659-4620
http://www.ibtta.org

Working Conditions

Bridge and lock tenders work eight-hour shifts, including nights, weekends, and holidays. Depending on their employers, they work thirty-two to forty hours per week.

Most tenders are attracted to the isolation that the job provides. It can be stressful when traffic is heavy—tenders are responsible for the safety of people and large boats and railroads. The job may involve climbing and other strenuous activities.

Earnings and Benefits

In 2004 the median salary for bridge and lock tenders was $37,050 per year. Benefits usually included health insurance and paid vacation and sick days.

Car Wash Worker

Definition and Nature of the Work

Although it takes a manager and at least two other workers to keep a car wash in operation, most companies have eight employees besides the manager. In large, busy car washes there may be even more. Because car washes specialize in fast service, workers must be willing to work quickly and steadily. Teamwork is important.

Workers see that cars are driven onto the washing-machine tracks properly and ensure that washing proceeds without problems. Some workers dry and polish the cars, while others vacuum the rugs and upholstery. Many car washes have cashiers who collect money from customers inside the car wash office; to speed service, workers at some businesses collect the money right at the car window before customers drive their cars into the washing machines. Most car washes also offer car waxing, and some sell gas.

Managers are responsible for hiring and supervising workers, buying supplies, and seeing that safety standards are met. Some managers maintain and fix their own car washing machines; others depend on outside mechanics. Broken machines can shut down their operations, so quick repairs are essential.

Education and Training Requirements

While most managers have no educational requirements for their workers, many prefer to hire high school graduates. Beginning workers are usually trained on the job.

Managers must have high school diplomas, plus business experience or business school training. Mechanical skill is also valuable.

A worker at an automated car wash adjust the tracks that carry the car into the washing machine, while a coworker prepares to vacuum the inside of the car. (© Martha Tabor/ Working Images Photographs. Reproduced by permission.)

Getting the Job

Job seekers can apply directly to local car wash managers. High school students may be able to get part-time jobs. Experienced workers who want to become managers can apply for cashier or assistant manager positions.

Advancement Possibilities and Employment Outlook

Car wash workers can become cashiers, assistant managers, or managers. Some workers become owners of one or more car washes.

Employment growth for car wash workers is expected to be as good as the average for all occupations through 2014. Openings regularly occur when workers become managers or leave the field. Turnover in the field is high.

Working Conditions

Weather is an important factor in the car wash business. On rainy days business may be slow. In clear weather workers may have busy, hectic days. Workers who polish and vacuum cars may be exposed to hot summer sun and winter weather. The work can be tedious.

Most employees work eight-hour days, sometimes in rotating shifts. Evening, weekend, and holiday work may be required.

Managers spend part of their time outside directing their workers, but they also perform office duties such as paying bills and interviewing job applicants. Their responsibilities may require more than eight hours each day.

Where to Go for More Information

International Carwash Association
401 N. Michigan Ave.
Chicago, IL 60611
(800) 422-8422
http://www.carwash.org

Earnings and Benefits

Earnings vary, depending on location. In 2004 the median wage for all car wash workers was $8.41 per hour. Managers earned significantly more, depending on the size of the operation and their specific duties.

Benefits vary greatly. Some employees receive health insurance after they have worked at the same car wash for more than one year.

Dockworker

Education and Training
None

Salary
Median—$9.67 per hour

Employment Outlook
Poor

Definition and Nature of the Work

Dockworkers operate machines that lift and move cargo on and off ships. Working in teams called gangs, they sometimes have to lift pieces of cargo by hand. However, more than ninety percent of all cargo is transported in containers that fit on trucks or railroad cars. Dockworkers are also called longshoremen.

Stevedoring companies, which contract to load and unload ships, hire dockworkers. The companies are either independent businesses that provide a service or divisions of large shipping companies. Both the safety of the cargo and the safety of the workers are the responsibility of these operations.

Dockworkers have several different tasks. Checkers inspect the cargo containers, noting any damage or unlocked containers, and handle shipping and receiving documents. This information is keyed into computer databases, which allow shipments to be tracked efficiently. Winch operators run the crane-like machines that move cargo between the ships and the dock. The winches have huge pincers that grab loose cargo or the sling—a heavy-duty net—used to hold it. Special mechanisms allow the winches to lift containers easily and quickly. Other dockworkers secure the slings around cargo so it can be lifted. Gear repairers keep all the equipment in working order.

Once the ships' cargo has been unloaded, dockworkers hand it over to truck drivers at what is called "the point of rest." It then becomes the truckers' responsibility.

Education and Training Requirements

There are no educational requirements for the job, but it does require agility, physical strength, and endurance. Good eyesight and hearing are important. Workers must be able to follow orders and to think quickly. Experienced workers train beginners to handle dockworkers' hooks, use rope and cable riggings, and stack cargo and containers.

Getting the Job

The procedure for becoming dockworkers varies according to port custom. Registration with the local union office or with privately owned stevedoring firms is the most common method. More than ninety-five percent of the nation's dockworkers are hired under union agreement. The International Longshoremen's Association is the major union, representing dockworkers at thirty-five ports.

Dockworkers unload cargo from ships using machines as well as their hands. (Copyright © 2003, Kelly A. Quin. Reproduced by permission.)

In the Gulf Coast and Great Lakes areas, workers are hired for daily work at a shape-up, a meeting place where all those desiring work gather at a specified time. The hiring supervisors, representing various contracting companies, select as many gangs as they need for the day's jobs. The main disadvantage of this system is that workers must go to the dock every day and spend time waiting without any guarantee of work.

Most other areas use a hiring hall system. Dockworkers register their availability at the hall. Each stevedoring company calls the hiring hall the night before ships are to be loaded or unloaded. The hall notifies the gang bosses by telephone. The bosses contact the gang members, who meet the next morning at the job sites. In some places, this system has been replaced by a computerized telephone system.

Advancement Possibilities and Employment Outlook

Advancement is slow and limited to the range of jobs on the dock. Occasionally, dockworkers start their own stevedoring companies or become pier superintendents.

The employment outlook varies by region. The Great Lakes area, for example, needs trained workers because its stevedoring industry is expanding. In other places automated loading procedures have reduced job opportunities. Los Angeles/Long Beach, New Orleans, and New York, the nation's busiest ports, employ the most dockworkers. Most openings occur as experienced workers retire or leave the field.

Working Conditions

When union members are called to jobs, they must work quickly and for long hours until the ships are loaded or unloaded. The work can be hazardous and continues regardless of the weather.

Earnings and Benefits

Earnings vary by region. In 2004 the median wage of all dockworkers was $9.67 per hour. Experienced workers on the East Coast earned more than $30,000 per year. Workers on the West Coast earned even more.

Longshoremen receive premium pay for overtime, holiday, and night work and for handling dangerous cargo such as explosives. Benefits include pensions, paid vacations, and medical insurance.

Where to Go for More Information

International Longshoremen's Association, AFL-CIO, CLC
17 Battery Pl., Ste. 930
New York, NY 10004
(212) 425-1200
http://www.ilaunion.org

International Longshore and Warehouse Union, AFL-CIO
1188 Franklin St., 4th Fl.
San Francisco, CA 94109
(415) 775-0533
http://www.ilwu.org

Gas Station Cashier

Education and Training
None

Salary
Median—$7.54 per hour

Employment Outlook
Good

Definition and Nature of the Work

Gas station cashiers process gas and product purchases. They also provide information and give directions to travelers.

Some cashiers work in small gas stations with only a few gas pumps; most work in larger stations that include convenience stores, which sell snacks, beverages, and car and travel accessories such as maps and window washing fluid. Many transactions require the handling of cash and making change, but the widespread use of credit cards has made the job easier and faster. Cashiers usually use cash registers and bar-code scanning devices.

In some establishments, cashiers control the gas pumps electronically. They may also monitor air pumps, vacuum cleaners, and automated car washing equipment.

Education and Training Requirements

While most employers prefer to hire high school graduates, the job has no formal educational requirements. Courses in math, accounting, and computers can be helpful. Because contact with the public is constant, applicants must enjoy working with people and be courteous and patient.

No work experience is necessary. New hires are trained on the job under the supervision of experienced employees. Training usually lasts only a few days.

Getting the Job

Job seekers can apply directly to gas station managers. Newspaper classified ads and Internet job sites may list opportunities in this field.

Advancement Possibilities and Employment Outlook

Gas station cashiers may advance to head cashier or be offered full-time work if they have part-time positions.

The employment outlook for gas station cashiers is good through 2014, especially for young workers who are willing to work part time. Turnover is high, so new workers are often needed to fill positions of workers who have taken other jobs.

Working Conditions

Cashiers can work part time or full time. Night, weekend, and holidays hours may be required.

Almost all cashiers work indoors, sometimes behind protective windows. While robberies occur, most gas stations have safety equipment and procedures to protect their employees. Work may be repetitive and may be include long periods of inactivity, especially late at night.

Earnings and Benefits

In 2004 the median salary of gas station cashiers was $7.54 per hour. Some full-time employees received benefits, such as health insurance.

Where to Go for More Information

Service Station Dealers of America/National Coalition of Petroleum Retailers and Allied Trades
1532 Pointer Ridge Pl., Ste. E
Bowie, MD 20716
(301) 390-4405
http://www.ssda-at.org

Industrial Truck Operator

Definition and Nature of the Work

Industrial truck operators use specially designed vehicles to move heavy boxes, crates, and drums. They work in many different places, from toy factories to steel mills to supermarkets. Even the federal government employs industrial truck operators for its warehouses.

Some of the vehicles have large forks attached to the front. By moving levers and pedals, the operators can slip the forks under pallets or skids, which are platforms made of wood or reinforced plastic. When the pallets are moved, the materials stacked on them are not disturbed and do not have to be restacked. Some trucks have scoops that pick up loose materials such as coal. Others are able to lift boxes high into the air to stack them on top of other boxes. Industrial trucks may also be fitted with tow bars to pull small trailers. Most industrial trucks run on large batteries; others run on gasoline.

Operators generally must be able to do minor repairs on their trucks. They also must keep records of the materials they move.

Education and Training
None

Salary
Median—$12.78 per hour

Employment Outlook
Poor

Education and Training Requirements

Some employers prefer to hire high school graduates, but diplomas or the equivalent are not required. Most companies require examinations to determine physical fitness, coordination, and depth perception.

Almost all industrial truck operators are trained on the job by experienced workers. It takes about three days to learn to maneuver the truck and to move materials safely; it can take considerably longer to become familiar with the layout of warehouses or storage areas.

Getting the Job

Job seekers can apply directly to large manufacturing firms, warehouses, storage depots, and dock terminals. State employment services, newspaper classified ads, and Internet job sites may provide employment leads.

Advancement Possibilities and Employment Outlook

Experienced industrial truck operators can become supervisors and managers.

Employment of industrial truck operators is expected to grow more slowly than other occupations through 2014. Improved technology and automation have eliminated the need for many positions. Although operators are employed nationwide, most work in large industrial cities in California, Illinois, Michigan, New York, Ohio, and Pennsylvania.

Working Conditions

Operators must be able to judge distances accurately so they do not drop large, heavy items, causing damage to the goods or injury to other workers. They must be strong and agile, because they sometimes must move materials by hand. The work can be dirty. Operators work both indoors and outside in all kinds of weather.

Most operators work forty hours per week, sometimes in rotating shifts. Overtime may be necessary. Many operators belong to unions.

Earnings and Benefits

In 2004 the median salary for all industrial truck operators was $12.78 per hour. Those who worked in large cities generally earned more.

Benefits usually include paid vacations, sick leave, health and life insurance, and retirement plans.

Where to Go for More Information

International Brotherhood of Teamsters, AFL-CIO
25 Louisiana Ave. NW
Washington, DC 20001-2198
(202) 624-6800
http://www.teamster.org

Industrial Truck Association
1750 K St. NW, Ste. 460
Washington, DC 20006
(202) 296-9800
http://www.indtrk.org

Intercity Bus Driver

Definition and Nature of the Work

Intercity bus drivers carry passengers from city to city, state to state. They work according to timetables and follow fixed routes. On shorter runs a single driver usually does all the driving; longer trips may have a series of drivers.

Bus drivers receive their assignments when they arrive at the terminal. They check their vehicles carefully, examining the tires, brakes, lights, and safety equipment. They are also responsible for fuel, oil, and water levels.

At the start of the trip and at each stop drivers take tickets from passengers and help them with their luggage. On some bus lines they collect fares from passengers. Drivers also supervise the unloading of any freight. While the buses are on the road, drivers may have to make small repairs. If buses need major repairs, drivers are responsible for moving passengers to other buses.

Bus drivers handle a fair amount of paperwork. The U.S. Department of Transportation and bus companies require that they keep logs of their work hours, miles driven, fares taken, and stops made. Drivers must also file detailed reports of any accidents.

Education and Training
License and training

Salary
Median—$14.30 per hour

Employment Outlook
Good

Education and Training Requirements

Basic requirements for intercity bus drivers are set by the government. In most cases drivers must be at least twenty-one years old; some companies require drivers to be older than twenty-four. They must be in good health, have good hearing and eyesight—at least 20/40 vision with or without glasses. Speaking, writing, and reading knowledge of English is also required.

Although not all intercity bus drivers have finished high school, most companies prefer to hire applicants who have. Prospective drivers must have good driving records and hold commercial driver's licenses (CDL). Information on how to apply for CDLs, which require written and driving tests, can be obtained from state motor vehicle agencies. Some companies prefer applicants who have experience driving local buses or trucks. Companies usually have applicants take driving tests, written tests, and physical examinations.

Newly hired drivers usually take company training courses that may last from two weeks to two months. In the classroom, drivers learn federal and state rules, company procedures, record keeping, and minor bus repairs. On the road, beginning drivers first observe experienced bus drivers. Soon they make their own runs, at first without passengers. During break-in periods, which usually last one to three months, trips with passengers are made under close supervision.

Once they have passed their break-in periods, new drivers are listed on the "extra board," which allows them to fill in for absent workers. It often takes months and sometimes even years for new drivers to get regular runs.

Getting the Job

Working as truck, taxi, or local bus drivers can lead to jobs as intercity bus drivers. Job seekers can apply directly to bus companies. State and local employment services and newspaper classified ads often provide employment leads.

Advancement Possibilities and Employment Outlook

As drivers build up seniority they get better routes and higher pay. They may also move into supervisory or management positions.

Employment of intercity bus drivers is expected to grow as fast as the average for all occupations through 2014. Opportunities should be best in group charter travel and in large, rapidly growing metropolitan areas. Intercity bus travel may increase as the population grows and the price of oil and gas rises. Openings regularly occur as drivers retire or leave the field. However, competition may be stiff because the occupation attracts many qualified applicants.

Working Conditions

Intercity drivers' schedules vary, but maximum hours have been set by law. They may drive up to ten hours at a time, followed by at least eight hours of rest. They are not allowed to work more than sixty hours in seven days.

Bus drivers who work for large companies often work fewer than thirty-nine hours per week. Many work split shifts, and weekend and holiday driving may be required.

The job can be stressful, because drivers are responsible for their passengers and must keep to schedules. They must be able to keep their attention focused during long trips. However, drivers have a certain amount of independence on the job. They should like working with people and enjoy driving.

Earnings and Benefits

Intercity bus drivers are usually paid according to the number of miles they drive. For short runs they may be paid by the hour. Almost all drivers are assigned a minimum number of miles or hours each week, so their weekly earnings are fairly stable. When drivers' routes take them away from home overnight, their companies pay for their meals and lodging. Drivers who are listed on the extra board get paid both by the hour and by the mile—when they are on duty but not actually driving, they are paid by the hour; when they drive, they are paid by the mile.

In 2004 the median wage for all intercity bus drivers was $14.30 per hour. The most experienced drivers earned more than $25.53 per hour.

Benefits usually include paid vacations, medical and life insurance, and retirement plans.

Where to Go for More Information

American Public Transit Association
1666 K St. NW
Washington, DC 20006
(202) 496-4800
http://www.apta.com

Transport Workers Union of America
1700 Broadway
New York, NY 10019
(212) 259-4900
http://www.twu.org

Local Transit Operator

Definition and Nature of the Work

Local transit operators run buses, subways, and, in some metropolitan areas, trolleys. They provide dependable transportation on fixed schedules. Some jurisdictions run their own transit systems, so operators work for government agencies. In many places, however, they work for private companies that have contracts with local government.

At the beginning of each shift, bus drivers check their vehicles for proper maintenance and pick up forms for refunds and transfers. Along their routes they gather fares from passengers—or, in areas where fares are handled electronically, see that passengers have paid the correct amount—and answer questions about stops and timetables.

Trolley drivers have many of the same duties. While few traditional trolleys are still in service, some cities have trackless trolleys, which are buses that run on electricity from overhead wires. Trolley operators also collect fares, give transfers, and answer questions.

Bus and trolley operators drive in street traffic. They obey the same laws that drivers of cars and trucks do. Operators fill out daily work reports, detailing any schedule delays, mechanical problems, or accidents.

Subways are trains that run on rails through tunnels under cities, on the surface, or on elevated tracks. While most subways are guided by computer systems, they usually have two operators on board. Drivers ride in the front of the first car, where they can start and stop the trains and watch for signals and lights along their routes. Conductors ride near the center of trains in small rooms with windows that allow them to observe passengers getting on and off. They open and close the doors and announce the stops over loudspeakers. Fares are collected and most information is provided at stations, not on the trains.

Most local transit operators work in cities, running public buses, subways, and trolleys. (© Martha Tabor/Working Images Photographs. Reproduced by permission.)

Education and Training Requirements

For most jobs, operators must be at least twenty-one years of age; be able to communicate well; and have good hearing and eyesight. Employers prefer applicants who have high school diplomas or the equivalent—educational requirements vary—and driving experience. Good driving records are essential. In most states transit operators must have commercial licenses, which require both written and skills tests.

Training may last several weeks. Classroom work usually covers bus and train operation, safety regulations, and company procedures. During practical instruction, beginning operators first observe more experienced workers and then make runs without passengers under close supervision.

At the end of the training period, most companies give both written and operating tests. Beginners may get routes as soon as they pass the tests. However, in many places operators are first put on an "extra list," which allows them to work when experienced workers are sick or on vacation.

Getting the Job

Job seekers can contact transit companies directly. State and private employment services, labor unions, Internet job sites, and newspaper classified ads can provide employment leads.

Advancement Possibilities and Employment Outlook

Many operators become drivers in other fields. Local bus drivers, for example, may become intercity bus drivers or long-haul truck drivers. Some operators become dispatchers or take on other supervisory roles.

Employment of local transit operators in most areas is expected to be good through 2014. Many cities are upgrading public transportation to increase ridership, which should mean more opportunities for operators. Openings occur each year when workers retire or leave the field. Because of the number of applicants, competition for full-time jobs can be stiff.

Working Conditions

Most local transit operators work forty-hour weeks, often in rotating shifts. Night, weekend, and holiday work may be necessary. Operators generally get extra pay for overtime work. Some operators work "swing shifts," which require several hours of work, followed by long breaks and then more work. This system puts extra vehicles in service during peak transit hours.

Transit operators must be patient, for they deal with people during the busiest times of the day, when tempers are likely to be short. Bus and trolley operators must drive in rain and snow and through traffic jams.

Earnings and Benefits

Earnings vary widely, depending on the size of the city, experience, and level of responsibility. In 2004 the median wage for all bus drivers was $13.49 per hour. Subway and trolley operators earned a median wage of $23.70 per hour.

Benefits usually include health insurance, paid vacation and sick days, and retirement plans. Most local transit operators belong to unions.

Where to Go for More Information

Amalgamated Transit Union
5025 Wisconsin Ave. NW
Washington, DC 20016-4139
(202) 537-1645
http://www.atu.org

American Public Transit Association
1666 K St. NW, Ste. 1100
Washington, DC 20006
(202) 496-4800
http://www.apta.com

Transport Workers Union of America
1700 Broadway
New York, NY 10019
(212) 259-4900
http://www.twu.org

Local Truck Driver

Definition and Nature of the Work

Local truck drivers transport goods over short distances, usually in light trucks or vans. Most drivers work for businesses that deliver their own products, such as department stores and meat packers, or for trucking companies. Some are employed by the federal government, the U.S. Postal Service, and states and municipalities. However, many local truck drivers are self-employed. Drivers who own one or two trucks account for a sizable number of the local for-hire trucking businesses.

Drivers' workdays begin at the terminal or warehouse, where they get their assignments and delivery forms. They may load their trucks themselves or have helpers. The goods are carefully arranged, often in the order of delivery. Heavy items are moved with hoists.

When they unload the goods, drivers have customers sign receipts and freight bills. They may also receive payment directly from customers.

Education and Training Requirements

Requirements vary, but companies generally prefer drivers who are at least twenty-one years old; are able to lift heavy objects; and have had some high school education. Courses in auto mechanics or driver education can be helpful. Operators usually need commercial driver's licenses, which require both written and driving tests. Good driving records are essential.

Job training is minimal—some companies offer one- or two-day courses. Usually new drivers ride with experienced operators until they get a sense of the job. Drivers of special trucks get extra help from workers who know the trucks well.

Getting the Job

Job seekers can apply directly to the personnel offices of trucking companies. State employment services, private agencies, newspaper classified ads, and Internet job sites often list openings.

Education and Training
License

Salary
Median—$11.80 per hour

Employment Outlook
Good

Local truck drivers transport goods over short distances in heavy trucks, such as this cement mixer, or in light trucks, such as the U.S. Postal Service trucks. (© Joseph Sohm; ChromoSohm Inc./Corbis.)

At some companies new drivers are put on an "extra list"; they are called to work when regular drivers are sick or on vacation. Extra drivers get regular routes fairly quickly.

Advancement Possibilities and Employment Outlook

After several years of driving, operators may become dispatchers or supervisors. Others move on to long-distance trucking or start their own companies.

Employment of local truckers is expected to grow as fast as the average for all occupations through 2014. Demand should increase as the amount of freight expands. However, many people are attracted to this field, so applicants may face stiff competition.

Working Conditions

Local truck drivers usually work forty-hour weeks, with shifts determined by the products they deliver. Those who transport food products for bakeries and grocery stores, for example, may work early in the morning or late at night. Some drive forty-eight hours over six days; they are paid extra for overtime. Most drive the same route each day, in all kinds of weather and during rush hours, so the job can be stressful. Many local drivers belong to unions.

Earnings and Benefits

Pay varies by the kind of truck driven and the location of the company. In 2004 the median wage for all local truck drivers was $11.80 per hour.

Benefits may include paid vacation and holidays, health and life insurance, and retirement plans.

Where to Go for More Information

American Trucking Associations
2200 Mill Rd.
Alexandria, VA 22314-4677
(703) 838-1700
http://www.truckline.com

International Brotherhood of Teamsters,
   AFL-CIO
25 Louisiana Ave. NW
Washington, DC 20001-2198
(202) 624-6800
http://www.teamster.org

Truckload Carriers Association
2200 Mill Rd.
Alexandria, VA 22314
(703) 838-1950
http://www.truckload.org

Long-Haul Truck Driver

Education and Training
License

Salary
Median—$16.11 per hour

Employment Outlook
Good

Definition and Nature of the Work

Long-haul truck drivers transport goods over hundreds and even thousands of miles. They may drive flatbed rigs, which are used for carrying steel, or tankers and tractor trailers. They usually drive at night when traffic is light. Long-haul routes are driven by the most experienced drivers because the trucks and cargo are extremely valuable.

When drivers report to the truck terminal, they are given their assignments—usually loaded trucks to be driven to specific destinations. They always inspect the cargo to make certain that it will not shift. They also check the truck itself—first to make sure it has been serviced properly and will run safely, then to be certain it has safety equipment, such as fire extinguishers and flares, in case of emergencies.

During their trips, long-haul drivers make rest stops every few hours, which is why they have lower accident rates than other drivers. On very long trips two drivers take turns. Many long-distance trucks have a small bunk in the cab where the off-duty driver can rest.

Long-haul truck drivers transport goods, such as oil, over long distances. They are responsible for the cargo as well as the truck. (© Earl Dotter. Reproduced by permission.)

When they have docked at their destinations, drivers complete paperwork required by the U.S. Department of Transportation. Their travel logs record exact routing; who drove; the length and location of all stops; and the condition of the truck. They must account for any breakdowns, repairs, or accidents. Drivers keep bills of lading—itemized lists of goods—for each shipment they carry.

Two types of firms hire long-haul drivers: private carrier firms, which are the trucking divisions of companies that transport the commodities they make, and common carrier firms (also called contract carriers), which transport the goods other companies make. Typically private and common carriers own their trucks. A growing number of long-haul truck drivers are owner-operators; they buy their own trucks and have to find cargoes to haul.

Moving van drivers are a special group of long-haul drivers. Like other drivers they carry freight over long distances, but their destinations usually are private homes. They also drive farther than most other long-distance drivers. Moving van drivers have several helpers who assist them in loading and unloading.

Education and Training Requirements

The U.S. Department of Transportation sets minimum requirements for long-haul truck drivers: they must be at least twenty-one years old; have normal blood pressure; and must pass physical examinations, which are usually paid for by employers. Applicants must also have at least 20/40 vision, with or without corrective lenses, and they must have good hearing.

In addition, drivers must take road tests in their particular type of truck. They must pass written tests on safety regulations given by the Department of Transportation. States require that drivers have state-issued commercial driver's licenses, which require written and driving tests.

Companies may have higher standards than those required by law. Many stipulate that their drivers be at least twenty-five years old or have several years of experience in long-haul trucking. Some firms require applicants to have completed at least two years of high school, and others require high school diplomas.

An increasing number of private vocational/technical schools and community colleges are offering courses in truck driving. High school courses in auto mechanics and driver training are helpful.

Drivers usually work as local truck drivers before they enter training programs for long-haul driving. Once hired, they take short courses on company policies. They make their first trips under the guidance of experienced drivers or teachers. Most drivers begin as substitute drivers on the "extra board," which is a list of alternates for regular drivers. With experience they become eligible for regular routes.

Getting the Job

Job seekers can apply directly to trucking companies and private carriers. State employment services, private agencies, newspaper classified ads, and Internet job sites are other sources of employment leads.

Advancement Possibilities and Employment Outlook

Full-time long-haul drivers are at the top of their profession. A few become dispatchers, safety supervisors, and driver supervisors. Others become owner-operators.

Employment of long-haul truck drivers is expected to increase about as fast as the average for all occupations through 2014. Long-distance trucks continue to be the most efficient means of transport for time-sensitive and perishable materials. Other forms of freight transportation—air, rail, and ship—also require trucks to move goods between airports, depots, ports, retailers, and warehouses. Job opportunities may fluctuate with the economy.

Working Conditions

While drivers have a good deal of independence in their workday, their routes keep them away from their families for extended periods. The hours can be long and the driving stressful and tiring.

The U.S. Department of Transportation regulates drivers' schedules. It stipulates that drivers may not work more than sixty hours in a seven-day period. The regulations also state that drivers may work no more than ten hours without resting for at least eight hours. Most long-haul truck drivers belong to unions.

Earnings and Benefits

Earnings depend on the number of miles driven and the total hours the drivers work. The type of truck, its weight, and the kind of cargo it carries also determine pay. For example, drivers of trucks carrying flammable materials are paid higher rates than are other drivers.

In 2004 the median wage for all heavy truck and tractor-trailer drivers was $16.11 per hour. The highest ten percent of drivers earned more than $24.07 per hour.

Benefits may include health insurance, retirement plans, and paid holidays and vacations.

Where to Go for More Information

American Trucking Associations
2200 Mill Rd.
Alexandria, VA 22314-4677
(703) 838-1700
http://www.truckline.com

International Brotherhood of Teamsters, AFL-CIO
25 Louisiana Ave. NW
Washington, DC 20001-2198
(202) 624-6800
http://www.teamster.org

Truckload Carriers Association
2200 Mill Rd.
Alexandria, VA 22314
(703) 838-1950
http://www.truckload.org

Marine Technician

Definition and Nature of the Work

Marine technicians inspect, maintain, and repair boats of all kinds. Using diagnostic equipment, they test and repair boat engines, hulls, propellers, rigging, masts, sails, and navigational equipment. They also install and test sanitation and refrigeration systems, cabinetry, electrical systems, steering gear, and accessories.

To efficiently inspect and repair boats, technicians must first remove them from the water using winches and tracks and set them up on blocks. Supervisors and technicians inspect the boats and decide on the type of work that needs to be done and estimate how long the repairs should take.

When repairing damaged hulls, technicians remove barnacles and loose paint using scrapers, power washers, and sandblasting equipment. They then replace any damaged or decayed sections of wood or fiberglass, sand the repairs smooth, and repaint.

Education and Training Requirements

Many employers prefer to hire applicants with high school diplomas or the equivalent, although they are not required. High school shop courses can be helpful. An increasing number of technicians get two years of training at vocational or technical schools. Useful courses include blueprint reading, machine repair, woodworking, and fiberglass repair.

Most new workers get on-the-job training from experienced technicians. Many employers send their technicians to short training courses offered by boat and engine manufacturers and distributors.

Getting the Job

Job seekers can apply directly to marinas and boat sales and service yards. School placement offices, newspaper classified ads, and Internet job sites may offer employment leads.

Advancement Possibilities and Employment Outlook

Advancement possibilities are limited. In large marinas and boatyards, technicians can become supervisors. Some experienced technicians open their own sales and service yards.

The employment outlook for marine technicians is good through 2014. As people have more leisure time, sales of boats are expected to increase. However, boat design is becoming more advanced, so those with the best training and experience may find the most job opportunities.

Working Conditions

The largest boatyards and marinas, which may employ up to ten marine technicians, are found in coastal areas. Smaller marinas, employing fewer people, are found near lakes and water-recreation facilities.

The number of hours marine technicians work varies. In spring and summer, technicians may be required to work more than forty hours per week, including

Education and Training
None

Salary
Average—$32,000 to $40,000 per year

Employment Outlook
Good

Where to Go for More Information

Association of Marine Technicians
513 River Estates Pkwy.
Canton, GA 30114-9419
(800) 467-0982
http://www.am-tech.org

National Marine Electronics Association
7 Riggs Ave.
Severna, MD 21146
(410) 975-9425
http://www.nmea.org

some weekend work. In the winter most of the work is routine maintenance, and some technicians may be laid off.

The shops and indoor areas where marine technicians work can be noisy and dirty. Technicians must take safety measures when working with fiberglass, resins, and other chemicals. Although technicians use machinery for many tasks, heavy lifting is often required.

Earnings and Benefits

Salaries vary, depending on skill, experience, and location. Average salaries for marine technicians range from $32,000 to $40,000 per year. Benefits may include paid holidays and vacations and health and retirement plans.

Motorboat Mechanic

Education and Training
High school plus training

Salary
Median—$14.74 per hour

Employment Outlook
Fair

Definition and Nature of the Work

Motorboat mechanics fix and service many kinds of boats. Most of them specialize in boats with outboard motors, which run on gasoline and can be taken off boats easily. Inboard motors, which are usually found in cabin cruisers and larger fishing boats, are not removed except for major repairs. Inboard motors often run on diesel fuel and are similar to truck motors.

In some shops, mechanics work only on motors, propellers, and other moving parts. They replace ignition points, adjust valves, and clean carburetors. In other shops mechanics have many duties, such as patching and painting hulls.

Most mechanics are employed by boat dealers and marinas. Those who work for manufacturers make final adjustments and repairs as equipment comes off the assembly line. A small number of mechanics work for boat rental companies. Marinas operated by federal, state, and local governments also employ motorboat mechanics.

Education and Training Requirements

Applicants with high school diplomas or the equivalent are preferred. High school courses in small engine repair, auto mechanics, and machine shop are helpful, as are classes in electricity, science, and math. Many mechanics enter the field by working during the summer as trainees for boat dealers.

Most mechanics learn their trade on the job. Trainees first do odd jobs around the shop, such as cleaning the boats and motors. They also learn routine jobs, such as changing spark plugs and ignition points. Eventually they learn to diagnose engine problems. Beginners need two to three years on the job to become skilled mechanics for gasoline-powered motorboats. Another year or so is needed to become skilled in diesel engine repair.

Some employers send mechanics to one- or two-week training courses sponsored by motorboat manufacturers. The programs usually focus on fixing advanced or specialized equipment. Experienced mechanics continuously upgrade their skills and learn about new kinds of boat motors.

Getting the Job

Job seekers can apply directly to boat dealers and marinas, which may have openings for trainees. Manufacturers may also be hiring. Newspaper classified ads, Internet job sites, or boating magazines may offer employment leads. State employment services may have information about jobs with government marinas.

Advancement Possibilities and Employment Outlook

Experienced mechanics can advance to supervisory positions, such as service manager. They can also open their own businesses if they can raise the capital.

Employment in this small field is expected to grow more slowly than other occupations through 2014. Openings should occur when experienced mechanics retire or leave the field. Demand may grow as the number of people over age forty increases—they buy the most boats.

Working Conditions

Most boat mechanics work near large bodies of water. Coastal areas in California, Florida, Louisiana, Massachusetts, New York, and Texas have many shops that employ one to three mechanics. Few shops have more than ten. They repair and service both inboard and outboard motors. Near smaller bodies of water mechanics usually fix outboard motors. Very small dealers and marinas often send their motors out to be fixed.

This work is not hazardous, but many mechanics get minor cuts and bruises. Shops can be noisy, and mechanics often have to work in cramped spaces.

In the spring and summer, boat mechanics generally work more than forty hours per week, including weekends. In the winter they usually work few hours or fix snowmobiles and other machinery.

Earnings and Benefits

In 2004 the median salary of motorboat mechanics was $14.74 per hour. Experienced mechanics often earn more. Some employers pay mechanics a weekly salary, while others pay a base salary plus an incentive, which is usually a percentage of the cost of labor. Under the incentive method, earnings depend on how much work mechanics are given and how quickly they complete it. Some motorboat mechanics are members of unions.

Benefits may include holiday and vacation pay and health and life insurance. Some mechanics receive paid sick leave and are covered under retirement plans.

A motorboat mechanic fixes an outboard motor for a small boat. He is employed by a boat dealer. (© Martha Tabor/ Working Images Photographs. Reproduced by permission.)

Where to Go for More Information

International Association of Machinists and
   Aerospace Workers
9000 Machinists Place
Upper Marlboro, MD 20772-2687
(301) 967-4500
http://www.iamaw.org

National Marine Manufacturers
   Association
200 E. Randolph Dr., Ste. 5100
Chicago, IL 60601
(312) 946-6200
http://www.nmma.org

Motorcycle Mechanic

Education and Training
On-the-job training

Salary
Median—$13.70 per hour

Employment Outlook
Good

Definition and Nature of the Work

Motorcycle mechanics service and repair many of the four million motorcycles on the roads. They perform routine tasks, such as adjusting and replacing spark plugs, ignition points, and brakes, as well as major repairs, such as overhauling engines.

Most mechanics work for motorcycle shops or dealers. Some are government employees who service motorcycles used by police. Others work in shops that customize motorcycles, adding instruments, changing engine parts, and altering the design.

Motorcycle mechanics use ordinary hand tools such as wrenches and screwdrivers, which they usually buy themselves. A full set of tools can cost as much as $500—beginners usually buy tools as their training progresses. Shops supply power tools, testing equipment, and hoists to lift heavy motorcycles.

Education and Training Requirements

Employers often look for applicants who have their own motorcycles and have already learned to make basic repairs. Sometimes they hire people with no experience if they are mechanically inclined and show interest in learning the work. While high school education is not required, employers prefer to hire applicants with high school diplomas or the equivalent. Courses in small engine repair, automobile mechanics, science, and mathematics can be helpful. High schools, vocational schools, and community colleges sometimes offer courses in motorcycle repair.

Most mechanics learn the trade on the job. Trainees first learn to assemble new motorcycles and perform routine maintenance. With experience they undertake major overhauls of electrical systems and engines. It usually takes two to three years for trainees to become experienced mechanics. Employers sometimes send mechanics to training courses offered by motorcycle manufacturers.

Motorcycle mechanics make major repairs and perform periodic maintenance. They usually work for motorcycle shops and dealers. (© Ariel Skelley/Corbis.)

Getting the Job

Job seekers should contact motorcycle dealers or manufacturers directly to inquire about trainee positions. State employment services, ads in motorcycle magazines, and Internet job sites may provide employment leads.

Advancement Possibilities and Employment Outlook

Advancement opportunities are limited. Mechanics with management ability may become service managers or general managers for motorcycle dealerships. Those with enough money open their own motorcycle shops. Some use their mechanical skills to fix other vehicles with internal combustion engines, such as snowmobiles and automobiles.

Employment of motorcycle mechanics is expected to grow as fast as the average for all occupations through 2014. Motorcycling is becoming increasingly popular, especially with adults between the ages of eighteen and twenty-four and those over forty, so demand for mechanics should increase. Openings regularly occur when experienced workers retire or leave the field.

Working Conditions

About nineteen thousand motorcycle mechanics are employed in the United States. Usually, they work for dealerships or for shops that fix all kinds of small engines. Most dealers employ fewer than five mechanics.

Shops are usually well lighted and well ventilated. Motorcycle work is cleaner than auto repair work, because mechanics do not have to crawl under motorcycles to work on them. Shops are often noisy, however. Although the work is not dangerous, mechanics do get minor cuts and bruises.

Motorcycling increases in warm weather, so mechanics may work more than forty hours per week during the summer months. Weekend hours may be necessary. Part-time and temporary mechanics are often hired to handle the workload.

Earnings and Benefits

Earnings vary, depending on skill and location. In 2004 the median wage for all motorcycle mechanics was $13.70 per hour. The most experienced mechanics earned more than $21.95 per hour. Some mechanics are paid a base salary plus an incentive. Under that system, earnings depend on how much work mechanics are given and how quickly they complete it. Some mechanics' wages are set by union contract.

Benefits may include holiday and vacation pay, life and health insurance, paid sick leave, and retirement plans. Mechanics who work for dealers are often given discounts on the purchase of motorcycles, parts, and accessories. Motorcycle mechanics who work in small shops usually receive fewer benefits.

Where to Go for More Information

American Motorcyclist Association
13515 Yarmouth Dr.
Pickerington, OH 43147
(800) 262-5646
http://www.ama-cycle.org

International Association of Machinists and
   Aerospace Workers
9000 Machinists Pl.
Upper Marlboro, MD 20772-2687
(301) 967-4500
http://www.goiam.org

Mover

Definition and Nature of the Work

Movers load household goods or office equipment onto trucks, transport it to a new location, and then unload it. The may move as few as one or two items or the contents of an entire house or office.

Some movers work for large companies that move cargo across the country. Smaller companies operate within state borders. Other movers work independently, using their own trucks or vans and operating within limited areas.

One of their main objectives is to transport items without damage, so they know the best way to pack delicate items such as china, glassware, and mirrors. They may disassemble furniture, such as beds, so it fits through doorways or into elevators. They may place furniture in special containers designed to protect it or build crates for irregularly shaped items. Movers also maintain inventories of the items they transport.

Because moving is a time-sensitive business, drivers must know how to make minor truck repairs.

Education and Training Requirements

Some companies offer on-the-job training, including driving instruction. Courses on packing and mechanics may also be available. The job has no educational requirements.

Interstate movers must comply with the guidelines of the Federal Motor Carrier Safety Administration. Many states have licensing standards for intrastate movers; for example, drivers may need commercial driver's licenses, which require written exams and driving tests.

Getting the Job

Job seekers can apply directly to moving companies, which are listed in the Yellow Pages. Many movers begin as helpers, loading and unloading cargo.

Advancement Possibilities and Employment Outlook

Movers may become dispatchers, responsible for overseeing the activities of vehicles in transit. Some may specialize in giving estimates, setting rates, responding to customer complaints, or maintaining safety standards. Others become owners of moving companies, who may also act as agents for large interstate moving businesses.

Employment is expected to increase about as fast as the average for all jobs through 2014. While economic conditions in some areas may affect the number of jobs, turnover in the field is fairly high. Openings regularly occur when experienced workers retire.

Movers may work for local businesses or for companies that move cargo across the country. The job requires physical strength and stamina. (© Michael Pole/Corbis.)

Working Conditions

The work requires physical strength, stamina, and good organizational skills. Hours tend to be long and irregular, and the job may involve a great deal of driving. Moving is a seasonal trade—the busiest months are June through September.

Earnings and Benefits

In 2004 the median income for all movers was $9.67 per hour. Self-employed movers may earn between $750 and $1,200 per week. Benefits for movers who work for large companies may include paid holidays and vacations, medical insurance, and retirement plans.

Where to Go for More Information

American Moving and Storage Association
1611 Duke St.
Alexandria, VA 22314-3482
(703) 683-7410
http://www.amconf.org

Parking Attendant

Definition and Nature of the Work

In some public and private parking lots, customers hand over their cars to attendants, who then park the cars. When customers return, the attendants quickly find the cars and return them to the customers. Sometimes they take payment and make change for customers, but more often the money is handled by cashiers.

When they are not parking cars, attendants usually stay inside a small booth near the entrance to the lot. When customers drive in, attendants give them numbered claim tickets, which they must turn in when they pick up their cars. In some lots the time of arrival is stamped on tickets by an automatic clocking machine. In others attendants write the time on the tickets by hand.

In crowded, single-level parking lots where space is limited, attendants make note of the time their customers plan to return. If customers intend to return quickly, attendants park their cars near the exit. Cars of customers who plan to be gone for several hours can be parked farther away from the exit.

If parking lots have many levels, attendants either drive the cars to other levels or move the cars to different floors by freight elevator.

During slow periods, attendants wash down the parking decks and do other maintenance work.

Education and Training
License

Salary
Median—$16,820 per year

Employment Outlook
Poor

Education and Training Requirements

Parking lot attendants must have driver's licenses and be able to drive all types of cars. Honesty is important because they sometimes handle large sums of money and are entrusted with customers' cars and belongings. In communities where special licenses are required, applicants' driving records are checked. They may be fingerprinted before getting jobs.

Companies often prefer applicants who have graduated from high school; diplomas are not required, however. Courses in auto mechanics can be helpful. Attendants should be able to do simple math and clerical work.

Attendants get little or no training. Large companies may offer brief on-the-job classes during which new workers are taught record keeping, customer relations, and driving and parking from experienced attendants.

Getting the Job

Job seekers can apply directly to managers of parking lots. Local government Web sites list job openings at municipal lots. State employment services, union offices, and newspaper classified ads may provide employment leads.

Advancement Possibilities and Employment Outlook

While opportunities for advancement are limited, some attendants become managers or supervisors. Parking lot chains may have jobs for regional or city managers. Some attendants become truck drivers, chauffeurs, or route delivery workers.

The job outlook for parking attendants is poor. Many parking facilities now rely on cashiers: customers get tickets from machines, park their own cars, and pay fees upon departure. Some large commercial parking facilities in urban areas are not equipped for such automation, however. They offer the best employment opportunities.

Working Conditions

Parking attendants work long shifts—sometimes ten hours at a stretch. They may work six days each week, and night, weekend, and holiday work may be required. Attendants are busiest during rush hours; at other times, they may have little to do.

Attendants have daily contact with people and cars, so they must enjoy working with both. They must be skilled drivers, for in many lots they must pay for any damage they do to cars while parking them. They must be in good health and agile because they must work quickly during peak hours.

Earnings and Benefits

In 2004 the median income of parking attendants was $16,820 per year. Union members and attendants who work in large cities earned more. Tips can add to attendants' earnings.

Some parking attendants, especially those who belong to unions, receive benefits such as health insurance and paid vacations.

Where to Go for More Information

International Brotherhood of Teamsters, AFL-CIO
25 Louisiana Ave. NW
Washington, DC 20001-2198
(202) 624-6800
http://www.teamster.org

National Parking Association
1112 Sixteenth St. NW, Ste. 300
Washington, DC 20036
(800) 647-7275
http://www.npapark.org

Parking Cashier

Definition and Nature of the Work

Parking cashiers issue claim tickets and collect fees when drivers use parking facilities. They also provide information, monitor security conditions in garages and lots, and contact tow trucks or police when needed. Most parking facilities are owned or managed by private companies, but some may be run by municipalities.

Cashiers usually sit in booths at the entrance or exit of parking garages or lots. In some facilities, they issue claim tickets that are stamped by a time clock when customers enter the lot. In others, customers simply take tickets from automatic ticket machines. When they drive to the exit of the parking facility, they present the tickets to the cashier, who calculates fees and takes payment. Cashiers may furnish receipts if requested.

Education and Training
None

Salary
Median—$7.81 per hour

Employment Outlook
Poor

Education and Training Requirements

The job has no formal educational or work requirements. Many employers prefer high school graduates, however. Courses in math, accounting, and computers can be helpful. Because contact with the public is constant, applicants must enjoy working with people and be courteous and patient.

New hires are trained on the job by experienced employees.

Getting the Job

Job seekers can apply directly to companies that own or manage parking facilities. Local government Web sites list openings at municipal garages or lots. State employment services, newspaper classified ads, and Internet job sites may provide employment leads.

Advancement Possibilities and Employment Outlook

Parking cashiers may advance to head cashier or full-time work if they are working part time. Parking lot chains may have openings for city or regional managers.

The employment outlook for parking cashiers is poor through 2014. More work is now automated, so fewer workers are needed in many parking facilities. Turnover is fairly high, so openings occur when experienced workers leave the field.

Working Conditions

Cashiers can work part time or full time. Night, weekend, and holiday work may be required. Hours vary, according to the needs of employers and availability of workers. For example, some cashiers may go to school during the day and work at night or on weekends.

Cashiers often work in booths with protective windows. Work can be repetitive, with long periods of inactivity, especially late at night.

Earnings and Benefits

In 2004 the median salary of parking cashiers was $7.81 per hour. Most started at minimum wage, which was $5.15 per hour in most states. Benefits, which varied widely, usually went to full-time employees.

Where to Go for More Information

National Parking Association
1112 Sixteenth St. NW, Ste. 300
Washington, DC 20036
(800) 647-7275
http://www.npapark.org

Railroad Clerk

Education and Training
High school

Salary
Median—$22,770 per year

Employment Outlook
Poor

Definition and Nature of the Work

Traditionally, railroad clerks worked in railroad stations, freight houses, yards, terminals, and company offices. But local railroad companies have merged, and most clerks have moved to central offices where data are computerized and procedures are more efficient. They turn out a steady stream of freight orders, tickets, train timetables, and statistics.

Clerks may collect bills, investigate complaints, adjust claims, trace shipments, compile statistics, sell tickets, and keep books. Thousands of clerks work in technical positions, preparing statistics on employment and traffic that are required by the federal government. Some clerks are dispatchers who relay orders to train conductors, detailing routes, timetables, cargo, and track conditions. For example, if a tree limb falls on a railroad track, the dispatcher tells the conductors on all the trains running on that track to stop or slow down. Sometimes dispatchers communicate with conductors and engineers by illuminating the colored lights along the tracks.

Education and Training Requirements

Railroad clerks must be high school graduates. Some may need special skills, such as proficiency in accounting, that require college or business school education. Many railroad companies require applicants to take clerical tests.

Computer and software skills are essential; knowledge of mathematics can be beneficial. On-the-job training is usually provided. Many clerks are first listed

Although most railroad clerks work at central offices preparing statistics on employment and traffic for the federal government, some still sell tickets at railroad stations. (© Richard T. Nowitz/Corbis.)

on the "extra board," which allows them to work when full-time employees are sick or on vacation. By filling in, they learn their duties before they get full-time jobs.

Getting the Job

Job seekers can apply directly to railroad companies. The Association of American Railroads provides a list of company addresses on request. Union offices, newspaper classified ads, and Internet job sites may provide employment leads.

Some job seekers start in lower-level jobs, such as office messenger, and work their way up to railroad clerk.

Advancement Possibilities and Employment Outlook

Railroad clerks can advance to higher-paying clerical jobs, such as dispatcher, or to administrative jobs, such as chief clerk and stationmaster. They can also become ticket, station, or traffic agents. With additional education and training, some clerks become auditors and statisticians.

Employment of railroad clerks is expected to decline through 2014, although qualified applicants may find opportunities when experienced clerks retire or leave the field. Demand for clerks should diminish as railroad companies computerize and centralize more of their operations.

Working Conditions

Railroad clerks generally work forty hours per week. Ticket sellers often have evening or night duty. Clerks who are on the extra board work irregular hours.

Most clerks work in large central offices, although clerks who check freight orders spend much of their workday outdoors. Ticket sellers have to deal mostly with rail passengers, while freight clerks deal with valuable goods and see that they are protected. Office conditions vary from busy—Pennsylvania Station in

New York City, for example—to small, quiet stations where trains stop once or twice a day. Many railroad employees are union members.

Earnings and Benefits

Earnings vary, depending on the kind of clerical work and level of skill and experience. In 2004 the median salary of all railroad clerks was $22,770 per year. Railroad dispatchers earned a median salary of $30,920 per year. Benefits vary by length of service, but generally include health insurance, paid vacations, and retirement plans.

Railroad Maintenance Worker

Education and Training
High school

Salary
Varies—see profile

Employment Outlook
Poor

Definition and Nature of the Work

To keep locomotives and other equipment in good working order, railroad companies hire maintenance workers: machinists, car repairers, boilermakers, blacksmiths, electrical workers, and sheet metal workers. In railroad language, these workers are called non-ops because they are not involved in the actual operation of trains.

Machinists make up one of the largest groups of non-ops. Although they work on many types of equipment, their specialty is engine and locomotive repair. They often disassemble, repair, and reassemble diesel engines. Car repairers make up the largest group of maintenance workers. They build and repair freight and passenger cars. Some work on moving parts, such as wheels, while others specialize in upholstery, painting, or carpentry.

Boilermakers repair and maintain the steam-heat units on diesel locomotives and in railroad stations. Workers sometimes disassemble boilers to determine whether defective sections need to be replaced or if adjustments can be made. Blacksmiths soften metal parts by heating them in a special furnace, called a forge, and repair them with chisels, hammers, and, if necessary, power tools. Many of their tasks have been automated, however. Electrical workers install and repair electrical systems in locomotives, passenger cars, and railroad buildings, while sheet metal workers install and fix pipes on all kinds of railway equipment.

Education and Training Requirements

Employers prefer to hire applicants with high school diplomas. They may test applicants on mathematical and mechanical skills.

Maintenance workers generally start as apprentices to specialists, such as blacksmiths. Apprenticeships usually last for three or four years. Some workers begin as observers and helpers and then advance to apprenticeship positions.

Getting the Job

Jobseekers should apply directly to railroad companies for apprentice positions. Railroad company Web sites can provide information on job opportunities and application procedures.

Advancement Possibilities and Employment Outlook

Advancement in this field is slow but steady. Apprentices become fully skilled workers after several years. Full-time workers sometimes advance to supervisory positions.

Employment of maintenance workers is expected to decline through 2014 because of improvements in equipment and procedures. Openings do occur when experienced workers retire or leave the field.

Working Conditions

Working conditions vary with each job. However, almost all maintenance jobs require outdoor work in all kinds of weather. Occasionally, electrical workers and others have to travel to make repairs. Railroad maintenance work is often dangerous, despite the strict safety regulations that have been enacted. Blacksmiths are often in danger from heated metals, and boilermakers can be hurt in explosions. Most of the jobs require physical strength and stamina. Maintenance employees have forty-hour workweeks, although they may be called on at any time to make emergency repairs. Higher wages are paid for overtime.

Earnings and Benefits

Wages vary according to the type of work, experience, and location. In 2004 the median wage for car repairers was $19.48 per hour. Machinists earned $16.33 per hour; boilermakers and blacksmiths, $21.68 per hour; electrical workers, $19.25 per hour; and sheet metal workers, $17.09 per hour. Apprentices usually earned lower wages, often a percentage of the skilled-worker wage. Benefits include health and dental insurance and retirement plans.

Where to Go for More Information

Brotherhood of Maintenance of Way
   Employees
20300 Civic Center Dr., Ste. 320
Southfield, MI 48076-4169
(248) 948-1010
http://www.bmwe.org

International Brotherhood of Boilermakers
753 State Ave.
Kansas City, KS 66101
(913) 371-2640
http://www.boilermakers.org

Railroad Signal or Switch Operator

Definition and Nature of the Work

Railroad signal operators install and maintain the signaling devices used by dispatchers to communicate with train crews. Switch operators control the track switches, usually two sections of rail, that divert the locomotive or cars from one track to another for coupling and uncoupling.

Signals are lights or other markers along the track that are controlled by train dispatchers, who work in the central railroad station. During construction of new signals, operators may mix and pour concrete tower bases and cut and weld the metal towers used to support the signals. Many of their duties have been taken over by technicians, who install and repair fiber-optic communication systems. Both signal operators and technicians check and repair lights, fiber-optic cables, or electrical lines.

Some railroads still use battery-powered and mechanical signals. Signal operators check the battery charge and moving parts of the older systems. After operators make inspections, they must complete written records of what they have seen and done.

Education and Training
High school and training

Salary
Median—$21.46 per hour

Employment Outlook
Poor

Railroad switch operators use two sections of track, known as switches, to transfer railroad cars. (© George H. H. Huey/Corbis.)

Switch operators may have to push or pull the switch tracks into place so that train cars can be diverted. Once the cars have moved into the switches, operators use brakes to stop them. They raise or lower levers to couple or uncouple cars and signal the engineer to move the locomotive into place to uncouple or couple other cars. Many of their duties have been mechanized or computerized.

Education and Training Requirements

A high school education is required. Courses in shop, mechanics, and math are helpful. Most railroads prefer to hire people who have training in electrical engineering from vocational or technical schools. Applicants must be between eighteen and thirty-five years old and in good health.

New workers undergo four- to 6-week training programs that combine classroom and on-site training. They also work under the supervision of experienced workers for some time. After about a year they become assistants in their departments. With more experience, they advance to jobs as signal or switch operators.

Getting the Job

Job seekers can apply directly to the personnel offices of railroad companies. State employment offices sometimes list railroad job openings.

Advancement Possibilities and Employment Outlook

Signal operators may become lead operators if they show leadership ability. They may also advance to gang supervisors, testers, inspectors, or railroad engineers. Switch operators may advance to supervisory or administrative positions.

Employment of signal and switch operators is expected to decline through 2014. Technical advances have led to increased productivity, so fewer operators are needed. Some positions become available when experienced workers retire, transfer to other railroad jobs, or leave the field.

Working Conditions

Once workers get jobs as signal or switch operators, their work is fairly steady. Signal installations and repairs are made outdoors in all kinds of weather and whenever and wherever equipment breaks. Signal operators travel to new construction sites, so they may be away from home frequently. Switch operators work in shifts in rail yards. Both jobs can be dangerous because of rolling machinery and electrical wiring.

Earnings and Benefits

In 2004 the median wage of signal and switch operators was $21.46 per hour. Benefits included health insurance, paid vacations and holidays, and pension plans. Many received passes entitling them to free travel on their rail lines.

Where to Go for More Information

Association of American Railroads
50 F St. NW
Washington, DC 20001-1564
(202) 639-2100
http://www.aar.org

Brotherhood of Railroad Signalmen
917 Shenandoah Shores Rd.
Front Royal, VA 22630-6418
(540) 622-6522
http://www.brs.org

United Transportation Union
14600 Detroit Ave.
Cleveland, OH 44107-4250
(216) 228-9400
http://www.utu.org

Railroad Track Worker

Definition and Nature of the Work

Railroad track workers build, inspect, maintain, and repair more than three hundred thousand miles of railroad track across the country. Working in crews called road gangs, they inspect the rails, railroad ties, and roadbeds for signs of wear. Other crew members then rebuild washed-out roadbeds, replace railroad ties, and lay new sections of rail. They use power equipment, such as spike-driving machines and bulldozers, as well as picks and shovels.

Regular crews maintain the tracks, also called the right-of-way, throughout the year. Extra crews are needed to repair large sections of track at certain times of the year, especially in the northern part of the country. The railroads in the Chicago area employ the greatest number of railroad track workers.

Education and Training
None

Salary
Median—$19.03 per hour

Employment Outlook
Poor

Education and Training Requirements

Applicants should be in good physical condition and know how to read and write. High school diplomas are not required. Track workers learn their skills through on-the-job training programs. Experienced crew members teach trainees proper repair methods and explain the use of such portable equipment as tie-tamping machines.

Getting the Job

Job seekers can apply directly to personnel offices of railroad companies. Job listings and application procedures can be found on railroad and labor union Web sites.

Crews of railroad track workers, called road gangs, build, inspect, maintain, and repair railroad tracks. (© Jonathan Blair/Corbis.)

Advancement Possibilities and Employment Outlook

Experienced track workers can advance by becoming skilled in operating the machines used to repair the railroad right-of-way. The most qualified track workers with the highest seniority may become track supervisors who oversee road gangs. High school diplomas or the equivalent may be required for supervisory positions.

Employment of railroad track workers is expected to decline through 2014. More and more repair work can be done by machines, reducing demand for track workers. Openings do occur when experienced crew members retire or leave the field.

Working Conditions

Railroad track workers spend most of their days outdoors, exposed to the elements. Some work time may be lost because of poor weather. Occasionally, workers are hurt on the job by power tools and machines, despite safety equipment and stringent safety procedures. The work is physically demanding and requires much stooping and standing.

Some track workers travel to job sites and live in trailers provided by the railroads. They belong to "floating crews." Whether they live at home or in railroad camps, most regular crew members work forty-hour weeks. Some overtime work may be available. Extra crews, on the other hand, work seasonally and may live on unemployment insurance the rest of the year. Many railroad track workers are members of unions.

Earnings and Benefits

In 2004 the median wage of railroad track workers was $19.03 per hour. Workers were paid higher wages for overtime work. Benefits include paid vacations and sick leave, health and life insurance, and retirement plans.

Route Delivery Driver

Definition and Nature of the Work

Route delivery drivers are truck drivers who sell and deliver goods along local routes. They may sell retail goods and services or wholesale products. Their specific duties vary according to their industries, the policies of their employers, and their role in sales.

Retail drivers work directly with people who buy and use goods and services. Drivers who deliver for laundries, for example, deliver clean linens, towels, and work clothes to customers on a regular basis. They also pick up soiled laundry, record work orders on computers or forms, and even collect money. Retail drivers may also be responsible for soliciting new customers along their routes.

Wholesale drivers, on the other hand, deliver goods to stores, such as grocery stores. They often stock the shelves with their goods and lobby for more prominent placement. They also describe upcoming specials to store managers; pitch new products; and take orders for the next delivery date.

Both retail and wholesale drivers handle paperwork, including invoices.

Education and Training Requirements

Employers prefer to hire applicants who are high school graduates and at least twenty-five years old, although younger people who start work in their warehouses may be promoted to driver positions. In most states, route delivery drivers must have commercial driver's licenses, which require written examinations, driving tests, and good driving records. Applicants should have good eyesight and hearing and be able to lift heavy objects. Prior work in sales and high school math courses can be helpful.

Most companies provide on-the-job training. New hires are taught business math, sales techniques, and defensive driving. Supervisors go with them on their first few trips to offer advice and to help them learn their routes.

Drivers often handle large sums of money, so companies may require them to be bonded. Companies generally pay for this kind of insurance, but sometimes workers have to pay the fees.

Getting the Job

Route delivery drivers who belong to unions may go to union hiring halls to find out about jobs. Others can apply directly to personnel offices of companies that need drivers. State employment services, newspaper classified ads, and Internet job sites are sources of employment leads.

Advancement Possibilities and Employment Outlook

Workers who drive retail trucks can move to wholesale routes, which have fewer customers but larger and more profitable accounts. Drivers can also become route or sales supervisors.

Some route delivery drivers deliver packages to customers within a certain local area. (AP Images.)

Employment of route workers is expected to increase slightly through 2014. Many companies are shifting sales duties away from route drivers to sales staffs in their offices.

Working Conditions

Route delivery drivers often finish their routes early and are allowed to return home without cuts in pay; on other days they may finish late and are not paid extra. Hours vary; milk delivery drivers, for example, begin and end the day early. Drivers should enjoy working with people, have good customer-service skills, and be patient and courteous.

Earnings and Benefits

Earnings for route delivery drivers vary, depending on the type of work and the size of their commissions. Large firms pay a minimum salary set by union contracts, which vary according to location and the kind of company. For example, companies that deal in wholesale goods generally pay higher wages. Firms that ask workers to drive big rigs such as gas and oil tankers also pay higher wages.

In 2004 the median wage of route delivery drivers, both retail and wholesale, was $9.96 per hour. The best salespeople earned much more.

Benefits may include health insurance, paid holidays and vacations, and retirement plans. Most companies provide uniforms.

Where to Go for More Information

American Trucking Associations
2200 Mill Rd.
Alexandria, VA 22314-4677
(703) 838-1700
http://www.truckline.com

International Brotherhood of Teamsters, AFL-CIO
25 Louisiana Ave. NW
Washington, DC 20001-2198
(202) 624-6800
http://www.teamster.org

Sailor

Education and Training
None

Salary
Median—$14 per hour

Employment Outlook
Poor

Definition and Nature of the Work

Sailors work on freighters, tankers, and passenger ships and are responsible for repairing, stowing, and preparing most deck equipment, such as cargo-handling gear. During docking or departing, sailors handle ships' mooring lines. At sea, they stand watch and steer the ship following instructions from the officer on watch. Sailors must be qualified to take charge of lifeboat crews and be familiar with fire safety and fire-fighting regulations. Many also have trades, such as welding or carpentry, that they use to help maintain the ships. Experienced sailors are usually called able seamen on oceangoing vessels or deckhands on boats that navigate inland waters.

Sailors with less experience, also known as ordinary seamen, perform routine maintenance work. They scrub deck areas and clean crew quarters, coil and splice lines and cables, and operate winches. Ordinary seamen may also take over able seamen's steering and lookout duties.

Education and Training Requirements

Employers have no specific educational requirements. However, certification as able seamen requires the ability to handle all gear and equipment, knowledge of all parts of ships, and the ability to tie common knots. Ordinary seamen learn and practice these skills for one year before they can apply for advancement to able seamen.

Although most sailors learn through on-the-job training, previous sea experience, such as service in the U.S. Coast Guard or the U.S. Navy, can be helpful. Many schools offer training for employment in the merchant marine. Federal and state marine academies are highly selective and are designed to train future officers. More appropriate for ordinary seamen are the schools run by labor unions; however, these schools accept only a limited number of young people without sea experience. The training they provide is not necessary to begin careers as able or ordinary seamen.

Getting the Job

In addition to health certificates, sailors must have government certificates known as merchant mariner's documents or seamen's papers. The certificates are obtained by furnishing the Coast Guard with proof of U.S. citizenship, three passport photographs, and either recommendations from recognized maritime training schools or written job commitments from shipping companies or unions. Most sailors get their first jobs by registering at union hiring halls, which are located in major ports.

Seamen's papers do not guarantee jobs, however. After registering at hiring halls, sailors must be present when job openings become available. The jobs go to the most highly qualified sailors with the greatest seniority.

Advancement Possibilities and Employment Outlook

After at least one year as ordinary seamen, sailors may apply for limited endorsement as able seamen. When they pass the appropriate Coast Guard examinations, sailors who are nineteen years of age or older can receive full endorsement. With endorsement and after years of experience, able seamen can advance to positions as boatswains, who are in charge of deck crews. To become boatswains, able seamen must also show the ability to supervise other seamen.

Employment for sailors is expected to grow more slowly than the average for all occupations through 2014. Although the number of U.S. ships is expected to increase slightly, newer ships are highly automated and require fewer sailors. Job openings may occur when experienced seamen retire or leave the field. Competition is likely to be stiff, with many experienced sailors vying for few job openings.

Working Conditions

While at sea, most sailors stand watch for four hours and then have eight hours off, seven days per week. Some sailors are day workers at sea, which means that they work eight hours per day, Monday through Friday. While in port, all sailors have forty-hour workweeks.

Despite safety regulations, sailors' work is hazardous. They are exposed to all kinds of weather and risk falls, fire, collisions, and sinkings.

Accommodations on ships are often cramped, and older ships offer little privacy. Mess halls provide opportunities for recreation. Sailors are usually away from home for long periods.

Earnings and Benefits

Earnings vary, depending on the type of vessel and experience. In 2004 the median wage for all sailors working on typical freighters was $14 per hour. Captains, pilots, and mates earned a median wage of $24.20 per hour. Experienced captains earned more than $35 per hour. Overtime and other premium wages usually equal fifty percent of base weekly wages. Sailors' duties are often seasonal; they often go for long periods without work and pay.

Benefits include room and board, comprehensive medical care, and hospitalization insurance. Sailors usually receive five to fifteen vacation days for every thirty days of employment. Pensions are available through unions.

School Bus Driver

Education and Training
License

Salary
Median—$11.18 per hour

Employment Outlook
Good

Definition and Nature of the Work

School bus drivers transport students to and from school and related events. In the morning, they pick students up at designated locations, such as private homes or street corners, and drop them off at school. In the afternoon, they drive back to the school, wait for students to board, and drive them back to the same designated locations. Drivers usually take the same routes every day.

Drivers also transport students and faculty on field trips and to extracurricular performances or sporting events. These trips may take place on weekends or at night.

Because the physical safety of students is paramount, drivers must be trustworthy and reliable and have excellent driving records. They must be alert in heavy traffic or bad weather and exercise great caution when children are getting on or off the bus. In some instances, they may have to maintain order and discipline unruly students, so they must know the school system's rules for student conduct. Sometimes they must prevent unauthorized persons from getting on their buses.

Education and Training Requirements

School bus drivers should have high school diplomas or the equivalent and good driving records. They must pass physical examinations, drug and alcohol screenings, and criminal background checks.

By federal regulation, school bus drivers are required to hold commercial driver's licenses, which require written exams and driving tests. They must also get "special endorsements" for their licenses, which require written exams and skills tests on the type of bus they will drive.

Drivers also receive one to four weeks of classroom training and driving instruction. Classroom work covers safe-driving practices; first aid; emergency procedures; state and local laws and regulations; school district policies; driver-student relations; and the special needs of disabled and emotionally troubled students.

Getting the Job

Job seekers can apply directly to school districts; openings are usually listed on their Web sites. Some school districts hire companies to drive school buses, so job seekers can apply directly to those businesses. Newspaper classified ads and Internet job sites may provide employment leads.

Advancement Possibilities and Employment Outlook

Experienced school bus drivers can apply for preferable routes or supervisory positions. Others become drivers for the public transportation system or for charter bus companies.

Employment of school bus drivers is expected to increase as fast as the average for all jobs through 2014. Growing suburban areas, in particular, need dependable drivers.

Working Conditions

Drivers work part time—many are on the road fewer than twenty hours per week—and only when school is in session. Some volunteer to drive buses for field trips or extracurricular activities so they can work more hours.

Driving can be stressful in bad weather or heavy traffic. While they may have to deal with unruly students at times, most drivers enjoy the interaction with children and take their responsibilities very seriously.

Earnings and Benefits

In 2004 the median wage for school bus drivers was $11.18 per hour. Experienced drivers earned more than $16.81 per hour.

Benefits vary by school district, but most receive health insurance, paid sick days, and retirement plans. They do not get vacation pay during the summer months when they are not working.

Where to Go for More Information

National Association for Pupil Transportation
1840 Western Ave.
Albany, NY 12203
(800) 989-6278
http://www.napt.org

National School Transportation Association
113 S. West St.
Alexandria, VA 22314
(703) 684-3200
http://www.yellowbuses.org

Service Station Attendant

Definition and Nature of the Work

Service station attendants perform a variety of tasks for motorists and boaters. They pump gasoline, check oil and water levels, clean windshields and other windows, and add air to tires. Most sell and install products, such as spark plugs and windshield-wiper blades. At some stations, attendants check transmission and brake fluid levels, charge batteries, and repair or change tires. They all take payments, make change, and give directions.

Duties vary from station to station. Smaller establishments may have only one attendant, who provides all services. Large stations may employ several attendants, each of whom has specific duties such as pumping gas and making minor repairs or replacing parts.

Education and Training
None

Salary
Median—$8.33 per hour

Employment Outlook
Poor

Service station attendants pump gasoline, clean windshields, and check oil and water levels. (© Tim Wright/Corbis.)

Some attendants make road calls to help stranded motorists by changing tires, recharging batteries, or making other minor repairs. Sometimes they tow vehicles to their stations for additional repair work.

Education and Training Requirements

Employers prefer to hire high school graduates, although the job has no specific educational requirements. No experience is required, and on-the-job training is common. Several large companies do offer training courses, however. Some high schools have vocational courses that combine students' last two years of school with part-time work as service station attendants.

Employers prefer applicants who have driver's licenses, a general understanding of how automobiles work, and some sales ability. They also should be familiar with local roads, highways, and points of interest so they can give directions to strangers and locate vehicles whose owners have called for road service. Marina service stations require employees to be familiar with basic boat maintenance, boat safety, and local waterways.

Attendants should be friendly, speak well, and be able to make change quickly and accurately and keep business records.

Getting the Job

Job seekers can apply directly to service stations. Newspaper classified ads may list job openings.

Advancement Possibilities and Employment Outlook

Advancement depends on individual goals. For attendants who are not interested in becoming supervisors, advancement is very limited. They may become expert in making certain kinds of repairs and advance to the job of mechanic's helper. With additional training, they can become automobile or boat mechanics. Those who have business management skills may advance to station manager. Many experienced station managers go into business for themselves by leasing stations from oil companies or buying their own stations. Oil companies hire some service station managers as sales workers or district managers.

Employment of service station attendants is expected to decline through 2014. Self-service gas stations have eliminated many jobs, and most motorists go to repair shops or oil-changing establishments. However, some drivers prefer to patronize full-service gas stations, so a certain number of attendants may always be needed.

Working Conditions

Service station attendants must be outdoors in all kinds of weather. Their work tends to be dirty, especially if they make repairs. Many attendants work forty to fifty hours per week, often at night and on weekends. Employees at larger stations usually work in shifts. Attendants get extra pay for overtime.

Earnings and Benefits

Earnings vary, depending on the station, its location, and the kind and amount of work done. In 2004 the median wage for service station attendants was $8.33 per hour. Attendants with more responsibility, such as those who do minor repairs and maintenance, earned more than $10 per hour. Attendants sometimes receive commissions on the goods they sell or bonuses.

Benefits for full-time personnel may include health insurance and paid vacations. Some employers furnish uniforms and pay for cleaning them.

Where to Go for More Information

Service Station Dealers of
 America/National Coalition of
 Petroleum Retailers and Allied Trades
1532 Pointer Ridge Pl., Ste. E
Bowie, MD 20716
(301) 390-4405
http://www.ssda-at.org

Special Service Bus Driver

Definition and Nature of the Work

Special service bus drivers are hired by groups or organizations to drive buses and their passengers to certain places, such as theaters or sports arenas. The businesses are usually called charter bus companies. The passengers do not pay the drivers directly; they arrange payment by the directors of their groups.

Bus drivers who work for charter companies make very few stops on their routes. Large groups of passengers board the bus at one or perhaps two stops. The drivers generally drop off all the passengers at the same destination and later make the return trips. Charter buses are hired for fairly long runs.

Sightseeing buses are also special service buses. Sometimes they are rented by groups, but often bus companies lease their vehicles to agencies that offer sightseeing tours. Drivers may guide the tours themselves, describing different points of interest while they drive.

There are also special service buses for people with disabilities. On these buses drivers must help each passenger on and off the bus.

Education and Training Requirements

Generally, special bus drivers must meet the same requirements as other bus drivers. They must be at least twenty-one years old and have good driving records.

Education and Training
High school and license

Salary
Median—$10.81 per hour

Employment Outlook
Good

Charter bus companies take all passengers to the same destination. (© Terry Wild Studio. Reproduced by permission.)

Most companies prefer to hire drivers who have high school diplomas or the equivalent. Almost all companies require new drivers to take written tests and have physical examinations.

Drivers must also have commercial driver's licenses, which allow them to drive vehicles that transport more than sixteen passengers. Applicants must pass both written tests on rules and regulations and skills tests on the type of bus they will drive on the job.

Company training programs vary, although most last several weeks. New employees work under the supervision of experienced drivers.

Special service bus drivers often get extra training. Sightseeing guides, for example, must learn details about the places on their routes.

Getting the Job

Special service drivers who run charter buses often get their jobs because they are on the "extra board," a list of substitute drivers, at bus companies. Job seekers can apply directly to the companies. State employment services, newspaper classified ads, and Internet job sites are all sources of employment leads.

Advancement Possibilities and Employment Outlook

When they advance, special service drivers get regular routes and their names are taken off the extra board. With experience, some become supervisors.

Employment in this field is expected to increase as fast as the average for all occupations through 2014. As people have more and more leisure time, demand for charter and tour drivers increases. Turnover can be high. Drivers who are willing to work part time may find the most opportunities.

Working Conditions

Special service bus drivers must enjoy working with people, because they have constant contact with passengers, especially on sightseeing tours. Driving can be tiring and stressful because of traffic snarls and weather conditions.

Special service bus drivers often work irregular hours. For example, charter bus drivers are needed for weekend and night work as well as regular day shifts. Many drivers belong to unions.

Earnings and Benefits

Earnings vary widely, depending on location and type of work. Special service drivers who are on the extra board are paid for each mile they drive. When they are on duty but not driving, they are paid by the hour. In most cases they are guaranteed minimum weekly salaries. In 2004 the median wage for charter bus drivers was $10.81 per hour.

Benefits vary, but most drivers can expect medical insurance and paid holidays and vacations.

Where to Go for More Information

International Brotherhood of Teamsters, AFL-CIO
25 Louisiana Ave. NW
Washington, DC 20001-2198
(202) 624-6800
http://www.teamster.org

United Transportation Union
14600 Detroit Ave.
Cleveland, OH 44107-4250
(216) 228-9400
http://www.utu.org

Taxi Dispatcher

Definition and Nature of the Work

Taxi dispatchers, also called starters, send cabs off to customers and keep records of all road-service calls. They may stay in touch with the drivers while they are on the road, communicating by phone, computer, or two-way radio.

Dispatchers help drivers with problems and answer their questions. For example, they may tell drivers which routes to take to avoid traffic jams. When drivers are involved in accidents, dispatchers call for assistance and send other taxis to the customers.

Education and Training Requirements

Taxi dispatchers usually have high school diplomas or the equivalent. Applicants must be organized and have the ability to work well under pressure. Clerical or customer service experience can be valuable.

Some dispatchers start out as taxi drivers. Others first perform clerical work and then advance to dispatch positions. New workers get on-the-job training.

Getting the Job

Job seekers should apply directly to taxi companies. Newspaper classified ads and Internet job sites may list openings.

Advancement Possibilities and Employment Outlook

Advancement opportunities are limited. Some dispatchers move to supervisory or administrative positions or start their own taxi companies.

Employment of dispatchers is expected to grow as fast as the average for all occupations through 2014. Openings occur when experienced workers retire or leave the field.

Education and Training
High school and on-the-job training

Salary
Median—$30,920 per year

Employment Outlook
Good

Working Conditions

Dispatchers must work well under pressure and respond to emergencies quickly and efficiently. Some work in offices at taxi companies; others work in small booths at airports and other transport hubs. Dispatchers work in all kinds of weather.

Forty-hour workweeks are standard; however, when emergencies occur or the workload is particularly heavy, dispatchers may be required to put in extra hours. Night, weekend, and holiday work may be necessary.

Where to Go for More Information

Taxicab, Limousine, and Paratransit
   Association
3849 Farragut Ave.
Kensington, MD 20895
(301) 946-5701
http://www.tlpa.org

Earnings and Benefits

Earnings vary, depending on experience and location. In 2004 the median salary of all taxi dispatchers was $30,920 per year. The most experienced workers earned more than $52,440 per year.

Benefits usually include paid vacations and holidays, life and health insurance, and retirement plans.

Taxi Driver

Education and Training
Licenses

Salary
Median—$10.68 per hour

Employment Outlook
Good

Definition and Nature of the Work

Taxi drivers transport passengers for hire. Almost all of them work in cities. Passengers may signal them by hand on the street or find them at hotels and airport terminals. When passengers call cab companies and request taxis, dispatchers contact drivers by two-way radios, cell phones, or computers.

At the start of their shifts, taxi drivers report to garages to pick up their cabs. They check the lights, brakes, and fuel level and start trip sheets, forms on which they record their destinations and fares. In some areas, taximeters determine fares based on distance and time. Drivers turn the taximeters on as soon as passengers announce their destinations and stop them when passengers are dropped off. In other cities, fares are determined by zones or by flat rate. Extra charges may be in effect at night, for handling luggage, or for additional passengers. Information placards in the cabs usually explain how fares are determined. Passengers sometimes give drivers tips. Taxi drivers must be expert at handling automobiles and know their cities thoroughly so they can make trips efficiently.

Education and Training Requirements

The job has no formal educational requirements, but most companies prefer to hire drivers with at least an eighth-grade education. Applicants must be twenty-one years of age, in good health, and have good driving records.

State governments set licensing requirements. In most states, cab drivers must obtain either state-issued chauffeur's licenses or special taxicab operator's licenses. Some states require both. Other states require commercial driver's licenses with "endorsements" to carry passengers. Licenses, which are issued by the motor vehicle or police department or by the Public Utilities Commission, must be renewed every year.

After receiving a call from the cab company telling him where the customer is located, a taxi driver picks up a woman and her seeing eye dog. (© Martha Tabor/Working Images Photographs. Reproduced by permission.)

Local governments set the standards for taxi driver training. In many jurisdictions, it includes up to eighty hours of classroom instruction, plus testing on local geography, motor vehicle laws, basic automotive repair, and safe driving practices. English proficiency tests may be required.

Some taxi companies also require on-the-job training. Lasting a week or so, this informal training is supervised by experienced drivers, known as lead drivers, and includes instruction on how to operate the taximeter and communications equipment and how to fill out paperwork. Drivers may get special guidance in helping passengers who are elderly or physically challenged.

Getting the Job

Job seekers can apply directly to taxicab companies. Newspaper classified ads and Internet job sites may provide employment leads.

Advancement Possibilities and Employment Outlook

Some taxi drivers buy and operate their own cabs. Relatively few supervisory jobs exist, although some drivers may be promoted to dispatcher, claim agent, or road supervisor.

Employment of taxi drivers is expected to increase about as fast as the average for all occupations through 2014. Turnover is high, so cab companies have frequent openings. Fuel prices may spur demand for taxi drivers. Opportunities should be best for those who are willing to work irregular hours.

Working Conditions

Taxi drivers' work is heaviest at rush hours, in bad weather, and on holidays. The job allows for a great deal of independence, but can be stressful if traffic is heavy. Cab drivers may work irregular hours; shifts often last ten hours or more per day with time for breaks. Workweeks run five or six days.

Earnings and Benefits

Earnings vary, depending on hours worked, fares completed, and tips received. In 2004 the median salary for taxi drivers was $10.68 per hour. Self-employed drivers and drivers who worked in large cities earned more.

Most taxi drivers do not receive the benefits available to workers in other occupations. Occasionally, full-time drivers get paid vacations and medical insurance.

Tire Changer and Repairer

Education and Training
None

Salary
Median—$9.99 per hour

Employment Outlook
Poor

Definition and Nature of the Work

Tire changers and repairers replace or fix the tires, treads, tubes, and related materials on automobiles, trucks, recreational vehicles, aircraft, bulldozers, and other types of vehicles. Also known as tire retreaders, tire-and-tube servicers, or tire fixers, they generally work for automotive service centers or retail or wholesale tire companies.

Tire changers and repairers remove and remount tires on vehicle wheels, test and repair tires and inner tubes, and balance tires and wheels. They use such equipment as hydraulic jacks, power hoists, mechanical tire changers, hot vulcanizing plates, and rubber mallets. Some rebuild worn tires using specialized retreading equipment.

Education and Training Requirements

The job has no formal educational requirements. High school courses in mathematics and industrial arts are helpful. Good motor coordination and manual dexterity are essential. Most employers provide on-the-job training that may last up to six months.

Getting the Job

Job seekers can apply directly to tire companies or automotive repair shops. State employment services, newspaper classified ads, or Internet job sites may provide employment leads.

Advancement Possibilities and Employment Outlook

Advancement within the automotive industry requires additional training and education. Enterprising workers can become service supervisors, open their own tire stores, or become involved in tire manufacturing.

Employment of tire changers and repairers is expected to grow more slowly than the average for all occupations through 2014. The popularity of RVs and high-performance, lightweight trucks may spur demand for workers skilled in replacing, repairing, retreading, and balancing tires for those vehicles.

Working Conditions

Most tire changers and repairers work in noisy, dirty service or retreading shops, where they may be exposed to hot temperatures. Some workers make emergency calls to repair tires on the roadside or in customers' driveways in all kinds of weather.

The work requires agility and strength. Heavy tires or equipment must be lifted, carried, moved, or handled. While safety equipment and procedures have been improved, workers can be injured on the job.

Earnings and Benefits

In 2004 the median salary for tire changers and repairers was $9.99 per hour. Those who worked with specialized tires, such as airplane or giant tires, earned more.

Benefits for full-time workers may include health insurance and paid vacation.

Where to Go for More Information

Tire Industry Association
1532 Pointer Ridge Pl., Ste. G
Bowie, MD 20716-1883
(800) 876-8372
http://www.tireindustry.org

Tow Truck Dispatcher

Definition and Nature of the Work

Tow truck dispatchers take calls for emergency service, relay the requests to local service stations or towing companies, and monitor the progress of the tow. Using computer-aided dispatch systems, they keep records and prepare detailed reports of all emergency calls and all communications with towing services.

Dispatchers usually stay in touch with drivers on the road, using phones, computers, or two-way radios, so they can solve problems and answer questions. For example, they can tell drivers which routes to take to avoid traffic jams. Dispatchers work for municipal governments, state or city police departments, the American Automobile Association (AAA), or private towing companies.

Education and Training
High school

Salary
Median—$30,920 per year

Employment Outlook
Good

Education and Training Requirements

Tow truck dispatchers usually have high school diplomas or the equivalent. They must be organized and able to work well under pressure. Clerical or customer service experience can be valuable. New dispatchers get on-the-job training.

Getting the Job

Job seekers can apply directly to municipal governments, police departments, AAA, or private towing companies. Some tow truck drivers and clerical workers get promoted to dispatcher. Newspaper classified ads and Internet job sites may provide employment leads.

Advancement Possibilities and Employment Outlook

Dispatchers have few advancement opportunities. Some move to supervisory or administrative positions. Others start their own towing companies.

Employment of dispatchers is expected to increase as fast as the average for all jobs through 2014. The increasing number of cars on the road should mean more job opportunities. Openings occur when experienced dispatchers retire or leave the field.

Working Conditions

Dispatchers must work well under pressure and respond to emergencies quickly and efficiently. They usually work in offices or call centers.

Forty-hour weeks are standard; however, when emergencies occur or the workload is particularly heavy, they may be expected to put in extra hours. Night, weekend, and holiday shifts may be required.

Earnings and Benefits

In 2004 the median salary for tow truck dispatchers was $30,920 per year. The most experienced workers earned more than $52,440 per year.

Benefits include paid vacations and holidays. Most companies offer retirement plans and life and health insurance.

Where to Go for More Information

American Trucking Associations
2200 Mill Rd.
Alexandria, VA 22314-4677
(703) 838-1700
http://www.truckline.com

Towing and Recovery Association of
  America
2121 Eisenhower Ave., Ste. 200
Alexandria, VA 22314
(800) 728-0136
http://www.towserver.net

Tow Truck Operator

Education and Training
High school and on-the-job training

Salary
Average—$18,000 to $25,000 per year

Employment Outlook
Good

Definition and Nature of the Work

Tow truck operators use specially equipped trucks to move vehicles that have broken down; have been damaged in accidents, abandoned, or impounded by the police; or cannot be driven for some other reason. Operators work for towing companies, service stations, or automobile salvage companies.

A tow truck operator may drive one of three kinds of trucks. Conventional tow trucks are equipped with a hook and sling that the operators use to raise one end of a disabled vehicle for towing. Operators of wheel-lift or full-float trucks use winches to lift cars and place support wheels under one or both axles for towing. Flatbed trucks are used for transporting more expensive cars. Operators lower the truck beds to the ground, winch disabled vehicles onto the beds, and then raise the beds for driving. In all cases, operators may attach steering locks, chains, or lights to disabled vehicles so they can be moved safely.

Sometimes operators diagnose and repair minor problems. They jump-start cars, replace spark plugs, connect loose wires, change flat tires, and add fuel. If vehicles have been involved in accidents, operators may need to remove, bend, or cut damaged parts before towing.

Many operators perform other tasks when they are not towing. Those working for service stations may fuel and service vehicles, perform repairs, and replace accessories and tires. Operators who work for automobile salvage companies may dismantle vehicles to salvage reusable parts.

Education and Training Requirements

Employers prefer to hire applicants with high school diplomas or the equivalent; however, the job has no specific educational requirements. Applicants must have good driving records. High school courses in automobile repair and bodywork can be useful. Many truck-driving schools offer training programs for tow truck operators.

A tow truck operator loads a damaged vehicle onto a truck bed. He is responsible for safely transporting it to a repair shop. (© Martha Tabor/Working Images Photographs. Reproduced by permission.)

New workers receive on-the-job training from experienced operators, who explain safety and business procedures, customer service techniques, and paperwork.

The Towing and Recovery Association of America offers certification programs for light, medium, and heavy-duty towing and recovery. Applicants are tested on customer service, safety procedures, incident management, and truck equipment.

Getting the Job

Job seekers can apply directly to towing companies, service stations, or automobile salvage and wrecking companies. State employment services, newspaper classified ads, or Internet job sites may provide employment leads.

Advancement Possibilities and Employment Outlook

Tow truck operators usually start by towing impounded or abandoned vehicles with conventional or wheel-lift trucks. With experience, they can move to flatbed trucks. Some operators become supervisors or managers of towing companies or service stations. Others start their own service stations, towing companies, or salvage companies.

Employment of tow truck operators is expected to grow as fast as the average for all occupations through 2014. The industry is moving toward more specialized towing companies, so trained and experienced operators should have the most opportunities. With more vehicles on the road each year, demand for tow truck operators should increase as well.

Working Conditions

Tow truck operators usually work forty-hour weeks. Overtime may be required, especially in bad weather. Many large towing companies have operators who work in shifts or who are on call for night, weekend, and holiday work.

Operators have to work outside in all kinds of weather. They use power equipment, chains, hoists, and tools and must take precautions to avoid possible injury. Small cuts and bruises are common.

Earnings and Benefits

Earnings vary, depending on experience, location, and type of company. Average salaries range between $18,000 and $25,000 per year. Flatbed truck operators can earn more. Instead of salaries, some operators receive a set fee for each car towed.

Full-time employees often receive paid holidays and vacations, health insurance, and retirement benefits.

Truck and Bus Dispatcher

Education and Training
High school and on-the-job training

Salary
Median—$30,920 per year

Employment Outlook
Good

Definition and Nature of the Work

Truck and bus dispatchers coordinate the movements of trucks and buses entering and leaving terminals. Truck dispatchers assign drivers to trucks and make sure they have the correct freight-charge bills for their loads. Bus dispatchers assign drivers to buses and ensure that the buses move out of the terminals on schedule.

Both truck and bus dispatchers stay in touch with drivers on the road, communicating by phone, computer, or two-way radio. Dispatchers answer drivers' questions and solve problems. For example, they may tell drivers which routes to take to avoid traffic jams. Progress of drivers along their routes is charted on large control boards in company offices. Dispatchers are required to keep the boards up to date.

When trucks and buses return to terminals, dispatchers check them in and handle their trip records. Dispatchers may also handle customers' requests and complaints.

Education and Training Requirements

Truck and bus dispatchers usually have high school diplomas or the equivalent. Initially, most truck and bus dispatchers are hired for driving jobs. As drivers, they become familiar with federal and state driving regulations, terminal procedures, and company operations. Once they have shown proficiency, they may be promoted to dispatcher positions and trained on the job.

Getting the Job

Drivers who show the necessary abilities may advance to dispatcher positions. A small number of truck dispatchers begin their careers as dockworkers or clerical workers and get promoted.

Job seekers can apply directly to truck or bus companies. Newspaper classified ads and Internet job sites may provide employment leads.

Advancement Possibilities and Employment Outlook

Advancement possibilities are good for dispatchers who remain with their companies for several years and demonstrate ability to handle assignments competently. Some dispatchers advance to truck terminal managers.

Employment of truck and bus dispatchers is expected to grow as fast as the average for all occupations through 2014. Economic conditions in some geographical areas may affect the number of job openings, especially new positions. Openings regularly occur when experienced dispatchers retire or leave the field.

Working Conditions

Dispatchers must work well under pressure and be able to respond to emergencies quickly and efficiently. Forty-hour weeks are typical. However, in emergencies or when the workload is particularly heavy, dispatchers may be expected to put in extra hours.

Earnings and Benefits

In 2004 the median salary of truck and bus dispatchers was $30,920 per year. The most experienced workers earned more than $52,440 per year.

Benefits often include paid vacations and holidays, life and health insurance, and retirement plans.

Where to Go for More Information

American Society of Transportation and
  Logistics
1700 N. Moore St., Ste. 1900
Arlington, VA 22209
(703) 524-5011
http://www.astl.org

Council of Supply Chain Management
  Professionals
2805 Butterfield Rd., Ste. 200
Oak Brook, IL 60523
(630) 574-0985
http://www.cscmp.org

Aircraft Dispatcher

Definition and Nature of the Work

Aircraft dispatchers, who are also called flight superintendents, schedule flights for airlines and make sure all Federal Aviation Administration (FAA) regulations are followed. They draw up flight plans and confer with pilots and flight engineers to determine that flights can be made safely. Dispatchers also maintain contact with crews after they are airborne to keep them advised of weather conditions, alternate landing plans, and necessary changes in altitude.

When drawing up flight plans, aircraft dispatchers check weather conditions and the amount of fuel to be loaded; determine the best routes and altitudes for flights; and select alternative landing sites if bad weather occurs. Dispatchers also examine mechanics' reports to make certain required maintenance has been completed.

If for any reason dispatchers or pilots decide that flights cannot be made, dispatchers must notify the passengers and crews and arrange for alternate flights. They also keep records of the availability of aircraft and equipment, weight of cargo, and the amount of time flown by each plane and each crew member.

Dispatchers may be in contact with as many as twelve planes at one time and must be able to coordinate action should emergencies arise. If any plans are changed, dispatchers must contact the dispatch centers at destination airports.

Dispatchers generally work for large airlines and are usually aided by assistant dispatchers, who help gather weather information.

Education and Training Requirements

High school diplomas are required. Many airlines prefer to hire applicants who have attended college for at least two years. Courses in mathematics, physics and meteorology can be useful. Flying experience and work history with airlines can be important when searching for employment.

Aircraft dispatchers must take FAA exams to become certified. To qualify for the exams, applicants must have 1) worked for a year or more under the supervision of experienced and certified dispatchers; 2) completed FAA-approved courses at airline schools or training centers; or 3) spent two of the preceding three years in commercial or military air traffic control. Written tests cover such subjects as federal aviation regulations, weather analysis, air navigational facilities, radio procedures, and airport and airway traffic procedures. Oral tests determine applicants' ability to interpret weather information and demonstrate knowledge of airline routes, navigational facilities, and landing and cruising speeds of aircraft.

Aircraft dispatchers must take continuing education courses at special training centers. At least once a year they are tested on new procedures and technology. In addition, they must "fly on the line" as observers for at least five hours each year.

Most aircraft dispatchers are former assistant dispatchers. Assistant dispatchers do not always have to be certified, but they must have had at least two years of college or two years of experience in ground or flight operations in jobs such as dispatch clerk or communications clerk.

Getting the Job

Job seekers can apply directly to airports or airlines for such positions as air traffic controller, dispatch clerk, radio operator, or meteorologist. Almost all dispatchers and assistant dispatchers have been promoted from these jobs. Many major airlines only hire dispatchers who have moved up within their own ranks.

Advancement Possibilities and Employment Outlook

Dispatchers can be promoted to such positions as chief flight dispatcher, flight dispatch manager, flight supervisor, chief flight supervisor, and superintendent of flight control. Advancement can be slow because the field is small and few vacancies occur.

The employment outlook for aircraft dispatchers is only fair through 2014. Although the airline industry continues to grow, improved communications equipment has increased productivity. Openings occur when experienced dispatchers retire or leave the field.

Working Conditions

Dispatchers are responsible not only for the lives of thousands of people but also for the safety of extremely valuable equipment. They must gather and analyze highly detailed information and make many decisions. Congestion at many airports has made the jobs of aircraft dispatchers more demanding. They must be able to work well with others and remain calm during emergencies.

Most dispatchers work rotating cycles of eight-hour day, evening, and night shifts. Overtime may be required. Many dispatchers belong to unions.

Earnings and Benefits

Salaries vary widely, depending on the size of airlines, location and size of airports, dispatchers' experience, and work schedules. In 2004 some smaller carriers offered beginning salaries around $20,000 per year. Meanwhile, some dispatchers at major airlines—most of whom had worked for those airlines for at least fifteen years—earned more than $100,000 per year. Over the next decade, salaries may be affected by the introduction of a two-tiered wage system: to compete with smaller, nonunion airlines, the major airlines have reduced their starting salaries for new employees.

Dispatchers usually receive paid sick leave and vacations, life and health insurance, and retirement benefits. In addition, they and their families may receive some free air transportation from their employers. They may also receive reduced fares on other airlines.

Where to Go for More Information

Airline Dispatchers Federation
2020 Pennsylvania Ave. NW, Ste. 821
Washington, DC 20006
(800) 676-2685
http://www.dispatcher.org

Air Transport Association of America
1301 Pennsylvania Ave. NW, Ste. 1100
Washington, DC 20004-1707
(202) 626-4000
http://www.air-transport.org

Aircraft Mechanic

Definition and Nature of the Work

Aircraft mechanics—also called airframe mechanics, power plant mechanics, and avionics technicians—service, repair, and inspect airplanes for commercial airlines, private firms, and the military. Although some mechanics are specialists, most have thorough knowledge of all parts of airplanes, including their engines, propellers, landing gear, hydraulic equipment, radio and radar instruments, and bodies.

Sometimes pilots report faulty equipment to maintenance crews. However, defects are usually discovered during the regular inspections made on all aircraft. The Federal Aviation Administration (FAA) requires that all planes be inspected and tested for safety after they have flown a certain number of hours. Mechanics must take full responsibility for any repairs that are required. They can lose their FAA licenses if the planes are not in perfect condition.

Line maintenance crews work at airports, making quick repairs on planes that are scheduled to take off. Major repairs are handled at an airline's overhaul base, where mechanics are usually more specialized. They may work on only one part of their companies' planes, such as the engine or the landing gear.

At smaller airports, airplane charter services, and general aviation repair shops, mechanics work on all parts of planes. Other aircraft mechanics work in plants where planes are manufactured. Sometimes they go on test flights to discover and correct any problems that new aircraft may have.

Aircraft mechanics must know all parts of an airplane and how they work together. (© Ralf-Finn Hestoft/ Corbis.)

Education and Training Requirements

Mechanics should be agile, work well with their hands and tools, and have good hearing and eyesight. Precision and attention to detail are important.

Employers require that applicants have high school diplomas or the equivalent. Useful subjects include mathematics, physics, chemistry, industrial drafting, auto and aircraft mechanics, machine shop, metal and wood shop, and welding. Applicants should be able to read and interpret blueprints, diagrams, electricity charts, and instructional manuals.

All aircraft mechanics must obtain government certification. Those with A licenses can work on airplane bodies; P licenses allow them to work on engines (also known as power plants). Some mechanics have both A and P licenses. Mechanics must pass written, oral, and practical tests to earn licenses. They must be at least eighteen years old and know how to read and write English.

Most mechanics study at FAA-approved schools for eighteen to twenty-four months. A growing number of companies require two- or four-year degrees in avionics, aviation technology, or aviation maintenance management from FAA-approved schools.

Graduates of those programs are eligible for licensing tests. Mechanics who have not taken such courses must have eighteen months of practical experience before they can take the tests. Applicants who desire both A and P certification must have thirty months of experience working with both the framework and engines of airplanes. Often untrained workers start out as helpers under skilled workers.

Technological advances require mechanics to continue their education during their careers. FAA rules state that certified mechanics must have at least one thousand hours of work experience in any two-year period or they must take refresher courses in aviation technology and repair.

Getting the Job

Job seekers can apply directly to employment offices of airlines. School placement offices, state employment services, and labor union offices can provide useful information on job opportunities and application procedures.

Advancement Possibilities and Employment Outlook

Advancement is easiest for mechanics with both A and P licenses. Mechanics can advance to lead mechanic or to the rank of crew chief. Some become supervisors and maintenance superintendents. Very good mechanics may become FAA inspectors after taking examinations.

Employment of aircraft mechanics is expected to increase as fast as the average for all occupations through 2014. However, while demand for air travel on both the large airlines and private and corporate aircraft may increase, demand for mechanics may be offset by technological advances that increase productivity. Still, openings can occur each year when workers retire or leave the field.

Working Conditions

Most mechanics work forty hours per week, usually in eight-hour shifts. Those who have worked the longest are given their choice of shifts. Beginning mechanics usually find themselves on night or weekend shifts.

Aircraft mechanics work with heavy equipment and are often required to lift or pull objects weighing more than seventy pounds. They may also work in precarious positions, such as on the tops of wings and fuselages of large jet planes. They may work outside in unpleasant weather. Because noise and vibration are constant, mechanics must take measures to protect their hearing.

Aircraft mechanics' jobs are often stressful. They are under pressure to identify and repair mechanical problems quickly so airlines can maintain strict flight schedules. More important, they are responsible for the safety of aircraft passengers and crew.

Earnings and Benefits

Salaries depend on the size of the company, the level of certification, and experience. In 2004 the median wage for all mechanics was $21.70 per hour. Benefits included paid vacations and holidays, medical insurance, and reduced air fares.

Where to Go for More Information

Air Transport Association of America
1301 Pennsylvania Ave. NW, Ste. 1100
Washington, DC 20004-1707
(202) 626-4000
http://www.air-transport.org

International Association of Machinists and Aerospace Workers
9000 Machinists Place
Upper Marlboro, MD 20772-2687
(301) 967-4500
http://www.iamaw.org

Professional Aviation Maintenance Association
400 Commonwealth Dr.
Warrendale, PA 15096
(724) 772-4092
http://www.pama.org

Airline Flight Attendant

Education and Training
High school plus training

Salary
Median—$43,440 per year

Employment Outlook
Good

Definition and Nature of the Work

Flight attendants are responsible for the safety and personal comfort of airline passengers. While some duties vary by airline and type of aircraft, many of their procedures are regulated by the Federal Aviation Administration (FAA).

Before flights they are briefed by the captain on emergency evacuation procedures, crew coordination activities, flying time, and weather. They check the passenger safety equipment and make sure the cabins are stocked with adequate supplies.

Flight attendants greet passengers as they board, check their tickets, direct them to their seats, and help them with their coats and small luggage. Before takeoff attendants demonstrate safety procedures. While airborne attendants check that safety belts are fastened when necessary; serve drinks, snacks, or precooked meals; distribute reading materials; and answer passengers' general questions.

Their most important duty is to provide assistance during emergencies, from reassuring passengers to opening doors and inflating emergency slides for evacuation. They are also trained to provide first aid.

Most flights have between one and ten attendants, depending on the size of planes and the proportion of economy to first-class passengers. Large aircraft such as the Boeing 747 may have as many as sixteen flight attendants.

Education and Training Requirements

Flight attendants must be high school graduates. Applicants with college backgrounds or experience dealing with the public are preferred. They must be at least nineteen years old and in excellent health. Good vision and hearing and clear speaking voices are required. Many international airlines require that their flight attendants be proficient in appropriate foreign languages. By FAA regulation, applicants must undergo thorough background checks.

Applicants must be tall enough to reach overhead bins, which contain emergency equipment, and their weight must be proportional to height. Applicants must also be clean shaven and have no visible tattoos, body piercings, or unusual hairstyles.

Most of the major airlines have established training schools for their new employees. Those that do not operate such schools generally send new employees to the schools of other airlines.

Most airline training programs last between four and eight weeks. Training covers flight regulations and duties, aircraft terminology, company policies, first-aid techniques, emergency procedures, and personal grooming. The courses include practice flights to accustom attendants to flight conditions.

Once trainees successfully pass their training programs, they receive the FAA's Certificate of Demonstrated Proficiency. They are then assigned to one of their airline's bases and are eligible to fly on reserve status, which means they can be called in to work for crew members who are sick, on vacation,

Airline flight attendants make sure that passengers are safe and comfortable. They may check passengers' safety belts, serve drinks and food, and provide pillows and blankets. (© Patrik Giardino/Corbis.)

or rerouted. Reserve status can last from one to ten years. Attendants graduate from reserve status by showing reliability and proficiency on the job.

Getting the Job

Job seekers can apply directly to personnel departments of airline companies. Names and addresses of airlines are available from the Web site of the Air Transport Association of America. Occasionally job openings for attendants are listed in newspaper classified ads or on Internet job sites.

Advancement Possibilities and Employment Outlook

Experienced flight attendants can become lead attendants, flight pursers, supervisory flight attendants, training inspectors, or recruitment representatives. Attendants who no longer want to fly sometimes transfer to other airline departments, such as public relations or sales.

Employment of flight attendants is expected to increase as fast as the average for all occupations through 2014. The FAA requires that there be at least one attendant for every fifty seats, so the increasing number of aircraft and the new, larger planes should drive demand for attendants. However, the economics of air travel can affect the number of flights, limiting the number of jobs. Openings usually occur when experienced workers retire or leave the field.

Working Conditions

Flight attendants usually have about sixty-five to ninety hours of scheduled flying time and up to fifty hours of ground duty per month. Hours may be irregular, requiring attendants to work at night, on weekends, or during holidays. Flight attendants have fifteen or more days off each month, sometimes away from their home bases. Attendants with the most seniority get the most desirable home bases and flight assignments.

Attendants' work involves exposure to many types of people, places, and cultures. However, the work can be strenuous. They are on their feet almost constantly, must complete many tasks quickly, and must deal with disruptive passengers or turbulent flights. Still, they must remain professional and pleasant in all situations.

Earnings and Benefits

Earnings depend on the airline, experience, and rank. In 2004 the median salary of experienced flight attendants was $43,440 per year, while senior flight attendants earned as much as $95,850 per year. Beginning attendants made $15,522 per year. Extra compensation was available for individuals willing to work additional hours or for working holidays and nights or on international flights. Living allowances are paid to flight attendants during their training and when they must stay away from their home bases. Most airlines require attendants to buy their own uniforms.

Benefits usually include paid sick leave, two to four weeks of paid vacation, tuition reimbursement, and reduced airfare for flight attendants and their immediate families. Hospitalization insurance and retirement plans are sometimes provided.

Where to Go for More Information

Air Transport Association of America
1301 Pennsylvania Ave. NW, Ste. 1100
Washington, DC 20004-1707
(202) 626-4000
http://www.air-transport.org

Association of Flight Attendants
501 Third St. NW
Washington, DC 20001
(202) 434-1300
http://www.afanet.org

Automobile Driving Instructor

Definition and Nature of the Work

Through a combination of classroom instruction and on-the-road practice, driving instructors prepare students for the exams they must pass to get their driver's permits and licenses. They teach students to operate vehicles and instill respect for state driving laws and parking regulations.

Driving instructors work in two kinds of schools: public high schools that offer courses in driver education and commercial driving schools open to the general public.

High schools offer driver education as an elective course for their sophomore or junior students. The course includes thirty hours of classroom study, which cover state laws and regulations and safe-driving practices. Students also observe another driver for six hours and practice driving for six hours with a licensed driver.

Some high schools offer adult driving classes in the evening. Instructors may teach others subjects as well.

Instructors who work for commercial schools generally teach driving full time. Their students are either adults or older teenagers. Typical courses include eight hours in the classroom combined with driving practice under the instructors' supervision.

Instructors in both types of schools teach driving in the same way. Students first learn about cars' instrument panels, the correct way to sit for driving, and how to use different controls. If students plan to drive cars with standard transmissions, they learn to use the gears and clutch before they begin driving. On the road students learn to park, turn, brake, and stop.

Instructors may administer practice exams to prepare students for the written tests they will be taking at the department of motor vehicles. They also provide feedback on student drivers' ability, pointing out skills they should practice before their final driving tests.

Automobile driving instructors teach students how to operate cars and prepare them to take tests to get their driver's licenses. (© Joe Bator/Corbis.)

Education and Training Requirements

Driving instructors must have finished high school and be at least twenty-one years old. They must be excellent drivers and have good driving records. In most states, they must have special licenses or certificates to teach driver education.

Some community colleges offer associate degrees for teachers of driver education. A minimum of thirty hours of classroom study is combined with on-the-job training, during which supervisors accompany trainees for their first few lessons. Some commercial driving schools charge fees to those who are training to be instructors, while other schools require trainees to work for free. High school driving instructors must have college degrees and be certified by the state in driver instruction.

Getting the Job

Local or state boards of education list openings in high school programs. Those who want to become commercial driving instructors should call local commercial schools. School placement services, newspaper classified ads, or Internet job sites may provide employment leads.

Advancement Possibilities and Employment Outlook

Part-time high school instructors can become full-time instructors and then directors of their programs. Instructors who want to be directors of commercial driving schools need advanced education in business and safety education. With experience and business training, some driving instructors open their own schools.

Employment of driving instructors is expected to increase as fast as the average for all jobs through 2014. Commercial schools, which are increasing in number, offer the best opportunities for instructors.

Working Conditions

Classrooms are usually clean and comfortable. However, on-the-road instruction can be stressful because instructors are responsible for beginning drivers who are operating machinery that can be dangerous. High school driving instructors follow the regular school schedule, while instructors in commercial schools arrange their own hours.

Earnings and Benefits

Salaries for commercial driving instructors vary by school. Most earn a percentage of what their students pay, so their earnings vary with the number of students. Some are paid salaries plus commissions. In 2004 the average salary of commercial driving instructors ranged from $14 to $19 per hour.

High school driving instructors are paid according to their schools' salary schedules, which can vary by size of school district and location. In 2004 the median salary of high school teachers ranged from $41,400 to $45,920 per year.

Benefits for commercial instructors vary according to the size, location, and policies of the companies. Some may get no benefits at all. High school driving instructors can expect paid vacations and holidays, health insurance, and retirement plans.

Where to Go for More Information

American Driver and Traffic Safety
  Education Association
Indiana University of Pennsylvania, R & P
  Bldg.
Indiana, PA 15705
(724) 357-4051
http://www.adtsea.iup.edu

Driving School Association of the
  Americas, Inc.
3090 E. Gause Blvd., Ste. 425
Slidell, LA 70461
(800) 270-3722
http://www.thedsaa.org

Automotive Exhaust Emissions Technician

Definition and Nature of the Work

Technicians who test vehicle exhaust emissions may work at service stations, at car dealerships, or for the automobile manufacturing industry. Some are employed by state governments in their vehicle inspection programs.

By connecting sensors to the exhaust systems of vehicles, the technicians can test the content of the exhaust and compare it to set standards for emissions. They may use gauges and dynamometers (instruments that measure the strength of the engine and related parts) during the tests. They may also repair exhaust malfunctions that the tests reveal. Technicians are responsible for cleaning, maintaining, and calibrating the test equipment.

Education and Training Requirements

Technicians are required to have postsecondary education, such as the two- and four-year programs offered by community colleges and technical schools. High school preparation should include courses in mathematics and laboratory science as well as automotive, metals, and electrical courses.

Certification is usually required for this profession, either through a state program or the National Institute for Automotive Service Excellence. Automobile dealers generally prefer to hire technicians who have certificates of special training from industry educational centers.

Technicians attach sensors and other equipment to automobiles to check the contents of engine exhaust. They work for service stations, car dealerships, or the automobile manufacturing industry. (© William Taufic/ Corbis.)

Getting the Job

Job seekers can apply directly to the personnel offices of auto dealerships or other automotive firms. School placement offices usually have up-to-date listings of job openings. Graduates may be recruited by the automotive industry during their final semesters.

Advancement Possibilities and Employment Outlook

With experience and, in some cases, additional education, technicians can be promoted to several advanced technical positions or to supervisory positions.

The employment outlook for automotive exhaust emissions technicians is only fair through 2014. The increased use of automation, which results in greater productivity, will limit the number of job openings.

Working Conditions

Most technicians work in garage facilities. Those who work for manufacturing companies may work in engineering design departments or laboratories. Technicians often work outdoors in all kinds of weather. They generally work forty hours per week. Overtime may be necessary.

Earnings and Benefits

Salaries vary, depending on the type of company or agency and location. In 2004 the median salary of specialty technicians employed by the automobile manufacturing industry was $15.68 per hour.

Benefits for full-time automotive exhaust emissions technicians usually include health insurance and paid vacations.

Automotive Mechanic

Definition and Nature of the Work

Automotive mechanics inspect, service, and repair the engines, brakes, and other parts of cars, buses, and trucks. They also perform routine maintenance to prevent future breakdowns.

Diagnosing problems quickly and accurately requires analytical ability. It also requires a thorough knowledge of cars' mechanical and electronic systems and competence with a variety of electronic tools, such as infrared engine analyzers and computers. Many mechanics consider diagnosing hard-to-find problems to be one of their most challenging and satisfying duties.

After locating the source of the malfunctions, mechanics often need to replace or repair faulty parts. Some mechanics specialize in particular kinds of repair, such as electrical or transmission problems. They usually work in special service shops.

Most mechanics work in automobile dealerships, automobile repair shops, and gasoline service stations. Many others are employed by federal, state, and local government agencies; taxicab and automobile leasing companies; and other businesses that repair their own cars and trucks. Automobile manufacturers hire mechanics to make adjustments and repairs after cars come off the assembly line. Other mechanics work for large department stores that have facilities for servicing automobiles.

Education and Training
Varies—see profile

Salary
Median—$15.60 per hour

Employment Outlook
Good

Education and Training Requirements

Employers prefer to hire applicants who are high school graduates. High school courses in metal work, mechanical drawing, science, mathematics, computer skills, and automobile maintenance are helpful. A number of advanced high school programs are part of the Automotive Youth Education Service, a certification program that prepares students for entry-level jobs. Participants often train under experienced mechanics for up to four years.

A growing number of employers require auto mechanics to complete training programs offered by trade, vocational, or community colleges. The programs

Automotive mechanics must be able to diagnose problems quickly and accurately and make the necessary repairs. (© Helen King/Corbis.)

last from six months to two years and combine classroom instruction and hands-on practical experience. Some trade schools partner with automotive dealerships, which allow students to work in their service departments.

Certification is important—but not mandatory—in this field. Automotive Service Excellence (ASE) certification, the nationally recognized standard, can be awarded in eight different areas of automotive service. Applicants must pass exams and have two years of relevant experience to become ASE-certified mechanics. To be recognized as master automobile technicians, mechanics must be certified in all eight areas of automotive service. Mechanics are retested every five years to renew certification. More than four hundred thousand service professionals have achieved ASE certification.

Getting the Job

School placement offices, job fairs, and apprenticeship programs can provide employment contacts and job leads. Job seekers can also apply directly to service stations, automotive dealerships, and repair shops. Newspaper classified ads and Internet job sites often list openings.

Advancement Possibilities and Employment Outlook

Experienced mechanics in large shops may advance to supervisory positions, such as repair shop supervisor or service manager. Mechanics who like to work with customers may become service estimators, who take clients' orders for repairs and write up job orders for mechanics. Many mechanics open their own repair shops or service stations.

Employment of automobile mechanics is expected to increase as fast as the average for all occupations through 2014. Turnover in this field is high, so many openings occur each year. Automotive technology is becoming increasingly complex, so mechanics who have had formal training may find the most opportunities. Demand should also be high for those who stay informed about new developments in this field, such as alternate fuels technology.

Working Conditions

Most mechanics work between forty and forty-eight hours per week, but many work longer hours during busy periods. Mechanics frequently get paid at higher rates for overtime.

Most mechanics work indoors, in shops with good ventilation, lighting, and heat. They frequently work with dirty, greasy parts and in awkward positions. Sometimes they must lift heavy objects. Minor cuts and bruises are common, but serious accidents are usually avoided by observing established safety procedures.

Earnings and Benefits

Salaries vary, depending on location and mechanics' experience. In 2004 the median wage of all automotive mechanics was $15.60 per hour. The most experienced mechanics earned more than $26.33 per hour. Apprentices started at about sixty percent of the standard wage and received increases throughout their training.

Benefits often include paid holidays and vacations. Mechanics may also get life, health, and accident insurance. Some employers supply uniforms.

Where to Go for More Information

Automotive Service Association
PO Box 929
Bedford, TX 76095-0929
(817) 283-6205
http://www.asashop.org

International Association of Machinists and
  Aerospace Workers
9000 Machinists Place
Upper Marlboro, MD 20772-2687
(301) 967-4500
http://www.iamaw.org

National Institute for Automotive Service
  Excellence
101 Blue Seal Dr. SE, Ste. 101
Leesburg, VA 20175
(703) 669-6600
http://www.asecert.org

Avionics Technician

Definition and Nature of the Work

Avionics is the application of electronics to the operation of aircraft, spacecraft, and missiles. Technicians inspect, test, and repair the electronic components of communication, navigation, and flight-control systems. For example, they may test and replace radar systems using such equipment as circuit analyzers and oscilloscopes.

Some technicians work with engineers to develop and install new electronics systems and calibrate them to specifications. Many specialize in particular systems, such as computerized guidance and flight-control equipment.

Technicians must complete and sign maintenance and installation documents for every piece of equipment. To keep up with technological advances, they read technical articles and attend seminars and training courses.

Education and Training
High school, training, and license

Salary
Median—$21.30 per hour

Employment Outlook
Fair

Education and Training Requirements

Avionics technicians must have high school diplomas and complete two- or four-year training programs at technical institutes or community colleges. Thorough understanding of the theory and practice of electronics is essential. Other useful courses are geometry, calculus, and technical writing.

Large aerospace companies and the armed services provide on-the-job training specific to their requirements. Avionics technicians are also required to obtain restricted radio-telephone operator's licenses, which are obtained from the Federal Communication Commission.

Getting the Job

College placement offices may have information about entry-level positions. Job seekers can also apply directly to aerospace companies and airlines. Some employment agencies specialize in placing technical staff.

Advancement Possibilities and Employment Outlook

Avionics technicians usually begin their careers as trainees, working under the supervision of skilled workers. As they gain experience they test and repair equipment independently. With more training they can become installers of new equipment or get jobs in research and development.

The employment outlook for avionics technicians is fair through 2014. The aerospace industry is closely tied to government spending and the economy, so overall employment can fluctuate. Those technicians with experience and knowledge of the latest technologies should find the most job opportunities.

Working Conditions

Avionics technicians generally work forty hours per week, sometimes in teams of technicians and engineers. Because electronic equipment must be kept very clean, they usually work indoors, often in the confined spaces of aircraft cockpits. The work is highly detailed, with exacting standards, and may include preparation and presentation of technical reports.

Earnings and Benefits

Salaries vary, depending on the type of company or size of airline. In 2004 the median wage of all avionics technicians was $21.30 per hour. The most experienced workers made more than $27.85 per hour.

Benefits usually include paid holidays and vacations and health and retirement plans. Technicians working for airlines may be eligible for free or greatly reduced fares when traveling.

Car Rental or Leasing Agent

Education and Training
High school or college plus training

Salary
Varies—see profile

Employment Outlook
Very good

Definition and Nature of the Work

Car rental agents usually work for large national companies and are stationed at airports, bus and train terminals, and car rental offices. They specialize in renting vehicles to travelers and others who need cars for short periods, such as businesspeople, vacationers, and drivers whose cars are being repaired.

Agents fill out forms, check driver's licenses, and collect deposits in cash or by credit card. When cars are returned, agents prepare the final bills for rental fees and mileage charges. Most of the mathematical computations have been computerized.

Supervisors, called station managers, run rental offices and supervise and train rental agents. Customer service representatives handle customers' complaints or problems.

Car rental agents often work at airports and bus and train terminals where travelers, such as businesspeople, need cars for short periods of time. (Judy Griesedieck/Time Life Pictures/Getty Images.)

Car leasing agents are usually salespeople who sell leasing services to individuals and businesses that need cars for long-term use. Many businesses and some individuals find it more economical to lease cars or trucks than to purchase them, partly because leasing companies often pay for repairs and maintenance on their vehicles. Customers pay a fixed leasing charge in return for the use of the vehicles and whatever services are listed in the lease. If customers lease fleets of trucks, salespeople negotiate the total price of the lease. Many salespeople get commissions on the leases they sell.

Car leasing salespeople work out of the regional offices of large leasing companies and in the leasing departments of large car dealerships. Many travel extensively to sell leasing services. They work under the supervision of sales managers and regional managers.

Many other people are employed in the business of renting cars and trucks. Some specialize in renting moving vans or construction equipment, while others maintain and repair the rental cars and trucks.

Education and Training Requirements

Car rental agents must have high school diplomas or the equivalent. Most of the large rental companies have short training programs.

Leasing salespeople must be college graduates with at least one year of sales experience; however, companies occasionally hire applicants who have only one or two years of college education but have been salespeople for several years. The large leasing companies have formal training programs that lead to assignments in specific sales territories.

Getting the Job

Job seekers can apply directly to rental and leasing companies. College placement offices, job fairs, newspaper classified ads, and Internet job sites are all sources of employment leads.

Advancement Possibilities and Employment Outlook

A car rental agent can become a station manager or a customer service representative. Experienced representatives sometimes move into the training departments of large rental companies.

Car leasing salespeople can become sales managers and regional managers. Some salespeople advance to supervisory jobs in the main offices of large leasing companies.

The employment outlook for car rental representatives and leasing salespeople is very good through 2014. Car and truck rental and leasing services are growing rapidly, creating new jobs. Despite overall growth in the industry, however, most openings occur as representatives are promoted or leave the field.

Working Conditions

Car rental agents usually work behind well-lighted, well-ventilated counters in airports and terminals. Some work in offices near car rental lots. They must maintain a professional manner and be patient, for their customers are often stressed from traveling. Many agents work part time. Evening, weekend, and holiday hours may be required.

Car leasing people spend much of their time on the road calling on customers. Because commissions make up part of their salaries, they work under pressure to sell as many leasing services as possible. The job can be stressful. Some workers are members of labor unions.

Earnings and Benefits

Wages and benefits vary widely, depending on location and union membership. In 2004 the median income for car rental agents was $10.42 per hour. The starting salary was usually $5.15 per hour, which is minimum wage in most states. Salaries for car leasing salespeople may fluctuate, depending on the commissions they are paid. In 2004 the median wage for car leasing agents was $17.87 per hour.

Benefits for full-time employees usually include health insurance and paid holidays, vacations, and sick days. Some employers may offer participation in 401K plans.

Diesel Mechanic

Education and Training
Varies—see profile

Salary
Median—$17.20 per hour

Employment Outlook
Good

Definition and Nature of the Work

Diesel mechanics repair, maintain, and rebuild diesel engines that power buses, trucks, ships, trains, and other vehicles. To repair engines, mechanics run diagnostic tests, find the sources of problems, and then remove and replace faulty parts. Mechanics who maintain engines may check water-cooling systems or clean air and oil filters to prevent engine parts from breaking down. Because diesel engines are expensive to replace, they are rebuilt at regular intervals, usually after vehicles have traveled more than one hundred thousand miles. Mechanics take the engines completely apart, replace worn parts, and put the engines back together.

At a city transit authority, a diesel mechanic performs routine maintenance on bus engines by checking the water-cooling system and the air and oil filters. (© Martha Tabor/ Working Images Photographs. Reproduced by permission.)

Diesel mechanics use many kinds of tools, including pliers, wrenches, screwdrivers, grinders, drills, and lathes. They also use testing equipment such as dynamometers, which measure engine power. Mechanics often lift heavy parts, so they should be in good physical condition.

Some mechanics do a variety of diesel engine repairs. Others specialize in rebuilding engines or in repairing fuel-injection systems, turbochargers, cylinder heads, or starting systems. Some also repair large natural gas engines used to power generators and other industrial equipment.

Mechanics are sometimes described by the type of equipment they repair. For example, those who repair diesel truck engines may be called diesel truck mechanics. Those who work on construction equipment, such as bulldozers and earthmovers, are usually called heavy equipment diesel mechanics.

Diesel mechanics work for equipment dealers, manufacturers, or companies that use and repair diesel equipment.

Education and Training Requirements

Employers prefer trainees and apprenticeship applicants who have high school diplomas and mechanical ability. Automobile repair and machine shop courses offered by many high schools and vocational schools are helpful, as are courses in science and mathematics.

Many diesel mechanics start by assisting experienced workers who repair gasoline-powered engines. That training lasts three to four years. New employees of companies that use or repair diesel equipment usually receive six to eighteen months of additional training.

Some mechanics enter formal apprenticeship programs, which generally last four years. They include classroom instruction and practical experience. Apprentices are paid for their work while they attend school at night.

A growing number of employers prefer to hire graduates of trade or technical schools. These programs generally last from several months to two years and provide practical experience and related classroom instruction. Graduates usually need additional on-the-job training before becoming skilled diesel mechanics.

Voluntary certification by the National Institute for Automotive Service Excellence (ASE) is recognized as the standard credential for diesel mechanics, who can be certified as master medium/heavy truck technicians, master school bus technicians, or master truck equipment technicians. To become certified, mechanics must pass one or more ASE-certified exams and have at least two years of hands-on experience in diesel engine repair. Because technology advances so quickly in this field, mechanics must be retested every five years to remain certified. Mechanics stay abreast of these advances through continuing education.

Getting the Job

Job seekers can apply directly to repair shops or manufacturing companies. School placement offices, state employment services, newspaper classified ads, and Internet job sites are all sources of employment leads.

Advancement Possibilities and Employment Outlook

Diesel mechanics with the most advanced training have the greatest opportunity for advancement. When vacancies occur, they can be promoted to shop supervisor or service manager. Locomotive specialists may advance to plant superintendent. Diesel engine mechanics on ships might become marine engineers. Experienced mechanics can also open their own repair shops.

The employment outlook for diesel mechanics is expected to be good through 2014. Diesel engines are more durable and economical than gasoline engines, so they may be used more extensively in trucks, buses, and other vehicles.

Working Conditions

Most larger repair shops are pleasant places in which to work, but some small shops have poor lighting, heating, and ventilation. Heavy parts are often supported by jacks or hoists, so proper safety measures must be taken. Mechanics handle greasy tools and engine parts and often stand or lie in awkward positions for extended periods. Sometimes they make repairs outdoors in all kinds of weather.

The typical workweek runs forty to forty-eight hours, although extra hours may be required for emergency repairs. Many shops have expanded their work hours to better serve their customers, so evening, night, and weekend work may be necessary. Many diesel mechanics belong to labor unions.

Earnings and Benefits

Earnings vary by industry. In 2004 the median wage for all diesel mechanics was $17.20 per hour. The most experienced mechanics earned more than $25.67 per hour. They were often paid time and a half for overtime. Inexperienced mechanics generally earned fifty to seventy-five percent as much as experienced mechanics.

Many mechanics receive paid holidays and vacations as well as health and life insurance. Railroad mechanics may receive free travel passes.

Where to Go for More Information

Association of Diesel Specialists
10 Laboratory Dr.
PO Box 13966
Research Triangle Park, NC 27709-3966
(919) 406-8804
http://www.diesel.org

International Association of Machinists and
   Aerospace Workers
9000 Machinists Place
Upper Marlboro, MD 20772-2687
(301) 967-4500
http://www.iamaw.org

International Brotherhood of Electrical
   Workers
900 Seventh St. NW
Washington, DC 20001
(202) 833-7000
http://www.ibew.org

National Institute for Automotive Service
   Excellence
101 Blue Seal Dr. SE, Ste. 101
Leesburg, VA 20175
(703) 669-6600
http://www.asecert.org

Merchant Marine Steward and Cook

Definition and Nature of the Work

Stewards and cooks see to the daily needs of passengers and crew aboard ship. They prepare and serve meals and maintain living quarters. All freighters, tankers, and passenger ships employ stewards.

Chief stewards supervise the preparation of food. They are also responsible for the maintenance of ships' living quarters and mess halls, keeping careful records of the use of food, linens, and furniture. On passenger ships chief stewards are in charge of the comfort of the passengers.

Chief cooks supervise the other kitchen employees. They plan menus in cooperation with chief stewards, issue supplies, and butcher and cut meat. They often cook the most demanding meals on the menu, and delegate other responsibilities to second cooks and bakers. In addition, they supervise the cleaning and maintenance of kitchens.

Second cooks support chief cooks in the preparation of food and maintenance of kitchen safety and cleanliness. Third cooks generally assist their superiors. Bakers are in charge of making desserts. Utility hands carry supplies, prepare vegetables, and wash and scour utensils. Mess attendants set tables, serve food, clean tables, and wash dishes. They also maintain the living quarters aboard ship.

Education and Training Requirements

The job has no formal educational requirements, although workers must have seaman's papers, which are issued by the U.S. Coast Guard. To receive these papers, workers must either participate in training programs or have promises of jobs from companies or unions. However, both companies and unions now promise jobs only in exceptional cases.

Several different kinds of schools provide training. Both the Seafarers International Union and the National Maritime Union sponsor schools for qualified candidates. The New York City school system offers maritime training at the Food and Maritime Trade High School. Some states have their own maritime academies. Workers are also trained at the U.S. Naval Academy, the U.S. Merchant Marine Academy, and the U.S. Coast Guard Academy.

Besides classroom training, any experience in the U.S. Coast Guard or U.S. Navy is useful, as is experience as a cook.

Getting the Job

Job seekers must first obtain seaman's papers from the Coast Guard and health certificates from the U.S. Public Health Service. Because very few companies or unions promise jobs, most new workers get their first jobs by registering at union or government hiring halls. The government hiring halls are run by the U.S. Navy's Military Sealift Command. These halls are located in major ports throughout the country.

Job openings go first to registered workers who have the most seniority and who have been out of work the longest. To get jobs workers must be present at the hiring halls when the openings occur.

Because seaman's papers do not guarantee continuing employment, all workers go to hiring halls between jobs. The waiting period may be only one week for those with seniority; new workers usually have to wait much longer.

Advancement Possibilities and Employment Outlook

Workers advance only on the recommendation of chief stewards to ship captains. New workers generally start as mess attendants or utility hands. With strong recommendations, mess attendants or utility hands can go on to such jobs as third cook, cook/baker, chief cook, and finally chief steward. The U.S. Coast Guard issues documents for each rank. The only requirement is age: third cooks must be at least nineteen years old; chief cooks and chief stewards must be at least twenty-one years old.

Job prospects are unfavorable. Most new ships are built to replace older ships, and the new vessels require fewer workers. Openings occur as workers retire or leave the field. However, there will be stiff competition for those jobs. Most openings will be filled by experienced workers who are unemployed.

Working Conditions

Living quarters on ships are clean and adequate. Like all merchant marine workers, cooks and stewards are away from home for long periods. Work aboard ships can be hazardous because of the constant risk of fire, falls, collisions, and sinking. Workers may be exposed to harsh weather while at sea.

The monthly pay of stewards and cooks is based on a forty-hour workweek. However, overtime work and other variations in hours occur regularly. Workers receive extra pay for this work.

Where to Go for More Information

Maritime Administration, U.S. Department
   of Transportation
400 Seventh St. SW
Washington, DC 20509
(800) 996-2723
http://www.marad.dot.gov

Seafarers International Union of North
   America
5201 Auth Way
Camp Springs, MD 20746-4275
(301) 899-0675
http://www.seafarers.org

Earnings and Benefits

Because of federal laws and the efforts of a strong union, employees of the U.S. merchant marine are among the highest-paid seamen in the world. In 2004 the median wage of chief stewards was $14.86 per hour; of chief cooks, $4,618 per month, including overtime pay; and of mess attendants and utility hands, $3,199 per month, including overtime. Overtime work increases most salaries by fifty percent. However, because employees of the merchant marine must often wait between jobs, their yearly income tends to be lower than the monthly figures would indicate.

Benefits include room and board, medical care, hospitalization insurance, pensions, and five to fifteen hours of paid vacation for each thirty days of employment.

Parking Analyst

Education and Training
Some college plus training

Salary
Median—$38,480 per year

Employment Outlook
Varies—see profile

Definition and Nature of the Work

Parking analysts, also called parking engineering technicians, develop plans for the construction and use of government-owned, multiple-vehicle parking facilities. These facilities may serve hospitals, libraries, or government offices, as well as general municipal parking.

To determine the best site for parking facilities, analysts conduct in-depth field surveys of possible locations, which take into account the effect the new facilities would have on their surroundings. Analysts also consider the necessary capacity, the possible turnover of vehicles, and the parking fees to be charged. Their last step is to prepare maps, graphs, tracings, and diagrams to demonstrate their findings.

Some analysts design parking facilities and prepare cost estimates for their construction. Their budgets must provide sufficient spaces and specify details of paving, lighting, and landscaping. At construction sites, parking analysts evaluate the contractors' work, ensuring that it conforms to their specifications. They keep logs as construction progresses and prepare final reports at the completion of projects.

Education and Training Requirements

High school diplomas are required. Most parking analysts have at least two years of training in engineering technology at the community college level. This training should include courses in statistics, methods of surveying, technical writing, oral communication, and economics. Additional training is received on the job.

Getting the Job

Parking analysts are employed by government agencies that operate large parking facilities. Job seekers should contact the federal, state, or local civil service commission.

Advancement Possibilities and Employment Outlook

Parking analysts advance by being promoted to higher grades. Each grade represents a different salary level and increased responsibility. With additional education, some parking analysts become engineers.

The employment outlook for parking analysts depends on the level of government spending through 2014. However, as the number of vehicles using government-owned parking facilities continues to grow, demand for new parking facilities should increase as well.

Working Conditions

Parking analysts' offices, usually located in government buildings, are pleasant, well lighted, and furnished with computers and drafting tables. Analysts travel to construction sites in all kinds of weather. Workweeks usually run forty hours.

Earnings and Benefits

Parking analysts are classified as engineering technicians in government service. In 2004 the median salary for all engineering technicians specializing in civil engineering work was $38,480 per year. The most experienced workers earned more than $57,550 per year. Those who worked for local governments earned about $43,700 per year, depending on their education and experience.

Benefits include health and life insurance, pension plans, and paid vacations.

Where to Go for More Information

International Brotherhood of Teamsters, AFL-CIO
25 Louisiana Ave. NW
Washington, DC 20001-2198
(202) 624-6800
http://www.teamster.org

International Parking Institute
PO Box 7167
Fredericksburg, VA 22404-7167
(540) 371-7535
http://www.parking.org

National Parking Association
1112 Sixteenth St. NW, Ste. 300
Washington, DC 20036
(800) 647-7275
http://www.npapark.org

Railroad Conductor

Education and Training
High school plus training

Salary
Median—$22.28 per hour

Employment Outlook
Poor

Definition and Nature of the Work

Railroad conductors supervise train crews and are responsible for the safety of the passengers and crew who ride on their trains. Some conductors, known as road service conductors, work on trains that carry passengers or freight locally or long distances. Other conductors work in the train yard and are called yard conductors or yardmasters.

Before trains leave the station, road service conductors receive train orders by telephone, fax, or computer from the dispatcher at the railroad's central office. These orders include listings of the cargo and their routes with the scheduled stops. Conductors must make sure that the crews of their trains understand these orders.

Conductors inspect each car of their trains, to make sure the operating mechanisms have been properly monitored and are working. If the repairs cannot be made during the run, conductors must instruct engineers to remove the defective cars. Conductors see that cars are added or removed at the proper points for picking up or unloading cargo.

Conductors signal to engineers when they want their trains to leave stations or train yards. On passenger trains they sometimes collect tickets and cash fares, and they may give information to passengers.

At the end of their trips road service conductors report to company officials, informing them of the number of passengers carried and the time their trains departed and arrived. If the trains carried cargo, they must report on its condition when their trains reach their destinations.

Yard conductors supervise all the workers and activities in the rail yard. Some cars are sent to special tracks to be unloaded of their cargo, and other cars must be prepared to leave at scheduled times. Yard conductors give engineers instructions to assemble, disassemble, and move cars. Usually, engineers direct cars by computer, but some cars may need to be moved manually by yard workers.

On passenger trains, railroad conductors collect tickets or cash for fares, provide passengers with information, and ensure that train cars are added or removed at the proper points. (© Martha Tabor/ Working Images Photographs. Reproduced by permission.)

Education and Training Requirements

It takes several years for conductors to get their positions because they must be promoted from other railroad jobs. Almost all are high school graduates. Helpful high school courses include electronics and manual arts, such as wood and metal shop. Part-time work on railroads during the summer and holiday seasons may be available and is valuable experience.

Many employers require aspiring conductors to complete training programs administered by either railroad companies or community colleges. Employers usually require job applicants to pass physical examinations, drug and alcohol screening, and criminal background checks.

Those who want to become conductors are tested on their knowledge of signals, timetables, operating rules, and other subjects. After passing these tests, potential conductors are made temporary conductors until full-time positions are available. Temporary conductors, also called "extra-board conductors," fill in for regular conductors who are sick or on vacation.

Railroads usually keep separate seniority lists for road service and yard conductors. However, depending on the railroad, some yard conductors may advance to freight work and eventually to passenger trains.

Getting the Job

Job seekers can apply directly to railroad employment offices or talk to the superintendents of railroads' local divisions. Newspaper classified ads and Internet job sites may provide employment leads.

Advancement Possibilities and Employment Outlook

Conductors are already at the top of their field. However, those who show special ability with people may become train masters or passenger agents.

The employment outlook for conductors is poor through 2014. The demand for railroad freight service will grow as the economy and transportation of goods expand; however, employment will decline because of technology that allows road service conductors and other workers to make more runs per day. In addition, new rules allow trains to travel with smaller crews. As a result, the industry is eliminating positions vacated by workers who retire. The number of yard conductors will also decline because coupling and uncoupling of cars is automated, and the amount of supervision needed for yard workers is being reduced.

Working Conditions

Railroad service conductors travel most of their working day and may spend a great deal of time away from home. While yard conductors generally work forty-hour weeks, service conductors often work longer hours. Full-time conductors have set schedules that they follow year after year. Extra-board conductors, on the other hand, usually have irregular schedules and work on short notice.

Conductors have responsible jobs and must be able to direct the work of others. They must be courteous to passengers and have working knowledge of how trains operate. In addition, they must have good eyesight and hearing and be in good health.

Earnings and Benefits

Pay for railroad conductors varies with the size of the railroad and the type of duties. In 2004 the median pay for railroad conductors was $22.28 per hour. Because most conductors are unionized, wages are usually guaranteed by contract. Generally, conductors who work in passenger or freight service get a full day's pay after they have made a run of a certain number of miles or have worked a certain number of hours. Conductors who work overtime receive time-and-a-half pay. However, many contracts limit the number of hours conductors can work or the amount of miles they can ride each month. After conductors have put in a certain number of miles or hours of work, they are often replaced by extra-board conductors. Extra-board conductors earn less than regular conductors because they work fewer hours each week.

Benefits usually include paid sick days and vacations, pensions, and disability plans. Conductors' families are usually able to travel at reduced rates or free of charge.

Where to Go for More Information

Association of American Railroads
50 F St. NW
Washington, DC 20001-1564
(202) 639-2100
http://www.aar.org

United Transportation Union
14600 Detroit Ave.
Cleveland, OH 44107-4250
(216) 228-9400
http://www.utu.org

Railroad Engineer

Education and Training
High school, training, and license

Salary
Median—$24.30 per hour

Employment Outlook
Poor

Definition and Nature of the Work

Railroad engineers are also called locomotive engineers. Some run the trains that carry freight or passengers across the country or locally. Yard engineers, by contrast, operate automated systems that move passenger and freight cars into place in rail yards. They add cars to trains before they leave the station and separate cars after trains have reached their destinations. They also use locomotives to switch cars around for loading and unloading freight.

Engineers must be able to operate any locomotive the train lines use. Before and after each run, they must check carefully for mechanical problems. They either make minor repairs themselves or return the locomotives to the yard for servicing.

Advanced technology has affected the way engineers do their jobs. Much of the information they were traditionally responsible for, such as knowing the proper speeds at curves and bridges along their routes, is now communicated to engineers by computers and telephones. For example, if a train is approaching a curve that requires a slower speed, computers relay that information from the central railroad station to the locomotive, alerting the engineer to make the necessary adjustments. Computerized devices also alert engineers to train malfunctions. Engineers still must know all the operating rules, including how signals are used, and the locations of rail sidings (platforms) and the number of cars each siding can hold.

Education and Training Requirements

It takes several years for railroad engineers to get their positions. Most aspiring engineers start as yard laborers. To be hired for these entry-level positions, workers must have high school diplomas or their equivalent. They must also have good vision and hearing and be in good physical condition—the job is physically strenuous. Besides physical examinations, applicants must undergo criminal background checks and drug screening. After several years in the rail yard, laborers can become eligible for additional training.

Federal regulations require that beginning engineers complete formal training programs, including classroom, simulator, and hands-on instruction. The programs are usually administered by railroad companies, but they may also be available through technical schools or community colleges. When they have completed the programs, workers must pass comprehensive exams to obtain engineering licenses.

Because rules and procedures change, engineers are retested periodically. They also undergo frequent drug and alcohol screening and physical examinations.

Getting the Job

Job seekers can apply directly to railroad companies for jobs as yard workers or—if they already have experience in the rail yard or other rail occupations—to be accepted into training programs. Job openings are sometimes listed by state or private employment agencies, on union Web sites, or on Internet job sites.

Railroad engineers must be able to run all locomotives used by the train line. (© Steve Crise/Corbis.)

Advancement Possibilities and Employment Outlook

Railroad engineers are at the top of their field. By accumulating seniority over many years, engineers can progress to more desirable jobs. For example, they may move to road service from assignments in the yard. Some may become railroad inspectors.

Employment of railroad engineers is expected to decline through 2014. While demand for service engineers to run freight trains should grow as the economy and transportation of goods expand, fewer yard engineers may be needed because of computerization. Opportunities could be plentiful, however, because a large number of engineers may retire in the next decade. More jobs for engineers may also become available if high-speed service expands in some rail corridors.

Working Conditions

Engineers who work in passenger service have fairly regular shifts in comfortable conditions. Those who work with freight have more difficult assignments. Especially on short runs, during which they must stop frequently to load and unload cars, the work can be physically demanding and sometimes dangerous. It often requires long hours, so strength and endurance are essential.

New engineers may wait years for regular assignments. In the meantime they are on call twenty-four hours a day to go where they are needed and may spend many nights away from home.

Earnings and Benefits

In 2004 the median salary for railroad engineers was $24.30 per hour. Overtime significantly increased many engineers' yearly income. (On some rail lines their earnings were curtailed by mileage limits that had been agreed to by the companies and the unions.) New engineers did not have regular hours, so they made much less money.

Benefits may include paid vacations, sick leave, health insurance, and pensions.

Traffic Technician

Education and Training
College plus training

Salary
Median—$38,480 per year

Employment Outlook
Good

Definition and Nature of the Work

Traffic technicians gather and analyze data about traffic flow, accidents, and proposed commercial and residential developments. For instance, they may use counters to measure vehicular and pedestrian traffic in specific places at specific times. Based on their findings, they make proposals to expedite traffic flow, such as additional traffic signs and better lighting to improve visibility. Also called traffic analysts or traffic-control technicians, they may assist traffic engineers on large civil engineering projects, such as highway overpasses.

Technicians often interact with the public, answering questions about traffic flow or discussing traffic-control plans, policies, or procedures. They may also visit the sites of commercial or residential developments to determine how the structures will affect current traffic patterns. They may design improvements to existing plans.

Traffic technicians work for federal highway agencies and for the highway or street departments of state, county, and city governments. Others work for private consulting firms, educational institutions, or businesses.

Education and Training Requirements

Traffic technicians must have high school diplomas. A growing number of technicians have college degrees in related fields. Useful courses include statistics, physics, city planning, and computer-aided design.

New hires participate in short training programs, which may involve both classroom instruction and practical experience. They are trained and supervised by experienced technicians until they can work independently.

Getting the Job

Civil service commissions can provide information about civil service tests and job opportunities in government. Job seekers can also apply directly to public transportation companies and engineering firms. College placement services, newspaper classified ads, and Internet job sites may offer employment leads.

Advancement Possibilities and Employment Outlook

With experience traffic technicians can become head technicians or move to supervisory positions. With additional education they can become traffic engineers.

Employment of traffic technicians is expected to grow as fast as the average for all jobs through 2014. As the population increases and continues to move to suburban areas, demand should grow for technicians who can analyze traffic flow and implement improvements.

Working Conditions

Traffic technicians usually work forty hours per week. Extra hours may be necessary to study evening or weekend traffic patterns or to assess commercial or residential development sites. Technicians spend much of their workday out on the roads analyzing traffic patterns.

Earnings and Benefits

In 2004 the median salary of traffic technicians was $38,480 per year. Benefits usually included paid holidays and vacations, health insurance, and retirement plans.

Where to Go for More Information

American Society of Civil Engineers
1801 Alexander Graham Bell Dr.
Reston, VA 20191-4400
(800) 548-2723
http://www.asce.org

Institute of Transportation Engineers
1099 Fourteenth St. NW, Ste. 300 W.
Washington, DC 20005-3438
(202) 289-0222
http://www.ite.org

Transportation Inspector

Definition and Nature of the Work

Transportation inspectors examine equipment and procedures to ensure that planes, public transportation systems, or railroads conform to federal or state safety regulations.

Aviation inspectors examine aircraft, maintenance procedures, air traffic controls, air navigational aids, and communications equipment. If they find the aircraft in compliance with federal safety regulations, they issue certificates of worthiness. Most aviation inspectors work for the Federal Aviation Administration (FAA).

Public transportation inspectors review the operation of public transportation systems to ensure that they comply with federal, state, and local regulations. They also investigate accidents and equipment failures and determine the need for repairs and changes in service.

Railroad inspectors monitor railroad equipment, roadbeds, and tracks to determine if repairs are needed. If repairs are made, they inspect again, testing equipment and facilities to ensure that they are in working order.

Education and Training
Varies—see profile

Salary
Median—$47,920 per year

Employment Outlook
Good

Education and Training Requirements

Educational and training requirements vary according to the job. In general, inspectors have advanced from other positions in their fields. For example, aviation inspectors usually start out as aircraft mechanics who have fulfilled the requirements for that job: two- to four-year degree, government certification, and eighteen to twenty-four months of instruction at an FAA-approved school. They then accumulate several years of experience before they qualify to become inspectors with the FAA, which may require a special authorization.

Railroad inspectors usually work their way up from railroad maintenance worker to signal operator and then to inspector. They must have years of experience in railroad maintenance and be very knowledgeable about safety procedures. They have been tested at every level of advancement to prove their skills and ability.

Public transportation inspectors usually advance from maintenance positions. They are experienced with the mechanics of subways, buses, trolleys, streetcars, and other forms of public transit. They have undergone substantial training, in the classroom and on the job, and are thoroughly acquainted with federal, state, and local safety regulations. They have been repeatedly tested on their knowledge and skills.

Getting the Job

Transportation inspectors usually start out in maintenance positions in their given fields and then advance to the job of inspector. Job seekers should first choose a field of interest and then apply for entry-level positions in that field. School placement offices can provide information on job opportunities.

Advancement Possibilities and Employment Outlook

Transportation inspectors can become chief inspectors or heads of their departments. They may also move into other administrative or supervisory positions within their companies or departments.

Employment of transportation inspectors is expected to grow as fast as the average for all occupations through 2014. Openings should occur as experienced inspectors retire or move into other positions.

Working Conditions

Transportation inspectors usually work forty-hour weeks. They work outside, in railroad yards, or inside, in garages and airplane hangars. Their tasks may be physically demanding, as inspectors have to climb and move into precarious positions to inspect some machinery and equipment. The job may be stressful, as their work can affect transportation schedules and the safety of passengers and crew.

Earnings and Benefits

Salaries vary, depending on the type of work and level of experience. In 2004 the median salary of all inspectors was $47,920 per year. Experienced inspectors earned much more.

Benefits include health and dental insurance and retirement plans.

Where to Go for More Information

American Public Transit Association
1666 K St. NW, Ste. 1100
Washington, DC 20006
(202) 496-4800
http://www.apta.com

Brotherhood of Maintenance of Way
   Employees
20300 Civic Center Dr., Ste. 320
Southfield, MI 48076-4169
(248) 948-1010
http://www.bmwe.org

National Air Transportation Association
4226 King St.
Alexandra, VA 22302
(703) 845-9000
http://www.nata.aero

Transport Workers Union of America
1700 Broadway
New York, NY 10019
(212) 259-4900
http://www.twu.org

Truck Terminal Manager

Definition and Nature of the Work

Terminal managers are responsible for the smooth operation of trucking centers, which are buildings where freight is loaded or unloaded. They coordinate, direct, and supervise all activities in the terminals.

Managers plan and direct operations, including the weighing of freight and choosing the lifts and crates that will be used to move it. They closely supervise the loading and unloading of cargo to avoid damage—their precautions save money and help maintain good reputations. Managers are also responsible for keeping equipment in good order and for making sure that working conditions are safe.

Terminal managers must be able to work effectively with all types of people. They handle customer complaints as well as interact with truck drivers and other terminal staff.

Education and Training Requirements

Terminal managers should have high school diplomas or the equivalent; most companies prefer applicants who have had some college education. High school and college courses in science, business administration, and personnel relations are helpful. Some community and junior colleges offer classes in warehouse organization, materials handling, and production control. Many of these courses combine classroom study with on-the-job training.

Companies also offer on-the-job training. New managers learn the routines of the terminal before they are given full responsibility. Some start out as truck drivers or dispatchers and are promoted.

Getting the Job

Most terminal managers start as truck drivers or dispatchers. Job seekers can apply directly to trucking terminals. School placement offices, state employment services, newspaper classified ads, and Internet job sites may provide employment leads.

Advancement Possibilities and Employment Outlook

Advancement depends on experience and education. Terminal managers who have some college training or degrees may have more opportunities than those with only high school diplomas, although experience is always a factor. Terminal managers can become company representatives or traffic managers.

Employment of terminal managers is expected to grow as fast as the average for all occupations through 2014. As general economic growth increases the amount of freight that needs to be moved, the trucking industry should expand, creating demand for terminal managers. Openings also occur when experienced managers retire or leave the field.

Working Conditions

Terminal managers usually work forty-hour weeks, often in shifts. Overtime may be necessary, especially if business gets heavy or in emergencies. The job can be stressful, because freight can be time-sensitive or perishable. Road condi-

> ### Education and Training
> Some college education
>
> ### Salary
> Median—$32.36 per hour
>
> ### Employment Outlook
> Good

Where to Go for More Information

American Society of Transportation and
   Logistics
1700 N. Moore St., Ste. 1900
Arlington, VA 22209
(703) 524-5011
http://www.astl.org

American Trucking Associations
2200 Mill Rd.
Alexandria, VA 22314-4677
(703) 838-1700
http://www.truckline.com

Council of Supply Chain Management
   Professionals
2805 Butterfield Rd., Ste. 200
Oak Brook, IL 60523
(630) 574-0985
http://www.cscmp.org

tions may delay arrival and departure of trucks. Managers usually have offices, but they are often outside in all kinds of weather.

Earnings and Benefits

Salaries vary, depending on education, level of responsibility, and experience. In 2004 the median wage of terminal managers was $32.36 per hour.

Benefits usually include paid vacations and holidays and health insurance. Some companies offer retirement plans.

Air Traffic Controller

Definition and Nature of the Work

Air traffic controllers coordinate the movement of aircraft in the air and at airports to prevent accidents and minimize delays. They usually work in teams, tracking planes using radar and visual observation. They consider the weather, including wind velocity and direction, and the number, size, and speed of all aircraft in the area.

Terminal controllers, also known as tower controllers, work in towers near the runways of major airports. They give pilots permission to taxi, take off, and land their aircraft. As planes approach airports, controllers in the radar room observe the planes and direct the pilots to runways. When airports are busy, the controllers may have to fit the planes into the traffic pattern of aircraft waiting to land. As planes approach runways, other controllers, who also are watching the planes on radar, monitor the aircraft the last mile, delaying any departures that would interfere with landings. Once the planes have landed, ground controllers in the tower direct the pilots to their assigned gates. Ground controllers usually work by sight; they use radar only if visibility is poor. For takeoffs, the procedure is reversed.

Once planes are airborne, their movement is controlled by en route controllers, who work in twenty air-route control centers throughout the country. Each cen-

Air traffic controllers work under great stress, coordinating the aircraft at airports to prevent accidents and minimize delays in taking off and landing. *(AP Images.)*

ter is responsible for a certain air sector and employs between three hundred and seven hundred controllers. En route controllers help pilots stay on course, advise them about other aircraft in the sector, and often reroute them around storms.

Air traffic controllers are also stationed at more than one hundred flight service stations, which provide pilots with information about weather and terrain, and at the Air Traffic Control Systems Command Center in Virginia, where they oversee the entire system.

The Federal Aviation Administration (FAA) has implemented the National Airspace System Architecture, a modernization of the entire air control system. As it replaces aging equipment with new technology and procedures, it should increase safety and controllers' efficiency.

Education and Training Requirements

Applicants must pass rigorous physical examinations, criminal background checks, and drug screening. Some applicants may also be required to take tests that indicate whether they have the aptitude for the job. Applicants must have the ability to work well under extreme pressure, speak clearly, and be under thirty-one years of age.

Some air traffic controllers qualify for their jobs through related military experience. Others qualify with four years of college in aviation administration; three years of work experience in aviation; or a combination of college and work experience. Fourteen colleges offer FAA-approved degrees in aviation administration with emphasis in air traffic control (the programs are listed on the National Air Traffic Controllers Association Web site). Appropriate experience would include work as a commercial pilot, an air dispatch operator, or an aircraft navigator.

Once selected, applicants undergo twelve weeks of intensive training at the Federal Aviation Administration Air Control Academy in Oklahoma. After graduating they are assigned to towers and centers throughout the United States as "developmental controllers." Additional class work and on-the-job training, with supervision, can last two to four years depending on their specialties and the complexity of the facility.

Getting the Job

Applicants are selected through the competitive federal civil service system. The FAA's job Web site and placement offices of FAA-approved aviation administration programs can provide applications. The Web sites of the National Air Traffic Controllers Association and the National Association of Air Traffic Specialists offer additional information.

Advancement Possibilities and Employment Outlook

New controllers usually begin by supplying pilots with basic flight and airport information. They can move up through the ranks of ground controller, local controller, departure controller, and arrival controller. At en route control centers, they serve as radar associate controllers and then radar controllers. Controllers may also transfer to different locations or advance to supervisory, management, or administrative positions at the FAA.

Employment of air traffic controllers is expected to increase about as fast as the average for all occupations through 2014. Although airports and aircraft are increasing in number and airspace is becoming more and more congested, improved technology may increase controllers' productivity and minimize the number of new positions. In addition, competition can be stiff because the number of qualified applicants exceeds the number of jobs available each year. Turnover is relatively low in this field because of the high pay and the young age of most workers.

Working Conditions

Air traffic controllers work forty hours per week. For night and weekend shifts, which are assigned on a rotating basis, controllers receive overtime pay or equal time off. Controllers work in clean, well-lighted, and well-ventilated facilities.

Air traffic controllers work under great pressure because every decision they make affects the lives of many people. They must be able to cope with this pressure on a day-to-day basis as well as in emergencies.

Earnings and Benefits

Salaries depend on the type and size of the airport—a large international airport has a different classification from a small regional facility. In 2004 the median salary for all air traffic controllers was $102,030 per year. Experienced and highly trained controllers earned more than $139,210 per year.

Besides health and life insurance, most controllers receive thirteen to twenty-six days of paid vacation and thirteen days of paid sick leave each year. Controllers who work for the federal government become eligible to retire earlier and with fewer years of experience than most other federal employees.

Where to Go for More Information

Air Traffic Control Association
1101 King St, Ste. 300
Alexandria, VA 22314
(703) 299-2430
http://www.atca.org

National Air Traffic Controllers Association
1325 Massachusetts Ave. NW
Washington, DC 20005
(202) 628-5451
http://www.natca.org

National Association of Air Traffic
    Specialists
PO Box 2550
Landover Hills, MD 20784-0550
(301) 459-5595
http://www.naats.org

Airplane Pilot

Definition and Nature of the Work

Pilots fly aircraft of all sizes, transporting passengers and cargo across the state and around the world. They are responsible for the safety of the airplane, its passengers, the crew, and any cargo on board.

Most pilots work for major airlines that carry passengers and cargo. Airlines require two pilots in the cockpit flying the plane: the captain and the copilot, also known as the first officer. Before a flight, they examine the airplane's control equipment, checking each item off a list. After determining the weather and flight conditions, the captain has their flight plans approved by the air traffic controllers. Meanwhile, the copilot charts the airplane's route and computes the flying time. By radio the captain then requests that the aircraft dispatcher give permission for them to taxi, or begin moving, to the runway. After receiving clearance for takeoff, the pilots accelerate the plane down the runway until it achieves lift and is airborne.

Once the plane is in the air, it usually flies itself by an electronic automatic pilot. The captain and copilot regularly report to air-route control stations by radio, reporting any problems they may have. They receive information about the

Education and Training
Varies—see profile

Salary
Varies—see profile

Employment Outlook
Good

weather and any traffic in their part of the sky. Near their destination airport, the captain rechecks the landing gear and requests clearance to land from the air traffic controllers. In poor visibility the landing may be performed entirely by instruments. After landing, the pilots must file a flight report. The plane is then turned over to the maintenance crew.

About one out of five pilots do not work for major airlines. Test pilots, for example, fly new or experimental planes to examine their flight performance and safety. Check pilots or pilot examiners regularly observe other pilots to review their flying ability. They are employed by the Federal Aviation Administration (FAA) and by large airlines. Business pilots fly aircraft—usually smaller jets—owned by private companies. Between flights, they may be in charge of maintenance. Agricultural pilots, or crop dusters, fly planes that drop chemical fertilizers and pest killers on crops. They sometimes work as firefighters, flying over forest fires to drop chemicals that douse flames.

Helicopter pilots fly over highways to report on traffic conditions and accidents. Others provide ambulance services, help fire departments extinguish fires, and assist rescue operations in wilderness and mountain areas. Private companies hire helicopter pilots to provide commuter services.

Education and Training Requirements

Most employers prefer college graduates for the job. Test pilots are usually required to have engineering degrees.

All pilots who are paid to transport passengers or cargo must have commercial pilot's licenses. Applicants must be at least eighteen years old and have at least 250 hours of flight experience. Fewer hours of flight experience are required of applicants who participate in certain FAA-approved flight schools. Applicants must also pass strict physical examinations to determine that they are in good health and have both good hearing and vision correctable to 20/20. The FAA also administers two tests for the license: one is a written test to check knowledge of FAA rules, navigation techniques, and the principles of safe flight; the other is a demonstration of flying skills, including flying by instruments, for an FFA check pilot. Licenses are granted for certain classes and types of airplanes. For example, all pilots must have ratings for the class of plane they can fly (such as single-engine, multiengine, or seaplane) and for the specific type of plane (such as DC-9s or Boeing 747s).

Some pilots need additional qualifications. For example, pilots must have instrument ratings to fly airplanes entirely by instrument when visibility is poor. The FAA rating requires that pilots have forty hours of experience in instrument flying. Helicopter pilots must have special helicopter ratings.

Airline pilots also need airline transport licenses. To qualify, pilots must be at least twenty-three years old and have a total of fifteen hundred hours of flight time, including night and instrument flying. Commercial pilots also need restricted radio operator's permits from the Federal Communications Commission. They must also pass psychological and aptitude tests.

The armed forces provide excellent pilot training. Flying can also be learned at one of the six hundred FAA-certified civilian flying schools. Either kind of training satisfies the flight experience requirements for commercial licensing.

Once hired, airline pilots must undergo a week of company orientation; three to six weeks of ground school and simulator training; and twenty-five hours of operating experience, culminating with a check ride with an FAA pilot examiner. Pilots must participate in additional training and simulator checks once or twice each year.

Getting the Job

Most airline pilots begin as flight engineers, who are stationed in the cockpit and make certain that the aircraft and all the instruments are in good working order. After one to five years, they can advance to first officer. The best opportunities for new airline pilots are with smaller, regional airlines.

Flight schools can offer job placement assistance in airline and commercial flying. Internet job sites as well as the FAA Web site also provide job listings.

Advancement Possibilities and Employment Outlook

Pilots are at the top of their profession, although they can advance through seniority: those who work for the same companies for many years receive higher pay and better routes. Some pilots take jobs as pilot examiners or airline administrators. Other pilots open their own flying schools. A few become air traffic controllers.

Employment of professional pilots is expected to increase about as fast as the average for all occupations through 2014. As smaller, no-frills airlines continue to grow and as the amount of cargo shipped by air expands, demand for pilots should increase. However, most passenger airlines have more qualified applicants than they have positions available, so competition is stiff. Jobs are likely to go to those pilots who have logged the greatest number of flying hours and have the most licenses and ratings. Those with military experience also have an advantage.

Working Conditions

Airline pilots work about sixteen days a month. They usually spend fewer than seventy hours a month actually flying, with the remaining time spent performing nonflying duties. By FFA rules, pilots may not fly more than one hundred hours per month or one thousand hours per year. The majority of flights involve layovers away from home.

While aircraft are usually clean and comfortable, the job involves considerable risk. For example, commercial pilots on international routes suffer from jet lag—a disorientation and fatigue caused by many hours of flying through different time zones. Test pilots have particularly dangerous jobs: if the planes they fly do not operate properly, they can be seriously injured or killed. Agricultural pilots often work with toxic chemicals.

Although flying does not involve much physical effort, pilots are subject to stress and must always be alert to make decisions quickly. They work under constant pressure, because they are responsible for the safety of their aircraft, passengers, and cargo. They can lose their jobs at any time if they do not pass demanding physical examinations.

Where to Go for More Information

Air Line Pilots Association, International
1625 Massachusetts Ave. NW
Washington, DC 20036
(703) 689-2270
http://www.alpa.org

Aircraft Owners and Pilots Association
421 Aviation Way
Frederick, MD 21701-4756
(301) 695-2000
http://www.aopa.org

Coalition of Airline Pilots Associations
1101 Pennsylvania Ave. NW, Ste. 6646
Washington, DC 20004
(202) 756-2956
http://www.capapilots.org

Earnings and Benefits

Pilots are paid according to the type, size, and speed of their airplanes and the number of hours and miles they fly. They receive extra pay for night work and for international flights. In 2004 the median salary of all airline pilots was $129,250 per year. Some senior captains of very large aircraft earned more than $200,000 per year. Many airline pilots are members of unions.

The median salary for commercial pilots was $53,870 per year. The most experienced commercial pilots earned more than $110,070 per year.

Benefits vary by employer, but usually include paid vacations, sick leave, retirement plans, and health and life insurance. Airline pilots and their immediate families can fly at reduced airfare. Living accommodations and allowances are provided when airline pilots are away from home.

Airport Manager

Education and Training
College

Salary
Median—$47,450 per year

Employment Outlook
Good

Definition and Nature of the Work

Airport managers oversee more than seventeen thousand airports in the United States. Some are large metropolitan airports with hundreds of scheduled flights arriving and departing every day. Others are private airfields with no scheduled flights and very little daily activity. Small airports are generally managed by their owners, but the operations of medium-sized and large airports are so complex that the airports need part-time or full-time managers.

While they generally have no direct control over flying activities, airport managers do make sure that Federal Aviation Administration regulations are enforced. They maintain good relations with the airlines that fly in and out of their airports and supervise the maintenance of runways and airport buildings. They oversee budgets, staffing, and public relations. Above all, airport managers must ensure that their airports run safely and efficiently and provide good service to their communities.

Depending on the size of the airport, managers may supervise small clerical staffs or large staffs of assistants and other workers. Alone or with their staffs, managers plan for the future needs of their airports and oversee new construction; meet with government officials and public representatives; and tackle the problems faced by passengers. Because businesses operating in the airport, such as food concessions and car rental companies, generate considerable income for airports, managers must negotiate contracts and make sure the vendors provide good service.

Airport managers do not need to be pilots, but they do need to understand aviation and business management. They must be able to work well with people and communicate effectively. Leadership and decision-making skills are essential.

Education and Training Requirements

Bachelor's degrees are required to enter this field. Most airport managers get degrees in business administration with special emphasis on air transportation or engineering. Many managers complete graduate studies in business administration.

High school courses in English, social studies, and mathematics can be helpful preparation. College courses should include management policies, economics, finance, public relations, business law, aviation legislation, and engineering. A few airports offer one- or two-year internship programs for college graduates. The programs provide experience in all phases of airport management.

Airport managers do not need to be pilots, but they must have expertise in aviation and business management. (© Martha Tabor/ Working Images Photographs. Reproduced by permission.)

Getting the Job

Most airport-manager jobs require extensive experience. The best route for new graduates is to develop work records in one or more fields of airline work, such as airline dispatching or airline public relations, and then apply for assistant manager positions. Experience in another field of management, such as bus transportation or sales management, can also be helpful. Job seekers can apply directly for assistant manager positions at smaller airports. Civil service commissions have information about the exams required for jobs at government-operated airports. They may also have lists of open positions.

Advancement Possibilities and Employment Outlook

Because airport managers are at the top of their field, they generally advance by moving to larger airports as assistant managers, department managers, and managers.

Employment of airport managers is expected to increase as fast as the average for all occupations through 2014. Growth of airports and air travel should increase the demand for airport managers. However, this is a comparatively small field, so job seekers can face strong competition for openings. Applicants with graduate degrees in business administration and diverse experience in the field should have the best opportunities.

Working Conditions

Airport managers usually work in clean, modern offices in airport administration buildings. They may supervise such outdoor activities as snow removal on runways.

Workweeks generally run forty hours, especially in large airports. Night and weekend work may be required. In emergencies managers must be available around the clock.

Earnings and Benefits

Salaries for airport managers vary widely according to the size and location of the airport. In 2004 the median salary for all airport managers was $47,450 per year. Managers of large international airports earned more than $80,000 per year.

Benefits usually include paid sick leave and vacations, life and health insurance, and retirement plans.

Fleet Manager

Education and Training
College

Salary
Varies—see profile

Employment Outlook
Good

Definition and Nature of the Work

Fleet managers are responsible for the vehicles owned by major corporations; government agencies; nonprofit organizations; or service organizations such as law enforcement agencies and educational institutions. They may be responsible for fleets ranging in size from several hundred to more than a thousand vehicles. Fleet managers are sometimes referred to as directors of fleet operations or administrators of corporate fleets.

Fleet managers often direct administrative staffs and report to transportation directors, vice presidents, or other administrative directors. Responsibilities generally include the development of fleet administration standards and vehicle operating policies; preparation of annual budgets and periodic reports on operating costs; purchase or lease of vehicles and equipment; and control over maintenance, repair, replacement, and disposal of vehicles.

In addition, managers may direct fleet-related risk management training, such as safety and accident prevention programs, and negotiate insurance matters. Some fleet managers create driver's manuals or newsletters to keep employees informed about their fleet programs.

Education and Training Requirements

Many employers prefer to hire applicants who have bachelor's degrees in science, marketing, or a technical field; some employers even require master's degrees. Fleet managers must have several years of experience working with the operation, maintenance, or administration of fleets of vehicles as well as supervisory experience. In addition, they need in-depth knowledge of auto rental and leasing programs, strong interpersonal skills, and excellent oral and written communication skills. Computer ability is essential.

Getting the Job

Workers must gain experience in the field before they can become fleet managers. Most managers have had several years of experience on fleet administration staffs or with car rental or leasing agencies. For entry-level positions in the field, job seekers can apply directly to companies that operate fleets of vehicles. Newspaper classified ads and Internet job sites may provide employment leads.

Advancement Possibilities and Employment Outlook

Fleet managers can advance by becoming managers of larger fleets. They can also become administrative directors, transportation directors, or vice presidents of companies.

Job openings for fleet managers are expected to increase as fast as the average through 2014. However, some companies may decide to contract with leasing firms to handle all aspects of fleet administration, thereby limiting the number of new openings for managers.

Working Conditions

Most fleet managers work for corporations or government agencies and have administrative staffs ranging in size from two to more than eleven employees. They generally work in comfortable offices, although they may spend some time checking vehicles outdoors.

Earnings and Benefits

Salaries for fleet managers vary, depending on the type of employer or geographic region. In 2004 salaries ranged from $30,000 per year to more than $70,000 per year.

Benefits usually include health insurance, retirement plans, and paid vacations and holidays. Many fleet managers get to drive company cars.

Where to Go for More Information

Automotive Fleet and Leasing Association
1000 Westgate Dr.
St. Paul, MN 55114
(651) 203-7247
http://www.aflaonline.com

National Association of Fleet
  Administrators
100 Wood Ave. S., Ste. 310
Iselin, NJ 08830-2709
(732) 494-8100
http://www.nafa.org

Flight Engineer

Definition and Nature of the Work

Flight engineers, sometimes called second officers, play almost as important a part in flying large aircraft as do pilots and copilots. Although they rarely take the controls to fly planes, flight engineers have many other responsibilities both on the ground and onboard aircraft.

Before a flight, the flight engineer inspects the outside of the plane to make sure there are no fluid leaks and that tires are inflated properly. If any problems are found, the engineer calls in mechanics to repair the plane.

Inside the aircraft, the flight engineer helps the pilot and copilot check the operation of more than a hundred instruments, including fuel gauges, oil pressure indicators, and switches to control wing flaps and landing gear. The flight engineer must also review the flight course and weather patterns to determine how much fuel should be loaded on the plane. If a plane is going to fly with a tailwind, it will need much less fuel than if it is going to be flying into a strong head wind.

Once the plane is airborne, the engineer advises the pilot, or captain, of any problems. The engineer monitors the instruments and may make minor re-

Education and Training
College, training, and license

Salary
Median—$129,250 per year

Employment Outlook
Fair

pairs, such as replacing fuses. The flight engineer also records fuel consumption during the flight and makes note of the performance of the engines.

After the plane has landed, the flight engineer inspects the plane again to make sure all equipment is functioning properly. If problems arose during the flight, the engineer reports them to the mechanics. The last task is to turn in the flight log of the trip.

The Federal Aviation Administration (FAA) now requires that most three- and four-engine airplanes and two-engine jet airplanes have flight engineers. Therefore, almost all flight engineers work for the major airlines that fly many large planes. Flight engineers are usually based in large cities that have major airports. Many are stationed in New York, California, Florida, Illinois, and Texas.

Education and Training Requirements

High school diplomas are required, although most airlines prefer to hire applicants with at least two years of college education. Flight engineers must have good vision and hearing and normal color perception. Physical exams are administered before applicants are hired.

Flight engineers also need commercial pilot's licenses and flight engineer's certificates from the FAA. To qualify for this certificate, applicants must have completed two-year courses in aircraft and engine maintenance or have three or more years of experience in this area of aviation.

Applicants can also qualify with at least one hundred hours of experience as a flight engineer or two hundred hours of flight time as a pilot in command of an aircraft with four or more engines. Another way to qualify is to complete FAA-approved courses on ground and flight procedures. In addition, applicants must pass written examinations covering flight theory, engine and aircraft performance, fuel requirements, the effect of weather on engine operation, and maintenance procedures. In-flight exams, which test the ability to perform both normal and emergency procedures, are also required.

Getting the Job

Flight schools can offer job placement assistance. Internet job sites as well as the FAA Web site provide job listings. Job seekers can also apply directly to the personnel departments of the major airlines. The Air Transport Association of America provides a list of the main offices of the airlines on request.

Advancement Possibilities and Employment Outlook

Advancement generally depends on flight engineers' qualifications and seniority. They can advance to copilot and pilot by obtaining the necessary licenses and flying the required number of hours.

Employment of flight engineers is expected to increase more slowly than the average for all occupations through 2014. Growth in this field will be limited because of the increasing use of computerized flight management systems. Many airlines are replacing older planes with newer models that do not require flight engineers.

Working Conditions

The work involves a certain amount of risk, but new procedures and technology make airplane travel safer every day. Flight engineers, like others in the airline industry, have irregular schedules. Employment is steady, but they must fly on late-night, cross-country, and international flights quite often. They are away from home much of the time.

Earnings and Benefits

Because most flight engineers are members of unions, their wages and benefits are set by contract. However, earnings depend on the type of flight, hours and miles flown, type of plane, and length of service. In 2004 the median salary for airline pilots and flight engineers was $129,250 per year.

The families of flight engineers generally receive a certain amount of free air transportation or reduced fares. Benefits include paid sick leave, between two and four weeks of vacation, life and health insurance, and retirement benefits.

Flight Instructor

Definition and Nature of the Work

Flight instructors teach students to fly airplanes and prepare them for tests to get licenses. Instructors are highly skilled pilots who have special ratings that allow them to teach.

In ground-school classes, they help their students learn specific flying skills—how to read airplane instrument panels, for example. They also explain the principles of math and physics that are important in flying. Other classes include supervised flying time, during which they provide feedback and may have students perform the same tasks or maneuvers many times. Some instructors use simulators or dual-controlled airplanes and helicopters.

Education and Training
Varies—see profile

Salary
Median—$31,530 per year

Employment Outlook
Good

Education and Training Requirements

The Federal Aviation Administration (FAA) requires flight instructors to have high school diplomas. High school courses in geography, science, math, and shop are good preparation. Airlines require that their instructors have at least two years of college. Many prefer instructors who have college degrees.

Instructors must have private pilot's licenses and commercial pilot's licenses, which have specific age, vision, and skill requirements. The licenses also require several FAA-administered examinations, including flight observation.

Applicants for flight instructor's ratings must pass FAA tests similar to those for commercial pilot's licenses: a rigorous physical examination; a written test that covers federal aviation rules, navigation techniques, radio operation, and meteorology; and a flying performance test. They must also pass tests in flight training maneuvers and both written and practical tests on flight instruction. Pilots who want to be instructors prepare for these tests by reading flight instruction

Flight instructors are highly skilled pilots who have special ratings that allow them to teach. *(Tim Boyle/Getty Images News/Getty Images.)*

handbooks and taking courses. Prospective instructors must have several hundred hours of flying experience as well.

Flight instructors receive ratings to fly and teach pilots of specific classes of aircraft. They must get additional ratings to fly and teach pilots of other kinds of planes.

Getting the Job

Flying schools usually have placement offices that help their students find jobs as instructors. Job seekers can also apply directly to airports, flying schools, and flying clubs.

Advancement Possibilities and Employment Outlook

Flight instructors can advance by taking courses that lead to additional credentials. For example, they may seek ratings to fly additional types of airplanes or qualify for instrument ratings. These advanced skills can be learned while they are already teaching basic flying courses. Some become chief instructors or directors of training for flight schools. Others become flight examiners for the FAA, giving licenses to students who pass various flying tests. With enough experience and flying hours, they can move to jobs as corporate or airline pilots.

Employment of flight instructors is expected to increase as fast as the average for all jobs through 2014. Anticipated growth of the airline industry, especially the growth in no-frills airlines and cargo traffic, should create a demand for more pilots, who need flight instructors.

Working Conditions

Flight instructors divide their time between classrooms on the ground and the cockpits of training planes. They must be patient and remain calm even in difficult situations. They work no more than eight hours per day, but their schedules are irregular: instructors work when their students are available. Weekend and evening work may be required.

Earnings and Benefits

Earnings for flight instructors vary according to the aircraft they use and whether they are freelance instructors or work for companies, airports, or flight schools. In 2004 the median salary of all flight instructors was $31,530 per year. Benefits varied by employer.

Where to Go for More Information

National Air Transportation Association
4226 King St.
Alexandria, VA 22302
(800) 808-6282
http://www.nata.aero

National Association of Flight Instructors
PO Box 3086
Oshkosh, WI 54903-3086
(920) 426-6801
http://www.nafinet.org

Industrial Traffic Manager

Definition and Nature of the Work

Businesses and manufacturers employ industrial traffic managers, also known as traffic managers, to decide how to transport their products. These employees arrange for the movement of raw materials into their factories and for the transportation of finished products to the markets where the goods are sold.

Industrial traffic managers must consider the kinds of raw materials and products their companies ship; the size and weight of their shipments; the safety factors involved in the transport; and time schedules. Sometimes they have to choose the containers and packaging materials. They then investigate the different transportation possibilities and choose the most cost-effective routes and carriers. Many of their calculations are made using computer software.

If delays in shipping occur, traffic managers must determine the reasons for the delays and arrange with carrier companies for faster service. When goods are lost or damaged in transit, they handle the claims and make the necessary arrangements with customers or carriers. Managers keep records of freight rates and shipments, usually by computer. Some traffic managers are responsible for approving bills, clearing shipments through customs, and leasing warehouse facilities for shipments. In large firms they often have assistants who do many of these tasks.

Some aspects of transportation are controlled by federal, state, and local regulations. Industrial traffic managers must be aware of the regulations and be prepared to argue cases for their companies before government regulatory agencies.

Industrial traffic managers work closely with the production, purchasing, marketing, and legal departments of their firms, conferring on such matters as importing raw materials inexpensively, planning shipping schedules, and purchasing goods. Sometimes they give advice on where to build warehouses and plants.

Education and Training Requirements

Employers prefer to hire college graduates with degrees in traffic management, logistics, or physical distribution. However, many people become managers with bachelor's degrees and courses in transportation, economics, management, marketing, and business law. Computer training is essential.

Education and Training
College

Salary
Median—$71,932 per year

Employment Outlook
Good

Although advanced degrees are not required, many traffic managers earn master's degrees.

Industrial traffic managers usually begin their careers as clerks or tracers in shipping rooms and traffic offices. With experience they can move into more technical positions, such as rate analyst, rate supervisor, senior rate clerk, and freight claims supervisor. All of these positions can be steps toward becoming assistant traffic manager and, eventually, traffic manager. At least seven years of experience in industrial transportation are required for qualified candidates to become traffic managers.

Getting the Job

Job seekers can apply directly to large companies for positions in their shipping or traffic departments. School placement offices can help graduates find openings. Internet job banks and newspaper classified ads may list available positions as well.

Advancement Possibilities and Employment Outlook

Traffic managers can advance by moving to larger companies or by specializing in one phase of traffic management. Advancement is usually based on experience and ability. However, education is becoming increasingly important. Chances for promotion to high-level jobs are better for those with advanced degrees and for those who participate in special studies related to the field.

Employment of industrial traffic managers is expected to grow as fast as the average for all jobs through 2014. Many large companies are separating their shipping and receiving activities into different departments, so more traffic management personnel and department heads should be needed. Employers may be selective, however, for they want expert traffic managers who can develop new ways to deliver raw materials and distribute finished products to larger and more distant markets.

Working Conditions

Many traffic managers work thirty-five to forty hours per week. However, they sometimes spend extra hours writing reports and traveling to branch offices. On occasion they may have to represent their companies before state or federal regulatory agencies.

Working conditions vary with the job and the company. Many managers have comfortable offices and visit factories often for consultation.

Earnings and Benefits

Salaries vary, depending on the size and type of company. In 2004 the median salary for industrial traffic managers was $71,932 per year. The most experienced managers, who worked at large companies and supervised large staffs, earned more than $82,755 per year.

Benefits usually include health and life insurance, paid vacations, and retirement plans.

Where to Go for More Information

American Society of Transportation and
   Logistics
1700 N. Moore St., Ste. 1900
Arlington, VA 22209
(703) 524-5011
http://www.astl.org

Council of Supply Chain Management
   Professionals Association
2805 Butterfield Rd., Ste. 200
Oak Brook, IL 60523
(630) 574-0985
http://www.cscmp.org

Merchant Marine Captain

Definition and Nature of the Work

Captains are in charge of all aspects of their ships' operations. They are responsible to the owners of their ships for the safety of the vessels, the crew, and the passengers or cargo. They maintain crew discipline and keep order. Captains are sometimes called masters.

Every captain rose through the ranks of the deck command, which is made up of first, second, and third mates. The first mate is the captain's most important assistant in assigning duties and maintaining order. A first mate also plans the loading and unloading of cargo and assists the captain in taking the ship in and out of port. The second mate is traditionally the navigation officer. The third mate oversees the navigating bridge and the chart room and maintains the signaling and lifesaving equipment.

While in port, the captain may act as the shipowner's agent in dealing with customs officials. The captain may pay and keep records of wages for the ship's other employees.

Education and Training Requirements

Captains have the most senior jobs in the merchant marine. They must attend officer training schools; qualify for their jobs in a series of examinations over a period of years; and possess the leadership qualities needed to run large, complex organizations.

Prospective captains should attend one of the maritime academies that provide officer training: the U.S. Naval Academy, the U.S. Coast Guard Academy, the U.S. Merchant Marine Academy, and the state academies in California, Maine, Massachusetts, Michigan, New York, and Texas. Candidates for the U.S. Naval Academy or U.S. Merchant Marine Academy must be nominated by members of Congress. Applications for the other academies are competitive. Applicants must be between seventeen and twenty-two years of age, single, high school graduates, U.S. citizens, and in good physical condition.

Education and Training
Advanced degree

Salary
Median—$24.20 per hour

Employment Outlook
Poor

Captains are in charge of all operations on their ships. They are the highest-ranking workers in the merchant marine. (© Martha Tabor/Working Images Photographs. Reproduced by permission.)

The academies provide three- and four-year training programs in nautical science and practical sea experience. The course of study includes navigation, mathematics, electronics, propulsion systems, electrical engineering, languages, history, and shipping management. Graduates are qualified to work as third mates in the merchant marine.

Graduates must then apply for U.S. Coast Guard certification to work on American ships—a legal requirement for seamen and officers alike. To be certified by the Coast Guard, applicants must be U.S. citizens and possess health certificates from the U.S. Public Health Service.

Third mates must be at least nineteen years old. To work their way up through the ranks of third, second, and first mate to captain, they must pass qualifying Coast Guard examinations at each rank. Length of service and the size of the ships on which they have trained are also factors in promotion to captain.

Getting the Job

Officers succeed to the rank of captain only after many years of service. Those looking for that experience may go to union hiring halls and apply to be mates.

Shipping companies maintain lists of those eligible for positions as captains. Officers who have seniority are hired first.

Advancement Possibilities and Employment Outlook

Captains are already the highest-ranking workers in the merchant marine. Some move to better ships or to ships with more desirable routes.

Employment of merchant marine officers is expected to grow more slowly than the average for all occupations through 2014. The size of the U.S. fleet should stabilize after several years of decline, and it should carry a larger proportion of international cargo because of increased regulations and insurance rates on foreign vessels. However, newer ships are designed to operate with much smaller crews. As a result, competition may be extremely strong for existing jobs—the demand for officers may be outweighed by the number of graduates of officer training schools.

Working Conditions

At sea, captains are on call twenty-four hours. While in port, a forty-hour workweek is standard. The work can be hazardous—the risk of falls, fire, collision, and sinking is always present. Harsh variations in temperature and violent storms are possible at sea.

Captains travel extensively, but they seldom have time to explore the ports they visit. They are away from their home ports for long periods.

Earnings and Benefits

The wages for captains are highest on the largest ships. In 2004 the median wage for captains was $24.20 per hour. The most experienced captains—captains of large container ships, oil tankers, or passenger ships—earned more than $100,000 per year.

Benefits include room and board; eighteen to thirty days of vacation for every thirty days of work; medical care; and hospitalization insurance. Captains usually receive pensions through the shipping companies that employ them.

Where to Go for More Information

Military Sealift Command
6353 Center Dr., Bldg. 8, Ste. 202
Norfolk, VA 23502
(877) 562-7672
http://www.sealiftcommand.com

National Marine Engineers Beneficial
    Association
444 N. Capitol St., Ste. 800
Washington, DC 20001
(202) 638-5355
http://www.d1meba.org

Seafarers International Union
5201 Auth Way
Camp Springs, MD 20746
(301) 899-0675
http://www.seafarers.org

Merchant Marine Engineer

Definition and Nature of the Work

Engineers in the merchant marine monitor and maintain ships' machinery, especially the engines that propel the vessels. They work on all kinds of ships, although most merchant marine ships are freighters or tankers that carry cargo.

Chief engineers supervise the seamen in engine departments and are responsible for main power plants and their auxiliary equipment. In addition, chief engineers direct and keep records of the repair and maintenance of the ships' equipment.

First assistant engineers are in charge of starting, stopping, and controlling the speed of the engines. Second assistant engineers are responsible for the fuel and water aboard ships, including all boilers and pumps. Third assistant engineers are in charge of lubrication systems and, on some ships, refrigeration and electrical equipment.

Engine departments have several other types of workers. Firers and water tenders check the flow of oil and water in the ships' oil-burning equipment and boilers. Oilers lubricate the moving parts in the mechanical equipment, while wipers clean engine rooms and the machinery.

Education and Training
Academy

Salary
Median—$26.42 per hour

Employment Outlook
Poor

Education and Training Requirements

Ship engineers start out as third assistant engineers and work their way up the ranks. Some third assistant engineers get their licenses without formal training: workers who have had three years of experience in engine rooms may take the licensing test if they are older than nineteen. However, the test is so difficult that few applicants pass it without formal training. That is why most ship engineers are graduates of approved training programs.

Graduates of marine academies receive U.S. Coast Guard licenses as third assistant engineers along with their bachelor's degrees. In school they take courses in marine steam systems and diesel engines. The marine academies in the United States include the U.S. Naval Academy, the U.S. Coast Guard Academy, the U.S. Merchant Marine Academy, and state academies in California, Maine, Massachusetts, Michigan, New York, and Texas.

To advance through the ranks to become chief engineers, workers must pass Coast Guard licensing tests at every level. Labor unions offer training programs to help employees pass promotional examinations.

Getting the Job

The best way to become marine engineers is to attend one of the marine academies. While candidates for the Naval Academy and the Merchant Marine Academy must be nominated by members of Congress, admission to the other academies is competitive. Graduates of the academies must pass the Coast Guard licensing test before they can become ship engineers at any level. New graduates, upon getting their licenses, usually get jobs as third assistant engineers.

Academy placement offices or unions can help new graduates find jobs.

Advancement Possibilities and Employment Outlook

Third assistant engineers may advance to second assistant engineers after one year of work. They must pass the Coast Guard test for the position and be at least twenty-one years old. With experience, second assistant engineers may progress to jobs as first assistants and then as chief engineers after they pass Coast Guard exams for each rank.

Employment of marine engineers is expected to grow more slowly than the average for all occupations through 2014. While the merchant marine fleet should expand over the next decade, engineers may face stiff competition for available positions because newer, more automated ships require fewer workers. Openings may occur when experienced engineers retire or leave the field.

Where to Go for More Information

Military Sealift Command
6353 Center Dr., Bldg. 8, Ste. 202
Norfolk, VA 23502
(877) 562-7672
http://www.sealiftcommand.com

National Board of Boiler and Pressure
  Vessel Inspectors
1055 Crupper Ave.
Columbus, OH 43229
(614) 888-8320
http://www.nationalboard.org

National Marine Engineers Beneficial
  Association
444 N. Capitol St., Ste. 800
Washington, DC 20001
(202) 638-5355
http://www.d1meba.org

Seafarers International Union
5201 Auth Way
Camp Springs, MD 20746
(301) 899-0675
http://www.seafarers.org

Working Conditions

Marine engineers are away from home for long periods. Accommodations on board ship are adequate and clean but not luxurious. Although conditions are better on newer ships, engine rooms are usually hot and cramped, and the work can be hazardous. Exposure to the weather and the risk of fire, collision, and sinking go with the job.

Engineers usually work two shifts lasting four hours during each day, with eight hours off between shifts. However, at sea they are on call twenty-four hours. In port engineers work forty hours per week.

Earnings and Benefits

Wages depend on rank and the size of the ship. In 2004 the median wage for all ship engineers was $26.42 per hour. The most experienced engineers earned more than $42.02 per hour. Overtime pay can increase engineers' wages considerably.

Benefits include room and board; eighteen to thirty days of paid vacation for each thirty days of work; and medical, dental, and hospital insurance. Partial pensions are available for engineers forced to retire prematurely by permanent disabilities.

Merchant Marine Purser

Education and Training
Varies—see profile

Salary
Average—$30,514 per year

Employment Outlook
Poor

Definition and Nature of the Work

All passenger ships and some freighters and tankers employ pursers, who do the complicated paperwork that is necessary each time ships enter ports. They keep their ships' accounts and prepare and keep records of payroll. Pursers also assist passengers whenever necessary.

One of the most important responsibilities of pursers is overseeing ships' documentation and customs declarations. They arrange for ship and document inspections by immigration officials and prepare passenger and crew lists for the appropriate governmental authorities. Ship pursers assist passengers in a number of ways: they arrange for room transfers; exchange currency; coordinate luggage transportation; and organize tours and sightseeing trips while ships are in port. They also answer questions and field complaints from passengers. In recent years, pursers have been trained as pharmacists' mates to improve health care onboard ships. They are in charge of the medicine chest and first-aid care and file injury reports. Passenger ships have fairly large purser departments; on cargo ships, fewer pursers are needed.

Education and Training Requirements

Most pursers attend maritime training schools, which include the U.S. Coast Guard Academy, the U.S. Merchant Marine Academy, the U.S. Naval Academy, and state academies in California, Maine, Massachusetts, Michigan, New York, and Texas. Other schools offer general seamanship training to a limited number of people with no experience at sea. Some pursers get their sea experience by serving in the U.S. Navy or U.S. Coast Guard.

To enter the federal academies, applicants must be between seventeen and twenty-two years of age, single, high school graduates, U.S. citizens, and in good physical condition. Candidates for the U.S. Merchant Marine Academy or the U.S. Naval Academy must be nominated by members of Congress. Admission to the other schools is competitive.

To qualify for their jobs, pursers need U.S. Coast Guard licenses, which require examinations. Prospective pursers should take commercial courses in high school or in business school. Experience in typing and bookkeeping can be useful.

Getting the Job

One of the most direct routes to becoming a purser is attending a marine academy. Most schools have job placement offices.

Advancement Possibilities and Employment Outlook

Assistant pursers may advance to jobs as tourist-class, cabin-class, and first-class pursers on passenger ships. With more experience, they can be promoted to pursers and executive pursers. The highest job in pursers departments is chief purser. Union training programs help candidates advance through the ranks.

Employment in the merchant marine is expected to grow more slowly than the average for all occupations through 2014. More important, the number of graduates of maritime training schools may exceed the growth in demand. Openings may occur when experienced pursers retire or leave the field, but applicants may find stiff competition.

Working Conditions

Pursers work long hours and irregular shifts. They are on call twenty-four hours when ships are at sea. As with all merchant marine occupations, the work can be hazardous. The risk of falls, fire, collision, and sinking is always present. Pursers are away from home for long periods and rarely have a chance to explore the ports they visit.

Earnings and Benefits

Salaries depend on the type and size of the ship, as well as pursers' experience and responsibility. In 2004 the average salary for pursers was $30,514 per year.

Benefits include eighteen to thirty days of vacation for each thirty days of work. Medical care, hospital insurance, and retirement plans are provided, as are room and board. Partial pensions are available for those who retire early because of permanent disabilities.

Where to Go for More Information

National Marine Engineers Beneficial
    Association
444 N. Capitol St., Ste. 800
Washington, DC 20001
(202) 638-5355
http://www.d1meba.org

Seafarers International Union
5201 Auth Way
Camp Springs, MD 20746
(301) 899-0675
http://www.seafarers.org

Merchant Marine Radio Officer

Definition and Nature of the Work

Radio officers work aboard cargo vessels and passenger ships. They use radio, Morse code, and other electronic and satellite communication devices to contact shore headquarters and other ships. In addition, radio officers receive and record time signals, weather reports, and other information important to the smooth operation of their vessels. They also maintain the radio equipment and depth-recording and electronic navigation devices on ships.

Education and Training Requirements

Radio officers must have either first- or second-class radio-telegraph operator's licenses from the Federal Communications Commission. To get such licenses, applicants must pass written examinations covering sea communication regulations, operating practices, and message routing. Passenger ships may have six radio officers; cargo ships have only one.

Radio officers get the best preparation at maritime academies. Without formal training the licensing examination may be difficult to pass. Marine academies include the U.S. Coast Guard Academy, the U.S. Merchant Marine Academy, the U.S. Naval Academy, and state academies in California, Maine, Massachusetts, Michigan, New York, and Texas. Candidates for the Merchant Marine Academy and the Naval Academy must be nominated by members of Congress. Admission to the other academies is competitive. To qualify for the federal academies, applicants must be between seventeen and twenty-two years old, single, high school graduates, U.S. citizens, and in good physical condition.

Radio operators may also get sea experience through training programs sponsored by one of the unions that represent seamen. However, the programs accept only a limited number of trainees who have no sea experience.

Getting the Job

Graduates of marine academies or training programs may take U.S. Coast Guard licensing exams. Once certified, radio officers can register at union hiring halls.

Advancement Possibilities and Employment Outlook

Career radio officers are members of a very specialized profession and have few chances for promotion. Some become head radio officers.

Employment of radio officers is expected to grow more slowly than the average for all occupations through 2014. The number of graduates of marine academies should slightly exceed the number of jobs available. Offshore oil and mineral exploration may offer the most job prospects. Openings do occur when career radio officers retire or leave the field.

Working Conditions

At sea, radio officers stand watch in the radio room. During every twenty-four hours, they work two shifts of four hours with eight-hour breaks between shifts. On some ships, radio officers work regular eight-hour days.

Clean and adequate accommodations are provided on board ship. Exposure to the weather and the risk of fire, collision, and sinking go with the job. Radio officers' work requires long periods away from home.

Earnings and Benefits

Earnings vary according to rank, type of ship, and location. In 2004 the median wage of all radio officers was $14 per hour. Overtime and bonus pay increased the earnings of some officers.

Room and board, medical care, and hospitalization insurance are provided. Vacation, ranging from eighteen to thirty days for every thirty days of work, and retirement plans are other benefits of the job. Officers who are forced to retire prematurely because of disabilities may be eligible for partial pensions.

Where to Go for More Information

National Marine Engineers Beneficial
    Association
444 N. Capitol St., Ste. 800
Washington, DC 20001
(202) 638-5355
http://www.d1meba.org

Seafarers International Union
5201 Auth Way
Camp Springs, MD 20746
(301) 899-0675
http://www.seafarers.org

Traffic Engineer

Definition and Nature of the Work

Traffic engineers are transportation engineers who specialize in the design and maintenance of safe roads and highways. They determine what kinds of roads are needed to make traffic flow smoothly and then find the most economical ways to build and maintain them.

Many engineers work in the highway or street departments of state or city governments; others work for federal highway agencies or county highway departments. Engineers can also work for private consulting firms, educational institutions, or industries.

Traffic engineers who work for state governments are mainly concerned with interstate highways or primary state roads, which carry heavy traffic over long distances. They do "need studies" to determine how many trucks, buses, and cars can be expected to use new roads and then work with highway engineers and location engineers to figure out the safest, most economical paths for them. Interstate turnpikes require careful planning of overpasses, exits, cloverleafs, and rest areas.

Traffic engineers who work for city governments try to solve parking problems and traffic jams and to choose the best public transit routes. In some large cities several traffic engineers may have the sole responsibility of timing the traffic lights.

To predict street and highway use in the future, engineers use statistical methods to analyze data about population, housing, commercial development, and existing traffic patterns. They are particularly concerned about accidents, so they keep records to identify possible causes. They may design new intersections, put up new signs, or remove trees that block vision.

Because highways and streets are funded by tax money, traffic engineers must present their plans to government officials for approval. They must prove that their new designs can benefit the public.

Education and Training Requirements

Traffic engineers must have bachelor's degrees in civil engineering. Some colleges offer specific traffic engineering programs. Courses should include trans-

Education and Training
College

Salary
Median—$64,230 per year

Employment Outlook
Good

Traffic engineers design roads, highways, and public transportation systems that allow traffic to flow smoothly. (© Martha Tabor/Working Images Photographs. Reproduced by permission.)

portation, statistics, city planning, highway economics, physics, systems analysis, computing, and computer-aided design. Graduate degrees may help in the search for employment. Advanced programs include courses on traffic-flow theory and freeway-exit design. Large highway departments sometimes have training programs for employees who have completed their degrees.

Getting the Job

School placement services may be able to help graduates find jobs. Civil service commissions can provide information about the tests required for government jobs and job listings. Job seekers can also apply directly to engineering consultants, public transportation companies, and automobile manufacturers. Newspaper classified ads and Internet job sites may offer employment leads.

Advancement Possibilities and Employment Outlook

Advancement depends on education and experience. Traffic engineers may start out by counting traffic or making charts and get promoted to traffic control, such as the regulation of stoplights. With experience they can become chief engineers or administrators of highway departments. Some start their own consulting businesses, while others take high-level jobs with automakers, redevelopment authorities, or safety commissions.

Employment of traffic engineers is expected to increase as fast as the average for all occupations through 2014. As the population increases and continues to move to suburban areas, demand should grow for traffic engineers who can design better roads and plan transit systems. New technologies, such as electronic toll collection and fiber optics, may also spur employment of engineers.

Working Conditions

Traffic engineers usually work forty hours per week, although extra hours may be required for special projects, such as studies of weekend traffic patterns. They usually have comfortable, well-lighted offices for preparing plans and analyzing data, but they also spend some time out on the roads, examining the sites of accidents or checking road conditions. Sometimes they observe traffic flow from helicopters. They often go before government officials to present plans and proposals, so they should be able to speak clearly and write precise reports. Some traffic engineers change employers frequently to work on highway projects in different parts of the country.

Earnings and Benefits

In 2004 the median salary for experienced traffic engineers was $64,230 per year. Many chief engineers or experienced consultants earned considerably more.

Benefits usually include health and life insurance, paid vacations, and retirement plans.

Where to Go for More Information

American Association of State Highway
  and Transportation Officials
444 N. Capitol St. NW, Rm. 249
Washington, DC 20001
(202) 624-5800
http://www.transportation.org

American Society of Civil Engineers
1801 Alexander Graham Bell Dr.
Reston, VA 20191-4400
(800) 548-2723
http://www.asce.org

Institute of Transportation Engineers
1099 Fourteenth St. NW, Ste. 300 W.
Washington, DC 20005-3438
(202) 289-0222
http://www.ite.org

Transportation Engineer

Definition and Nature of the Work

Transportation engineers are civil engineers who design highways, airports, and railway and bus systems. They work for governmental agencies; for consulting firms that troubleshoot for the government; and for private firms that produce materials and equipment used in transportation. Engineers are also teachers and researchers at colleges and universities.

Some transportation engineers specialize. For example, traffic engineers plan new roads or traffic patterns, while railroad engineers plan for high-speed rail service. Some engineers develop entire transportation systems, including roads, subways, commuter trains, and buses. Engineers also supervise the construction or repair of transportation systems.

Municipal, county, or state officials hire engineers to develop new transportation systems or to find alternative routes to relieve congestion on existing highways. Sometimes the engineers draw up plans for new multilane highways to be built in places where only local roads exist. In other cities they may decide whether buses or trains can best provide commuter service.

In planning projects, engineers consider costs, the needs of the town or state, and the availability of land. They determine whether the land is good for building—marshland may have to be filled or treated before construction begins—and how the projects could affect the environment. Once these factors have been analyzed, engineers make detailed proposals.

Some transportation engineers oversee construction. They invite contractors to submit bids and then choose the best bid. Once work begins, engineers make sure that schedules are met and building standards are followed. When a highway is being constructed, for example, engineers check the building materials to

Education and Training
College

Salary
Median—$64,230 per year

Employment Outlook
Good

Transportation engineers often specialize. Some plan new roads, while others develop or restructure public transit systems. (© Martha Tabor/Working Images Photographs. Reproduced by permission.)

make sure the contractors are following highway department standards. Engineers also inspect the completed road to make sure it is safe for drivers.

Education and Training Requirements

Transportation engineers must have bachelor's degrees in civil engineering. Nearly half of those working today hold master's degrees or doctorates, which may be required for teaching and research positions.

Prospective transportation engineers should take high school courses in mathematics and science. Courses in computer-aided design are also helpful. College courses in English and the natural and social sciences, including political science, can be as important as specialized courses in surveying, specifications writing, traffic control, and the mechanics of fluids and materials. Some engineers get graduate degrees in business administration to improve their chances for advancement.

Transportation engineers continue their education by reading technical publications and attending seminars and conferences.

Getting the Job

College placement offices may be able to help graduates find employment. Job seekers can also apply directly to construction companies and to consulting firms that do engineering work. Civil service commissions have information about civil service tests and job openings in government agencies. Other good sources of job leads are newspaper classified ads, Internet job sites, and engineering journals.

Advancement Possibilities and Employment Outlook

With experience and ability transportation engineers can advance to a number of positions, such as construction supervisor, project engineer, or designer of transportation systems. In addition, they may become supervisors of engineering departments, chief engineers for construction firms, or consulting engineers.

Employment of transportation engineers is expected to grow as fast as the average for all occupations through 2014. Many new roads need to be built and existing roads need to be redesigned. Demand should also be strong over the next decade for engineers who can design better public transportation systems.

Working Conditions

Transportation engineers work in offices or at construction sites in all kinds of weather. They generally work forty hours per week, although overtime may be necessary if construction deadlines must be met.

Because their work affects public behavior and policy, transportation engineers must be able to communicate effectively with diverse groups of people—from government officials to machine operators to the general public. They must be willing to make and advocate unpopular decisions.

Earnings and Benefits

In 2004 the median salary of transportation engineers was $64,230 per year. The most experienced engineers earned more than $94,660 per year. Salaries were higher for those with master's degrees and doctorates.

Benefits usually include paid holidays and vacations, health insurance, and retirement plans.

Where to Go for More Information

American Society of Civil Engineers
1801 Alexander Graham Bell Dr.
Reston, VA 20191-4400
(800) 548-2723
http://www.asce.org

American Association of State Highway
    and Transportation Officials
444 N. Capitol St. NW, Ste. 249
Washington, DC 20001
(202) 624-5800
http://www.transportation.org

Institute of Transportation Engineers
1099 Fourteenth St. NW, Ste. 300 W
Washington, DC 20005
(202) 289-0222
http://www.ite.org

Books

Exploring the Working World

American Salaries and Wages Survey, 8th ed., Helen S. Fisher. Farmington Hills, MI: Thomson Gale, 2005.

America's Fastest Growing Jobs: Detailed Information on the 140 Fastest Growing Jobs in Our Economy, 8th ed., Michael Farr. Indianapolis, IN: JIST Publishing, 2004.

America's Top 101 Jobs for College Graduates, 6th ed., Michael Farr. Indianapolis, IN: JIST Publishing, 2005.

America's Top 101 Jobs for People without a Four-Year Degree, 7th ed., Michael Farr. Indianapolis, IN: JIST Publishing, 2004.

America's Top 300 Jobs, 9th ed., U.S. Department of Labor. Indianapolis, IN: JIST Publishing, 2004.

Best Career and Education Web Sites: A Quick Guide to Online Job Search, 4th ed., Rachel Singer Gordon and Anne Wolfinger. Indianapolis, IN: JIST Publishing, 2004.

Best Entry-Level Jobs, Ron Lieber and Tom Meltzer. New York: Princeton Review, 2006.

Best Jobs for the 21st Century, 4th ed., Michael Farr and Laurence Shatkin. Indianapolis, IN: JIST Publishing, 2006.

Big Book of Jobs, 2003–2004, U.S. Department of Labor. New York: McGraw-Hill, 2003.

Career Discovery Encyclopedia, 5th ed., 8 vols. Chicago: Ferguson, 2003.

Enhanced Occupational Outlook Handbook, 5th ed., Indianapolis, IN: JIST Publishing, 2005.

Job Hunter's Sourcebook: A Thomson Gale Career Information Guide. Farmington Hills, MI: Thomson Gale, biennial.

Jobs Rated Almanac, 6th ed., Les Krantz. Fort Lee, NJ: Barricade, 2002.

The National JobBank, 2006. Avon, MA: Adams Media, 2006.

Occupational Outlook Handbook series. Washington, DC: United States Government Printing Office, biennial. Briefs, separately published.

Occupational Outlook Quarterly. Washington, DC: United States Government Printing Office. Quarterly publication.

Professional Careers Sourcebook, 7th ed. Farmington Hills, MI: Thomson Gale, 2002.

200 Best Jobs for College Graduates, 3rd ed., Michael Farr and Laurence Shatkin. Indianapolis, IN: JIST Publishing, 2006.

Recommended

Best Jobs for the 21st Century, 4th ed., Michael Farr and Laurence Shatkin. Indianapolis, IN: JIST Publishing, 2006. Lists five hundred jobs and categorizes them into sixty-five "Best Jobs for..." lists. Organizes jobs by category, education required, best growth potential.

Jobs Rated Almanac, 6th ed., Les Krantz. Fort Lee, NJ: Barricade, 2002. Rates 250 jobs and sorts into "best for" and "worst for" rankings. Factors include salary, benefits, and stress level.

300 Best Jobs without a Four-Year Degree, 2nd ed., Michael Farr and Laurence Shatkin. Indianapolis, IN: JIST Publishing, 2006.

VGM's Career Encyclopedia, 5th ed., New York: McGraw-Hill, 2002.

Vocational Careers Sourcebook, 5th ed., Farmington Hills, MI: Thomson Gale, 2002.

Education and Training Opportunities

Acing the College Application: How to Maximize Your Chances for Admission to the College of Your Choice, Michele Hernandez. New York: Ballantine, 2002.

Admission Matters: What Students and Parents Need to Know about Getting Into College, Sally P. Springer and Marion R. Franck. San Francisco: Jossey-Bass, 2005.

Barron's Guide to Graduate Business Schools, Eugene Miller and Neuman F. Pollack. Hauppauge, NY: Barron's Educational Series, revised regularly.

Barron's Guide to Law Schools. Hauppauge, NY: Barron's Educational Series, revised regularly.

Barron's Guide to Medical and Dental Schools, Sol Wischnitzer and Edith Wischnitzer. Hauppauge, NY: Barron's Educational Series, revised regularly.

Barron's Profiles of American Colleges. Hauppauge, NY: Barron's Educational Series, annual.

Bear's Guide to College Degrees by Mail and Internet, 10th ed., John Bear. Berkeley, CA: Ten Speed Press, 2005.

Best 109 Internships, 9th ed., Mark Oldman and Samer Hamadah. New York: Princeton Review, 2003.

The Best 361 Colleges. New York: Princeton Review, annual.

Chronicle Vocational School Manual. Moravia, NY: Chronicle Guidance Publications, annual.

The College Application Essay, Sarah Myers McGinty. New York: The College Board, 2004.

The College Board Book of Majors, 2nd ed. New York: The College Board, 2006.

The College Board Scholarship Handbook. New York: The College Board, annual.

The College Cost and Financial Aid Handbook. New York: The College Board, annual.

College Financial Aid: How to Get Your Fair Share, 6th ed., Peter V. Laurenzo. Albany, NY: Hudson Financial Press, 2002.

The College Handbook. New York: The College Board, annual.

College Majors Handbook with Real Career Paths and Payoffs, 2nd ed., Neeta P. Fogg. Indianapolis, IN: JIST Publishing, 2004.

College Planning for Gifted Students, 3rd ed., Sandra L. Berger. Waco, TX: Prufrock Press, 2006.

College Success Guide: Top 12 Secrets for Student Success, Karine Blackett and Patricia Weiss. Indianapolis, IN: JIST Publishing, 2005.

Complete Book of Colleges. New York: Princeton Review, annual.

Recommended

Acing the College Application: How to Maximize Your Chances for Admission to the College of Your Choice, Michele Hernandez. New York: Ballantine, 2002. Written by former Dartmouth College admissions officer. Frank but reassuring advice on application, essay, and personal interview.

The Insider's Guide to Colleges. New York: St. Martin's Griffin, annual. Surveys students at 320 U.S. and Canadian schools on dorm life, class size, and other campus-related topics.

Vault Guide to Top Internships, Samer Hamadah. New York: Vault, 2005. Provides information on internships offered by 700-plus companies, including Fortune 500 corporations. Nonprofit and government programs also listed.

Fiske Guide to Colleges, Edmund Fiske. Naperville, IL: Sourcebooks, annual.

The Gourman Report: A Rating of Undergraduate Programs in American and International Universities, Jack Gourman. Los Angeles: National Educational Standards, revised regularly.

Guide to College Majors. New York: Princeton Review, 2006.

Guide to the Most Competitive Colleges. Hauppauge, NY: Barron's Educational Series, revised regularly.

How to Choose a College Major, Linda Landis Andrews. New York: McGraw-Hill, 2006.

How to Write Your College Application Essay, Kenneth Nourse. New York: McGraw-Hill, 2001.

The Insider's Guide to Colleges. New York: St. Martin's Griffin, annual.

The Internship Bible, 10th ed. New York: Princeton Review, 2005.

The National Guide to Educational Credit for Training Programs. Washington, DC: American Council on Education, revised regularly.

100 Successful College Application Essays, 2nd ed. New York: New American Library, 2002.

Peterson's Best College Admission Essays, 3rd ed. Princeton, NJ: Thomson Peterson's, 2004.

Peterson's College Money Handbook. Princeton, NJ: Thomson Peterson's, annual.

Peterson's College and University Almanac. Princeton, NJ: Thomson Peterson's, annual.

Peterson's Competitive Colleges. Princeton, NJ: Thomson Peterson's, annual.

Peterson's Financial Aid Answer Book. Princeton, NJ: Thomson Peterson's, annual.

Peterson's Guide to Four-Year Colleges. Princeton, NJ: Thomson Peterson's, annual.

Peterson's Guide to Two-Year Colleges. Princeton, NJ: Thomson Peterson's, annual.

Peterson's Internships. Princeton, NJ: Thomson Peterson's, annual.

Quick Guide to College Majors and Careers, Laurence Shatkin. Indianapolis, IN: JIST Publishing, 2002.

Rugg's Recommendations on the Colleges, Frederick Rugg. Fallbrook, CA: Rugg's Recommendations, annual.

Students' Guide to Colleges: The Definitive Guide to America's Top 100 Schools Written by the Real Experts—the Students Who Attend Them, Jordan Goldman and Colleen Buyers. New York: Penguin, 2005.

The Truth about Getting In: A Top College Advisor Tells You Everything You Need to Know, Katherine Cohen. New York: Hyperion, 2002.

US News Ultimate College Guide. Naperville, IL: Sourcebooks, annual.

Vault Guide to Top Internships, Samer Hamadah. New York, Vault, 2005.

Career Goals

The Career Adventure: Your Guide to Personal Assessment, Career Exploration, and Decision Making, 4th ed., Susan M. Johnston. Upper Saddle, NJ: Prentice-Hall, 2005.

Career Guide to America's Top Industries, 6th ed., U.S. Department of Labor. Indianapolis, IN: JIST Publishing, 2004.

Career Warfare: 10 Rules for Building a Successful Personal Brand and Fighting to Keep It, David F. D'Alessandro and Michele Owens. New York: McGraw-Hill, 2003.

College Majors and Careers: A Resource Guide for Effective Life Planning, 5th ed., Paul Phifer. Chicago: Ferguson, 2003.

Cool Careers for Dummies, Marty Nemko, Paul Edwards, and Sarah Edwards. Foster City, CA: IDG Books, 2001.

Customize Your Career, Roz Usheroff. New York: McGraw-Hill, 2004.

Do What You Are: Discover the Perfect Career for You through the Secrets of Personality Type, 3rd ed., Paul D. Tieger and Barbara Barron-Tieger. New York: Little, Brown, 2001.

50 Best Jobs for Your Personality, Michael Farr and Laurence Shatkin. Indianapolis, IN: JIST Publishing, 2005.

Finding a Career That Works for You: A Step-by-Step Guide to Choosing a Career and Finding a Job, Wilma Fellman. Plantation, FL: Specialty Press, 2000.

Finding Your Perfect Work: The New Career Guide to Making a Living, Creating a Life, 2nd ed., Paul Edwards and Susan Edwards. New York: Penguin, 2003.

The 5 Patterns of Extraordinary Careers: The Guide for Achieving Success and Satisfaction, James M. Citrin and Richard Smith. New York: Crown Business, 2003.

The Global Citizen: A Guide to Creating an International Life and Career, Elizabeth Kruempelmann. Berkeley, CA: Ten Speed Press, 2002.

Guide to Your Career, 5th ed., Alan B. Bernstein. New York: Princeton Review, 2004.

How Hard Are You Knocking? The Job Seeker's Guide to Opening Career Doors, Timothy J. Augustine and Rona Curcio. Winchester, VA: Oakhill Press, 2005.

Job Search and Career Checklists: 101 Proven Time-Saving Checklists to Organize and Plan Your Career Search, Arlene S. Hirsch. Indianapolis, IN: JIST Publishing, 2005.

Recommended

Finding Your Perfect Work: The New Career Guide to Making a Living, Creating a Life, 2nd ed., Paul Edwards and Susan Edwards. New York: Penguin, 2003. Lists types of careers, with emphasis on self-employment opportunities.

What Color Is Your Parachute? A Practical Manual for Job-Hunters and Career-Changers, Richard Nelson Bolles. Berkeley, CA: Ten Speed Press, revised annually. The classic in the genre, and the top-selling career-advice book consistently since the mid-1970s. Updated to reflect twenty-first-century concerns.

Monster Careers: How to Land the Job of Your Life, Jeffrey Taylor and Douglas Hardy. New York: Penguin, 2004.

New Guide for Occupational Exploration: Linking Interests, Learning and Careers, 4th ed., Michael Farr and Laurence Shatkin. Indianapolis, IN: JIST Publishing, 2006.

The Play of Your Life: Your Program for Finding the Career of Your Dreams—And a Step-by-Step Guide to Making It a Reality, Colleen A. Sabatino. New York: Rodale, 2004.

What Color Is Your Parachute? A Practical Manual for Job-Hunters and Career-Changers, Richard Nelson Bolles. Berkeley, CA: Ten Speed Press, revised annually.

What Should I Do with My Life? The True Story of People Who Answered the Ultimate Question, Po Brosnan. New York: Random House, 2002.

Where's My Oasis? The Essential Handbook for Everyone Wanting the Perfect Job, Rowan Manahan. New York: Vermillion, 2004.

Getting the Job and Getting Ahead

Almanac of American Employers, Jack W. Plunkett. Galveston, TX: Plunkett Research Ltd., biennial.

e-Resumes: A Guide to Successful Online Job Hunting, Pat Criscito. Hauppauge, NY: Barron's Educational Series, 2004.

Guide to Internet Job Searching, Margaret Riley Dikel. New York: McGraw-Hill, 2004.

How to Earn What You're Worth: Leveraging Your Goals and Talents to Land Your Dream Job, Sunny Bates. New York: McGraw-Hill, 2004.

How to Get Any Job with Any Major: Career Launch & Re-launch for Everyone Under 30 (or How to Avoid Living in Your Parents' Basement), Donald Asher. Berkeley, CA: Ten Speed Press, 2004.

How to Get Your First Job and Keep It, 2nd ed., Deborah Perlmutter Bloch. New York: McGraw-Hill, 2002.

Insider's Guide to Finding a Job: Expert Advice from America's Top Employers and Recruiters, Wendy S. Enelow and Shelly Goldman. Indianapolis, IN: JIST Publishing, 2004.

International Job Finder: Where the Jobs Are Worldwide, Daniel Lauber and Kraig Rice. River Forest, IL: Planning/Communications, 2002.

International Jobs: Where They Are and How to Get Them, 6th ed., Nina Segal and Eric Kocher. New York: Basic Books, 2003.

Job-Hunting on the Internet, 4th ed., Richard Nelson Bolles and Mark Emery Bolles. Berkeley, CA: Ten Speed Press, 2005.

Job Savvy: How to Be a Success at Work, 3rd ed., LaVerne L. Ludden. Indianapolis, IN: JIST Publishing, 2002.

Job Search Magic: Insider Secrets from America's Career and Life Coach, Susan Britton Whitcomb. Indianapolis, IN: JIST Publishing, 2006.

The Job Search Solution: The Ultimate System for Finding a Great Job Now!, Tony Bashara. New York: AMACOM, 2005.

Job Seeker's Online Goldmine: A Step-by-Step Guidebook to Government and No-Cost Web Tools, Janet E. Wall. Indianapolis, IN: JIST Publishing, 2006.

Knock 'Em Dead 2006: The Ultimate Job Seekers Guide, Martin Yate. Avon, MA: Adams Media, 2006.

National Job Hotline Directory: The Job Finder's Hot List, 3rd ed., Sue Cubbage and Marcia Williams. River Forest, IL: Planning/Communications, 2003.

1000 Best Job Hunting Secrets, Diane Stafford and Moritza Day. Naperville, IL: Sourcebooks, 2004.

Super Job Search: The Complete Manual for Job-Seekers & Career-Changers, 3rd ed., Peter Studner. Los Angeles: Jamenair Ltd., 2003.

10 Insider Secrets to a Winning Job Search: Everything You Need to Get the Job You Want in 24 Hours—Or Less, Todd Bermont. Franklin Lakes, NJ: Career Press, 2004.

Very Quick Job Search: Get a Better Job in Half the Time, 3rd ed., Michael Farr. Indianapolis, IN: JIST Publishing, 2003.

Recommended

How to Get Any Job with Any Major: Career Launch & Re-launch for Everyone Under 30 (or How to Avoid Living in Your Parents' Basement), Donald Asher. Berkeley, CA: Ten Speed Press, 2004. Counsels liberal arts degree-holders on how to package their education and strengths to land a high-paying position.

Knock 'Em Dead 2006: The Ultimate Job Seekers Guide, Martin Yate. Avon, MA: Adams Media, 2006. Offers range of advice for job-hunters at all levels, including resume-building, interview strategies, and salary negotiation tips.

Resumes and Interviews

Adams Job Interview Almanac, 2nd ed., Richard Wallace. Avon, MA: Adams Media Corp., 2005.

Adams Resume Almanac, 2nd ed., Richard Wallace. Avon, MA: Adams Media Corp., 2005.

Amazing Resumes: What Employers Want to See—and How to Say It, Jim Bright and Joanne Earl. Indianapolis, IN: JIST Publishing, 2005.

Competency-Based Resumes: How to Bring Your Resume to the Top of the Pile, Robin Kessler and Linda A. Strasburg. Franklin Lakes, NJ: Career Press, 2004.

Cover Letter Magic, 2nd ed., Wendy S. Enelow and Louise Kursmark. Indianapolis, IN: JIST Publishing, 2004.

Cover Letters That Knock 'Em Dead, 6th ed., Martin Yate. Avon, MA: Adams Media, 2004.

The Elements of Resume Style: Essential Rules and Eye-opening Advice for Writing Resumes and Cover Letters That Work, Scott Bennett. New York: AMACOM, 2005.

Expert Resumes for Career Changers, Wendy S. Enelow and Louise M. Kursmark. Indianapolis, IN: JIST Publishing, 2005.

Fearless Interviewing: How to Win the Job by Communicating with Confidence, Marky Stein. New York: McGraw-Hill, 2002.

Ferguson Guide to Resumes and Job-Hunting Skills, Maurene J. Hinds. Chicago: Ferguson, 2005.

Gallery of Best Resumes: A Collection of Quality Resumes by Professional Resume Writers, 3rd ed., David F. Noble, Ph.D. Indianapolis, IN: JIST Publishing, 2004.

Get the Interview Every Time: Fortune 500 Hiring Professionals' Tips for Writing Winning Resumes and Cover Letters, Brenda Greene. Chicago: Dearborn Trade Publishing, 2004.

How to Interview Like a Top MBA: Job-Winning Strategies from Headhunters, Fortune 100 Recruiters, and Career Counselors, Shel Leanne. New York: McGraw-Hill, 2003.

How to Turn an Interview into a Job, Jeffrey G. Allen. New York: Simon and Schuster, 2004.

McGraw-Hill's Big Red Book of Resumes. New York: McGraw-Hill, 2002.

Monster Careers: Interviewing—Master the Moment That Gets You the Job, Jeffrey Taylor and Doug Hardy. New York: Penguin Books, 2005.

The Resume.com Guide to Writing Unbeatable Resumes, Warren Simons and Rose Curtis. New York: McGraw-Hill, 2004.

Recommended

Resume Magic: Trade Secrets of a Professional Resume Writer, 2nd ed., Susan Britton Whitcomb. Indianapolis, IN: JIST Publishing, 2003. Before and after resume samples provide a how-to on crafting the perfect resume. Includes tips on e-resumes and tricks for scannable-text submissions.

301 Smart Answers to Tough Interview Questions, Vicky Oliver. Naperville, IL: Sourcebooks, 2005. Advice on how to handle the questions designed to unsettle, from explaining gaps in work history to acing arcane trivia volleys.

The Resume Handbook: How to Write Outstanding Resumes & Cover Letters for Every Situation, 4th ed., Arthur D. Rosenberg and David V. Hizer. Avon, MA: Adams Media, 2003.

Resume Magic: Trade Secrets of a Professional Resume Writer, 2nd ed., Susan Britton Whitcomb. Indianapolis, IN: JIST Publishing, 2003.

Resumes for Dummies, 4th ed., Joyce Lain Kennedy. Indianapolis, IN: Wiley, 2003.

Resumes That Knock 'Em Dead, 6th ed., Martin Yate. Avon, MA: Adams Media, 2004.

301 Smart Answers to Tough Interview Questions, Vicky Oliver. Naperville, IL: Sourcebooks, 2005.

201 Best Questions to Ask on Your Interview, John Kador. New York: McGraw-Hill, 2002.

Winning the Interview Game: Everything You Need to Know to Land the Job, Alan H. Nierenberg. New York: AMACOM, 2005.

Mid-Career Options

Change Your Job, Change Your Life: Careering and Re-Careering in the New Boom/Bust Economy, 9th ed., Ron Krannich. Manassas Park, VA: Impact, 2004.

Fearless Career Change, Marky Stein. New York: McGraw-Hill, 2005.

Fire Your Boss, Stephen M. Pollan and Mark Levine. New York: HarperCollins, 2004.

I Don't Know What I Want, But I Know It's Not This: A Step-by-Step Guide to Finding Gratifying Work, Julie Jansen. New York: Penguin Books, 2003.

Over-40 Job Search Guide: 10 Strategies for Making Your Age an Advantage in Your Career, Gail Geary. Indianapolis, IN: JIST Publishing, 2004.

Radical Careering: 100 Truths to Jumpstart Your Job, Your Career, and Your Life, Sally Hogshead. New York: Gotham, 2005.

Second Acts: Creating the Life You Really Want, Building the Career You Truly Desire, Stephen M. Pollan and Mark Levine. New York: HarperCollins, 2003.

Working Identity: Unconventional Strategies for Reinventing Your Career, Hermania Ibarra. Boston: Harvard Business School Press, 2003.

Equality of Opportunity

Dancing on the Glass Ceiling, Nancy Frederick and Candy Deemer. New York: McGraw-Hill, 2004.

Job-Hunting for the So-Called Handicapped or People Who Have Disabilities, 2nd ed., Richard Nelson Bolles and Dale Susan Brown. Berkeley, CA: Ten Speed Press, 2001.

Job Search Handbook for People with Disabilities, 2nd ed., Daniel J. Ryan. Indianapolis, IN: JIST Publishing, 2004.

Lavender Road to Success: The Career Guide for the Gay Community, Kirk Snyder. Berkeley, CA: Ten Speed Press, 2003.

Resources for People with Disabilities, 2nd ed., Shawn Woodyard. Chicago: Ferguson, 2001.

Lists and Indexes of Career and Vocational Information

Encyclopedia of Careers and Vocational Guidance, 13th ed., 5 vols. Chicago: Ferguson, 2006.

O*Net Dictionary of Occupational Titles, 3rd ed. Indianapolis, IN: JIST Publishing, 2004.

Recommended

I Don't Know What I Want, But I Know It's Not This: A Step-by-Step Guide to Finding Gratifying Work, Julie Jansen. New York: Penguin Books, 2003. Experienced career coach identifies the top six reasons people are dissatisfied with their jobs and provides a step-by-step process for finding a career that suits every personality.

Working Identity: Unconventional Strategies for Reinventing Your Career, Hermania Ibarra. Boston: Harvard Business School Press, 2003. Help for those considering a mid-life career change.

Recommended

Dancing on the Glass Ceiling, Nancy Frederick and Candy Deemer. New York: McGraw-Hill, 2004. A former advertising executive teams with a professional executive coach to provide practical as well as inspirational advice for women in the workplace.

Job-Hunting for the So-Called Handicapped or People Who Have Disabilities, 2nd ed., Richard Nelson Bolles and Dale Susan Brown. Berkeley, CA: Ten Speed Press, 2001. From the author of *What Color Is Your Parachute?* Advice for the physically or mentally challenged on finding a career niche.

Internet Sites

Sites with Extensive Links

About.com
http://careerplanning.about.com

Beyond.com
http://www.beyond.com

Jobweb.com
http://www.jobweb.com

JIST Publishing
http://www.jist.com

Job Hunt: Online Job Search Guide and Resource Directory
http://www.job-hunt.org

Vault.com
http://www.vault.com

Vocational Information Center
http://www.khake.com

Career Development Resources

Career Magazine
http://www.careermag.com

Career Resource Homepage
http://www.careerresource.net

Job Hunters Bible
http://www.jobhuntersbible.com

Princeton Review
http://www.princetonreview.com

Quintessential Careers
http://www.quintcareers.com

Online Information and References

AT&T Toll-Free Internet Directory
http://www.tollfree.att.net

The Best Jobs in the USA Today
http://www.bestjobsusa.com

Careers.org
http://www.careers.org

Federal Jobs Digest
http://www.fedworld.gov/jobs/jobsearch.html

Job Finders Online
http://www.planningcommunications.com/jf

Job Safari
http://www.jobsafari.com

Monster Career Center
http://content.monster.com

Occupational Outlook Handbook
http://www.bls.gov/oco

SpherionExchange
http://employee.spherionexchange.com/start.cfm

U.S. Bureau of Labor Statistics Homepage
http://www.bls.gov/home.htm

US News and World Report Career Center
http://www.usnews.com/usnews/biztech/career/career_home.htm

Wall Street Journal Career Journal
http://www.careerjournal.com

Yahoo! Business and Economy
http://dir.yahoo.com/Business_and_Economy

Job Databases and Resume Posting

After College
http://www.aftercollege.com

America's Job Bank
http://www.ajb.org

Career Builder
http://www.careerbuilder.com

Career Mart
http://www.careermart.com

Employment Guide
http://www.employmentguide.com

Yahoo! Hot Jobs
http://hotjobs.yahoo.com

Idealist Nonprofit Career Center
http://www.idealist.org

Job.com
http://www.job.com

JobBank USA
http://www.jobbankusa.com

Job Web
http://www.jobweb.org

Monster Jobs
http://www.monster.com

Monstertrak
http://www.monstertrak.monster.com

NationJob.com
http://www.nationjob.com

Now Hiring
http://www.nowhiring.com

Audiovisual Materials

The following titles include, where possible, the developer's name and location or else the name and location of a distributor. Audiovisual titles may be available through several distributors.

Exploring the Working World

Career Advantage: Strategies for Success series. Video, guide. Princeton, NJ: Films Media Group.

Career Clusters series. Video. Charleston, WV: Cambridge Educational.

Career Exploration series. Video. South Charleston, WV: Meridian Education Corp.

Career Guidance Videos series. Video. South Charleston, WV: Meridian Education Corp.

Career S.E.L.F. Assessment: Finding a Career That Works for You. Video. Charleston, WV: Cambridge Educational.

Careers, Careers, Careers! Video, guide. Princeton, NJ: Films Media Group.

Careers for the 21st Century series. Video, guide. South Charleston, WV: Meridian Education Corp.

Careers without College. Video. Charleston, WV: Cambridge Educational.

The Changing Workplace: Technology and Globalization. Video. Princeton, NJ: Films Media Group.

Choices Today for Career Satisfaction Tomorrow. Video, guide. Charleston, WV: Cambridge Educational.

Complete Job Search System. Video. Charleston, WV: Cambridge Educational.

Connect on the Net: Finding a Job on the Internet. Video. Charleston, WV: Cambridge Educational.

Educational Planning for Your Career. Video. South Charleston, WV: Meridian Education Corp.

The 50 Best Jobs for the 21st Century series. Video. Indianapolis, IN: JIST Publishing.

The JIST Video Guide for Occupational Exploration series. Video. Indianapolis, IN: JIST Publishing.

Internet Careers: College Not Required. Video. Charleston, WV: Cambridge Educational.

Introduction to Career and Educational Exploration. Video. Princeton, NJ: Films Media Group.

JIST TV Series: The Job Search Channel. Video. Indianapolis, IN: JIST Publishing.

Jobs for the 21st Century. Video. Mt. Kisco, NY: Guidance Associates.

Learning for Earning. Video, guide. South Charleston, WV: Meridian Education Corp.

Log On for Success: Using Internet Job Sites. Video, guide. Charleston, WV: Cambridge Educational.

Researching Career Options: New Technologies and Current Techniques. Video. Princeton, NJ: Films Media Group.

School-to-Work Transition. Video. South Charleston, WV: Meridian Education Corp.

Ten Fastest Growing Careers: Jobs for the Future. Video. Mt. Kisco, NY: Guidance Associates.

What Would I Be Good At? Video. Mt. Kisco, NY: Guidance Associates.

What's Out There: How the World of Work is Organized. Video. Princeton, NJ: Films Media Group.

Your Career Search: Taking the First Step. Video. Mt. Kisco, NY: Guidance Associates.

Your Future: Planning Through Career Exploration. Video. South Charleston, WV: Meridian Education Corp.

Getting the Job and Getting Ahead

Career Evaluation. Video. Charleston, WV: Cambridge Educational.

Common Mistakes People Make in Interviews. Video, guide. Charleston, WV: Cambridge Educational.

Exceptional Employee: A Guide to Success on the Job. Video. Charleston, WV: Cambridge Educational.

Exceptional Interviewing Tips: A View from the Inside. Video, workbook. Charleston, WV: Cambridge Educational.

Extraordinary Answers to Common Interview Questions. Video. Charleston, WV: Cambridge Educational.

Finding a Job. Video. Charleston, WV: Cambridge Educational.

First Impressions: Etiquette and Work Habits for New Employees. Video, guide. Charleston, WV: Cambridge Educational.

From Pinkslip to Paycheck: The Road to Reemployment series. Video. Indianapolis, IN: JIST Publishing.

Getting Good Answers to Tough Interview Questions. Video. Indianapolis, IN: JIST Publishing.

Getting the Job You Really Want series. Video, workbook, guide. Indianapolis, IN: JIST Publishing.

How to Find a Job on the Internet. Video. Indianapolis, IN: JIST Publishing.

How to Be a Success at Work series. Video. Indianapolis, IN: JIST Publishing.

The Ideal Resume. Video. Charleston, WV: Cambridge Educational.

If at First: How to Get a Job and Keep It. Video. Mt. Kisco, NY: Guidance Associates.

Interview to Win Your First Job. Video. Indianapolis, IN: JIST Publishing.

Interviewing for a Job. Video. Charleston, WV: Cambridge Educational.

Job Survival Kit. Video. Charleston, WV: Cambridge Educational.

On-the-Job Success series. Video. Indianapolis, IN: JIST Publishing.

Planning Your Career. Video. Charleston, WV: Cambridge Educational.

The Portfolio Resume series. Video. Charleston, WV: Cambridge Educational.

"Quick" Job Search series. Video. Indianapolis, IN: JIST Publishing.

Succeeding on the Job. Video. Charleston, WV: Cambridge Educational.

Success in the Job World series. Video. Indianapolis, IN: JIST Publishing.

Staying on Track in Your Work Search. Video. Princeton, NJ: Films Media Group.

Power Interviewing Skills: Strategies for the Interviewee. Video. Charleston, WV: Cambridge Educational.

Take This Job and Love It: Keys to Surviving Your New Job. Video. Charleston, WV: Cambridge Educational.

Ten Commandments of Resumes. Video. Charleston, WV: Cambridge Educational.

Tough Times Job Strategies. Video, guide. Charleston, WV: Cambridge Educational.

*Understanding and Using the O*NET*. Video, guide. Charleston, WV: Cambridge Educational.

The Very Quick Job Search Video. Video. Indianapolis, IN: JIST Publishing.

The Video Guide to JIST's Self-Directed Job Search series. Video. Indianapolis, IN: JIST Publishing.

Web Resumes. Video. Charleston, WV: Cambridge Educational.

Computer Software

The following titles include, where possible, the developer's name and location or else the name and location of a distributor. Software titles may be available through several distributors.

Ace the Interview: The Multimedia Job Interview Guide. CD-ROM. Charleston, WV: Cambridge Educational.

Adams Media JobBank FastResume Suite. CD-ROM for Windows. Avon, MA: Adams Media.

Barron's Profiles of American Colleges on CD-ROM. Windows or Macintosh. Hauppauge, NY: Barron's Educational Series.

Cambridge Career Center. CD-ROM. Charleston, WV: Cambridge Educational.

Career Discovery Encyclopedia. CD-ROM. Chicago, IL: Ferguson.

Career Explorer. CD-ROM for Windows. Indianapolis, IN: JIST Publishing.

Career Finder Plus. CD-ROM. Indianapolis, IN: JIST Publishing.

CareerOINKs on the Web. Network. Indianapolis, IN: JIST Publishing.

Careers without College. CD-ROM. Indianapolis, IN: JIST Publishing.

Complete Resume Designer. CD-ROM. Charleston, WV: Cambridge Educational.

Custom Resume Creator. CD-ROM for Windows. Indianapolis, IN: JIST Publishing.

Decisions. CD-ROM. Indianapolis, IN: JIST Publishing.

Electronic Career Planner. CD-ROM for Windows. Indianapolis, IN: JIST Publishing.

Exploring the World of Work. CD-ROM. New York: McGraw-Hill.

JIST Presents Interview Mastery. CD-ROM. Indianapolis, IN: JIST Publishing.

Job Search series. CD-ROM. Indianapolis, IN: JIST Publishing.

Job Survival series. CD-ROM. Indianapolis, IN: JIST Publishing.

The Keys to Interviewing Success: Unlocking Your Professional Future. CD-ROM. Charleston, WV: Cambridge Educational.

Moving on Up: An Interactive Guide to Finding a Great Job. CD-ROM for Windows. Charleston, WV: Cambridge Educational.

Multimedia Career Center. CD-ROM. Charleston, WV: Cambridge Educational.

The Multimedia Career Path. CD-ROM. Charleston, WV: Cambridge Educational.

The Multimedia Guide to Occupational Exploration. CD-ROM. Charleston, WV: Cambridge Educational.

Multimedia Job Search. CD-ROM for Windows. Charleston, WV: Cambridge Educational.

Multimedia Take This Job and Love It. CD-ROM. Charleston, WV: Cambridge Educational.

OOH Career Center. CD-ROM. Charleston, WV: Cambridge Educational.

School-to-Work Career Center. CD-ROM. Charleston, WV: Cambridge Educational.

Success in the World of Work: Succeeding on the Job. CD-ROM. South Charleston, WV: Meridian Education Corp.

Targeting Success. CD-ROM. Indianapolis, IN: JIST Publishing.

General

Books

Careers for Courageous People and Other Adventurous Types, 2nd ed., Jan Goldberg. Lincolnwood, IL: NTC Publishing, 2005.

Careers for Travel Buffs and Other Restless Types, 2nd ed., Paul Plawin. New York: McGraw-Hill, 2003.

Inside Secrets to Finding a Career in Travel, Karen Rubin. Indianapolis: JIST Publishing, 2001.

Opportunities in Travel Careers, 2nd ed., Robert S. Milne and Marguerite Backhausen. New York: McGraw-Hill, 2003.

Transportation, Careers in Focus series, 2nd ed., Ferguson Publishing Staff, eds. New York: Ferguson, 2002.

Vault Guide to Technology Careers, Tod Emko and Evan Koblentz. New York: Vault, 2005.

Vault Guide to the Top Transportation Industry Employers, Laurie Pasiuk et al., eds. New York: Vault, 2006.

Audiovisual Materials

Mechanical Careers. Three videos. Indianapolis: JIST Publishing.

Transportation, Distribution, and Logistics. Video. South Charleston, WV: Meridian Education Corp.

TransTech: A Tour of Transportation Technology. CD-ROM. South Charleston, WV: Cambridge Educational.

Automotive, Bus, and Truck Transportation

Books

Career Opportunities in the Automotive Industry, G. Michael Kennedy. New York: Ferguson, 2005.

Careers for Car Buffs and Other Freewheeling Types, 2nd ed., Richard S. Lee and Mary Price Lee. New York: McGraw-Hill, 2004.

Careers in Trucking, rev. ed., Donald D. Schauer. New York: Rosen Publishing, 2002.

Opportunities in Automotive Service Careers, rev. ed., Robert M. Weber and Philip A. Perry. New York: McGraw-Hill, 2002.

Internet Sites

1-800-Drivers
http://www.1800drivers.com

Autojobs.com: The Bulletin Board for Automotive Employment
http://www.autojobs.com

etrucker.net
http://www.etrucker.net

TruckNet: The Insiders Guide to Trucking
http://www.truck.net

Ward's Auto
http://www.wardsauto.com

Audiovisual Materials

Automotive Technicians, Career Encounters series. Video. South Charleston, WV: Meridian Education Corp.

Innerview: Automotive. Video. Fresno, CA: Edgepoint Productions.

Aviation and Air Transportation

Books

Airline Pilot Interviews: How You Can Succeed in Getting Hired, 2nd ed., Irv Jasinski. Seattle: Aviation Book Company, 2002.

Career Opportunities in Aviation and the Aerospace Industry, Susan Echaore-McDavid. New York: Checkmark, 2005.

Checklist for Success: A Pilot's Guide to the Successful Airline Interview, rev. ed., Cheryl A. Cage. Newcastle, WA: Aviation Supplies and Academics, Inc., 2002.

Flight Attendant Job Finder & Career Guide, 77th ed., Tim Kirkwood. River Forest, IL: Planning/Communications, 2002.

Flight Guide for Success: Tips and Tactics for the Aspiring Airline Pilot, 3rd ed., Karen M. Kahn. Santa Barbara, CA: Cheltenham, 2004.

Job Hunting for Pilots: Networking Your Way to a Flying Job, 2nd ed., Gregory N. Brown. Ames, IA: State Press, 2001.

Vault Guide to Flight Attendant Careers, Mark Gazdik et al. New York: Vault, 2005.

Welcome Aboard! Your Career as a Flight Attendant, rev. ed., Becky S. Bock and Cheryl A. Cage. Newcastle, WA: Aviation Supplies and Academics, 2005.

Internet Sites

AvCrew
http://www.avcrew.com

Aviation and Aerospace Jobs Page
http://www.nationjob.com/aviation

Aviation Employee Placement Service
http://www.aeps.com

Avjobs.com
http://www.avjobs.com

Find a Pilot
http://www.findapilot.com

Maritime Careers

Books

Opportunities in Marine and Maritime Careers, rev. ed., William Ray Hietzmann.
New York: McGraw-Hill, 2006.

Internet Sites

Maritime Global Net
http://www.mgn.com

The information in this directory was generated from the IPEDS (Integrated Postsecondary Education Data System) database of the U.S. Department of Education. It includes only regionally or nationally accredited institutions offering postsecondary occupational training in transportation. Because college catalogs and directories of colleges and universities are readily available elsewhere, this directory does not include institutions that offer only bachelor's and advanced degrees.

Aircraft Maintenance and Operations

ALABAMA

Alabama Aviation and Technical College
US Hwy. 231
Ozark 36360

Community College of the Air Force
130 West Maxwell Blvd.
Montgomery 36112

ALASKA

Take Flight Alaska
1740 East Fifth Ave.
Anchorage 99501-2897

University of Alaska, Anchorage
3211 Providence Dr.
Anchorage 99508

University of Alaska, Fairbanks
Signers Hall
Fairbanks 99775

ARIZONA

Chandler-Gilbert Community College
2626 East Pecos Rd.
Chandler 85225-2499

Glendale Community College
6000 West Olive Ave.
Glendale 85302

ARKANSAS

Black River Technical College
Hwy. 304
P.O. Box 468
Pocahontas 72455

Pulaski Technical College
3000 West Scenic Dr.
North Little Rock 72118

CALIFORNIA

Cypress College
9200 Valley View
Cypress 90630

Gavilan College
5055 Santa Teresa Blvd.
Gilroy 95020

Glendale Community College
1500 North Verdugo Rd.
Glendale 91208-2894

Kings River Community College
995 North Reed Ave.
Reedley 93654

Long Beach City College
4901 East Carson St.
Long Beach 90808

Mount San Antonio College
1100 North Grand
Walnut 91789

Orange Coast College
2701 Fairview Rd.
Costa Mesa 92626

Sacramento City College
3835 Freeport Blvd.
Sacramento 95822

San Diego Mesa College
7250 Mesa College Dr.
San Diego 92111-4998

Sierra Academy of Aeronautics
Technicians Institute
9465 Earhart Rd.
Oakland 94614

COLORADO

Colorado Aero Tech
10851 West 120th Ave.
Broomfield 80021

Colorado Northwestern Community College
500 Kennedy Dr.
Rangely 81648-3598

Pikes Peak Community College
5675 South Academy Blvd.
Colorado Springs 80906-5498

DELAWARE

Delaware Technical and Community College, Terry
1832 North Dupont Pkwy.
Dover 19901

FLORIDA

Embry-Riddle Aeronautical University
600 South Clyde Morris Blvd.
Daytona Beach 32114-3900

Florida Institute of Technology
150 West University Blvd.
Melbourne 32901-6975

George T Baker Aviation School
3275 Northwest 42nd Ave.
Miami 33142

Lively Technical Center
500 North Appleyard Dr.
Tallahassee 32304

National Aviation Academy A & P School
5770 Roosevelt Blvd.
Ste. 105
Clearwater 33760

GEORGIA

Atlanta Area Technical School
1560 Stewart Ave. SW
Atlanta 30310

Heart of Georgia Technical Institute
560 Pinehill Rd.
Dublin 31021

Macon Technical Institute
3300 Macon Tech Dr.
Macon 31206

Middle Georgia Technical Institute
1311 Corder Rd.
Warner Robins 31088

South Georgia Technical Institute
1583 Souther Field Rd.
Americus 31709

IDAHO

Aero Technicians, Inc.
P.O. Box 7
Rexburg 83440

Idaho State University
741 South Seventh Ave.
Pocatello 83209

ILLINOIS

Belleville Area College
2500 Carlyle Rd.
Belleville 62221

City Colleges of Chicago, Richard J Daley College
7500 South Pulaski Rd.
Chicago 60652

Lewis University
Rte. 53
Romeoville 60446

Rock Valley College
3301 North Mulford Rd.
Rockford 61114

Southern Illinois University, Carbondale
Faner Hall 2179
Carbondale 62901

INDIANA

Vincennes University
1002 North First St.
Vincennes 47591

IOWA

Hamilton Technical College
1011 East 53rd St.
Davenport 52807

Indian Hills Community College
525 Grandview
Ottumwa 52501

Iowa Western Community College
2700 College Rd.
P.O. Box 4C
Council Bluff 51502

KANSAS

Cowley County Community College
125 South Second St.
Arkansas City 67005

Wichita Area Technical College
201 North Water
Wichita 67202-1292

KENTUCKY

Kentucky Technical, Somerset Regional Technology Center
230 Airport Rd.
Somerset 42501

MAINE

Air Tech, Inc.
Access Rd.
Sanford Airport
Sanford 04073

MARYLAND

Frederick Community College
7932 Opossumtown Pike
Frederick 21702

MICHIGAN

Kirtland Community College
10775 North Saint Helen Rd.
Roscommon 48653

Lansing Community College
419 North Capitol Ave.
Lansing 48901-7210

Macomb Community College
14500 Twelve Mile Rd.
Warren 48093-3896

Michigan Institute of Aeronautics
47884 D St.
Willow Run Airport East Side
Belleville 48111

MINNESOTA

Anoka-Ramsey Community College
11200 Mississippi Blvd.
Coon Rapids 55433-3470

Minneapolis Community and Technical College
1501 Hennepin Ave.
Minneapolis 55403-1779

Red Wing-Winona Technical College, Winona
1250 Homer Rd.
P.O. Box 409
Winona 55987

MISSISSIPPI

East Mississippi Community College
P.O. Box 158
Scooba 39358

MISSOURI

Linn Technical College
One Technology Dr.
Linn 65051

Maple Woods Community College
2601 Northeast Barry Rd.
Kansas City 64156

Saint Louis University, Main Campus
221 North Grand Blvd.
Saint Louis 63103

MONTANA

Helena College of Technology of the
University of Montana
1115 North Roberts St.
Helena 59601

NEBRASKA

Western Nebraska Community College
1601 East 27th St. NE
Scottsbluff 69361-1899

NEW JERSEY

Mercer County Community College
1200 Old Trenton Rd.
Trenton 08690

Teterboro School of Aeronautics
80 Moonachie Ave.
Teterboro 07608-1083

NEW MEXICO

Eastern New Mexico University, Roswell
Campus
52 University Blvd.
Admin Center
Roswell 88202

NEW YORK

College of Aeronautics
La Guardia Airport
Flushing 11371

NORTH CAROLINA

Guilford Technical Community College
Box 309
Jamestown 27282

Wayne Community College
3000 Wayne Memorial Dr.
Goldsboro 27533-8002

OHIO

Davis College
4747 Monroe St.
Toledo 43623

OKLAHOMA

Metro Area Vocational Technical School
District 22
1900 Springlake Dr.
Oklahoma City 73111

O T Autry Area Vocational Technical
Center
1201 West Willow
Enid 73703

OREGON

Lane Community College
4000 East 30th Ave.
Eugene 97405

Portland Community College
P.O. Box 19000
Portland 97280-0990

PENNSYLVANIA

Community College of Beaver County
One Campus Dr.
Monaca 15061

Pennsylvania College of Technology
One College Ave.
Williamsport 17701

Quaker City Institute of Aviation
98 Ashton Rd.
Northeast Philadelphia Airport
Philadelphia 19114

SOUTH CAROLINA

North American Institute of Aviation
Conway-Horry Co. Airport
P.O. Box 680
Conway 29528

SOUTH DAKOTA

Lake Area Technical Institute
230 11th St. NE
Watertown 57201

TENNESSEE

Nashville State Technical Institute
120 White Bridge Rd.
Nashville 37209

Tennessee Technology Center at
Memphis
550 Alabama Ave.
Memphis 38105-3604

TEXAS

Hallmark Institute of Technology
8901 Wetmore Rd.
San Antonio 78216

Houston Community College System
22 Waugh Dr.
P.O. Box 7849
Houston 77270-7849

International Aviation and Travel
Academy
4846 South Collins
Arlington 76018

Mountain View College
4849 West Illinois
Dallas 75211

North Harris Montgomery Community
College District
250 North Sam Houston Pkwy. E
Ste. 300
Houston 77060

Rice Aviation, A Division of Northrop
Rice USA, Inc.
205 Brisbane
Houston 77061

San Jacinto College, Central Campus
8060 Spencer Hwy.
Pasadena 77505

Tarrant County Junior College
1500 Houston St.
Fort Worth 76102

Texas State Technical College, Waco
3801 Campus Dr.
Waco 76705

UTAH

Dixie College
225 South, 700 East
Saint George 84770

Salt Lake Community College
P.O. Box 30808
Salt Lake City 84130

WASHINGTON

Green River Community College
12401 Southeast 320th St.
Auburn 98092

Seattle Community College, South
Campus
6000 16th Ave. SW
Seattle 98106

WISCONSIN

Blackhawk Technical College
P.O. Box 5009
Janesville 53547

Gateway Technical College
3520 30th Ave.
Kenosha 53144-1690

Milwaukee Area Technical College
700 West State St.
Milwaukee 53233-1443

WYOMING

Laramie County Community College
1400 East College Dr.
Cheyenne 82007

Automotive Mechanics

ALABAMA

Alabama Aviation and Technical
College
US Hwy. 231
Ozark 36360

Chauncey Sparks State Technical
College
Hwy. 431 S
Eufaula 36027

Community College of the Air Force
130 West Maxwell Blvd.
Montgomery 36112-6613

ARIZONA

Central Arizona College
8470 North Overfield Rd.
Coolidge 85228-9778

Clinton Technical Institute
2844 West Deer Valley Rd.
Phoenix 85027

Universal Technical Institute, Inc.
3121 West Weldon Ave.
Phoenix 85017

ARKANSAS

Northwest Technical Institute
709 South Old Missouri Rd.
Springdale 72764

Pulaski Technical College
3000 West Scenic Dr.
North Little Rock 72118

Quapaw Technical Institute
200 Mid America Blvd.
Hot Springs 71913

CALIFORNIA

Cosumnes River College
8401 Center Pkwy.
Sacramento 95823-5799

Marin Regional Occupational Program
P.O. Box 4925
San Rafael 94913

Southwestern College
900 Otay Lakes Rd.
Chula Vista 91910

COLORADO

Denver Automotive & Diesel College
460 South Lipan St.
Denver 80223-9366

DELAWARE

Delaware Technical and Community
College, Owens
Box 610
Georgetown 19947

FLORIDA

American Motorcycle Institute
3042 West International Speedway Blvd.
Daytona Beach 32124

Broward Community College
225 East Las Olas Blvd.
Fort Lauderdale 33301

Pensacola Junior College
1000 College Blvd.
Pensacola 32504

Pinellas Technical Education Center,
Clearwater
6100 154th Ave. N
Clearwater 34620

GEORGIA

Atlanta Area Technical School
1560 Stewart Ave. SW
Atlanta 30310

Savannah Technical Institute
5717 White Bluff Rd.
Savannah 31405-5594

ILLINOIS

Carl Sandburg College
2232 South Lake Storey Rd.
Galesburg 61401

Illinois Valley Community College
815 North Orlando Smith Ave.
Oglesby 61348-9692

Lincoln Land Community College
Shepherd Rd.
Springfield 62194-9256

Sauk Valley Community College
173 Illinois Rte. 2
Dixon 61021

Triton College
2000 Fifth Ave.
River Grove 60171

Universal Technical Institute, Inc.
601 Regency Dr.
Glendale Heights 60139

IOWA

Hawkeye Community College
1501 East Orange Rd.
Waterloo 50704

Iowa Lakes Community College
19 South Seventh St.
Estherville 51334

Kirkwood Community College
P.O. Box 2068
Cedar Rapids 52406

KANSAS

Kansas City Area Vocational Technical
School
2220 North 59th St.
Kansas City 66104

Kansas State University
Anderson Hall
Manhattan 66506

KAW Area Technical School
5724 Huntoon
Topeka 66604

LOUISIANA

Louisiana Technical College,
Alexandria Campus
4311 South MacArthur Dr.
Alexandria 71302-3137

MAINE

Eastern Maine Technical College
354 Hogan Rd.
Bangor 04401

MICHIGAN

Michigan Institute of Aeronautics
47884 D St.
Willow Run Airport East Side
Belleville 48111

MINNESOTA

Alexandria Technical College
1601 Jefferson St.
Alexandria 56308

Minnesota West Community and
Technical College
1011 First St. W
Canby 56220

North Hennepin Community College
7411 85th Ave. N
Brooklyn Park 55445

Northwest Technical College, Detroit
Lakes
900 Hwy. 34 E
Detroit Lakes 56501

Saint Paul Technical College
235 Marshall Ave.
Saint Paul 55102

MISSISSIPPI

Jones County Junior College
900 South Court St.
Ellisville 39437

Northwest Mississippi Community
College
510 North Panola Hwy. 51 N
Senatobia 38668

MISSOURI

Maple Woods Community College
2601 Northeast Barry Rd.
Kansas City 64156

NEVADA

All Rite Trade School
93 West Lake Mead Dr.
Henderson 89015

NORTH CAROLINA

Central Carolina Community College
1105 Kelly Dr.
Sanford 27330

Halifax Community College
P.O. Drawer 809
Weldon 27890

NORTH DAKOTA

North Dakota State College of Science
800 North Sixth St.
Wahpeton 58076

OKLAHOMA

Central Oklahoma Area Vocational
Technical School
Three Court Circle
Drumright 74030

Metro Area Vocational Technical School
District 22
1900 Springlake Dr.
Oklahoma City 73111

OREGON

Lane Community College
4000 East 30th Ave.
Eugene 97405

PENNSYLVANIA

Pennco Tech
3815 Otter St.
Bristol 19007

Pennsylvania College of Technology
One College Ave.
Williamsport 17701

SOUTH CAROLINA

Greenville Technical College
Station B
P.O. Box 5616
Greenville 29606-5616

TENNESSEE

Tennessee Technology Center at
Knoxville
1100 Liberty St.
Knoxville 37919

TEXAS

Austin Community College
5930 Middle Fiskville Rd.
Austin 78752

Blinn College
902 College Ave.
Brenham 77833

Cedar Valley College
3030 North Dallas Ave.
Lancaster 75134

Tarrant County Junior College
1500 Houston St.
Fort Worth 76102

Texas State Technical College, Waco
3801 Campus Dr.
Waco 76705

Universal Technical Institute, Inc.
721 Lockhaven Dr.
Houston 77073

UTAH

Bridgerland Applied Technology Center
1301 North, 600 West
Logan 84321

VIRGINIA

Danville Community College
1008 South Main St.
Danville 24541

J Sargeant Reynolds Community
College
P.O. Box 85622
Richmond 23285-5622

Northern Virginia Community College
4001 Wakefield Chapel Rd.
Annandale 22003

Thomas Nelson Community College
P.O. Box 9407
Hampton 23670

Tidewater Community College
121 College Pl.
Norfolk 23510

WASHINGTON

Bates Technical College
1101 South Yakima Ave.
Tacoma 98405

Lake Washington Technical College
11605 132nd Ave. NE
Kirkland 98034

Seattle Community College, South
Campus
6000 16th Ave. SW
Seattle 98106

Spokane Community College
North 1810 Greene Ave.
Spokane 99207

WISCONSIN

Chippewa Valley Technical College
620 West Clairemont Ave.
Eau Claire 54701

Madison Area Technical College
3550 Anderson St.
Madison 53704

ALABAMA

Bevill State Community College
100 State St.
Sumiton 35148

Douglas MacArthur State Technical
College
1708 North Main St.
Opp 36467

Gadsden State Community College
1001 George Wallace Dr.
Gadsden 35902-0227

George C Wallace State Community
College, Dothan
Rte. 6
Box 62
Dothan 36303-9234

George C Wallace State Community
College, Hanceville
801 Main St. NW
Hanceville 35077-2000

Harry M Ayers State Technical College
1801 Coleman Rd.
Anniston 36202

J F Ingram State Technical College
5375 Ingram Rd.
Deatsville 36022

John M Patterson State Technical
College
3920 Troy Hwy.
Montgomery 36116

Trenholm State Technical College
1225 Air Base Blvd.
Montgomery 36108

ALASKA

Alaska Vocational Technical Center
809 Second Ave.
Seward 99664

People Count, Inc.
P.O. Box 1310
Kenai 99611

University of Alaska, Anchorage
3211 Providence Dr.
Anchorage 99508

ARIZONA

Glendale Community College
6000 West Olive Ave.
Glendale 85302

Mesa Community College
1833 West Southern Ave.
Mesa 85202

National Education Center, Arizona
Automotive Institute
6829 North 46th Ave.
Glendale 85301-3579

Pima Community College
2202 West Anklam Rd.
Tucson 85709-0001

Universal Technical Institute, Inc.
3121 West Weldon Ave.
Phoenix 85017

ARKANSAS

Arkansas Valley Technical Institute
Hwy. 23 N
P.O. Box 506
Ozark 72949

Black River Technical College
Hwy. 304
Box 468
Pocahontas 72455

Cossatot Technical College
183 Hwy. 399
De Queen 71832

Crowley's Ridge Technical Institute
I40 Crowley's Ridge Rd.
Forrest City 72336-0925

Foothills Technical Institute
1800 East Moore St.
Searcy 72143

Great Rivers Vocational Technical
School
P.O. Box 747
Hwy. 1 NE
McGehee 71654

Northwest Technical Institute
709 South Old Missouri Rd.
Springdale 72764

Ozarka Technical College
218 South Dr.
P.O. Box 10
Melbourne 72556-0010

Pulaski Technical College
3000 West Scenic Dr.
North Little Rock 72118

Quapaw Technical Institute
200 Mid America Blvd.
Hot Springs 71913

Westark College
P.O. Box 3649
Fort Smith 72913

CALIFORNIA

American River College
4700 College Oak Ave.
Sacramento 95841

California Career School
1100 Technology Cir.
Anaheim 92805

Center for Employment Training,
Redwood City
2821 Middlefield Rd.
Redwood City 94063

Chabot College
25555 Hesperian Blvd.
Hayward 94545

Chaffey Community College
5885 Haven Ave.
Rancho Cucamonga 91737-3002

Citrus College
1000 West Foothill Blvd.
Glendora 91741-1899

College of Alameda
555 Atlantic Ave.
Alameda 94501

College of Marin
835 College Ave.
Kentfield 94904

College of the Redwoods
7351 Tompkins Hill Rd.
Eureka 95501-9302

DMC Automotive Training School
530 Cameron
Placentia 92870

East Los Angeles Skill Center
3921 Selig Place
Los Angeles 90031

El Camino College
16007 Crenshaw Blvd.
Torrance 90506

Electronics Learning Center
13321 Garden Grove Blvd.
Unit M
Garden Grove 92643

Escuelas Leicester
1940 South Figueroa St.
Los Angeles 90007

Fresno City College
1101 East University Ave.
Fresno 93741

Gavilan College
5055 Santa Teresa Blvd.
Gilroy 95020

Golden West College
15744 Golden W
Huntington Beach 92647

Imperial Valley College
P.O. Box 158
Imperial 92251-0158

Kings River Community College
995 North Reed Ave.
Reedley 93654

Los Angeles Trade Technical College
400 West Washington Blvd.
Los Angeles 90015-4181

Marin Regional Occupational Program
P.O. Box 4925
San Rafael 94913

Merced College
3600 M St.
Merced 95348-2898

Mira Costa College
One Barnard Dr.
Oceanside 92056-3899

Modesto Junior College
435 College Ave.
Modesto 95350-5800

Oxnard College
4000 South Rose Ave.
Oxnard 93033

Pasadena City College
1570 East Colorado Blvd.
Pasadena 91106

Rio Hondo College
3600 Workman Mill Rd.
Whittier 90601-1699

San Diego City College
1313 12th Ave.
San Diego 92101

San Joaquin Delta College
5151 Pacific Ave.
Stockton 95207

Sequoia Institute
420 Whitney Place
Fremont 94539

Solano County Community College
District
4000 Suisun Valley Rd.
Suisun 94585-3197

Victor Valley College
18422 Bear Valley Rd.
Victorville 92392-9699

Yuba College
2088 North Beale Rd.
Marysville 95901

COLORADO

Aims Community College
Box 69
Greeley 80632

Arapahoe Community College
2500 West College Dr.
Littleton 80160-9002

Denver Automotive & Diesel College
460 South Lipan St.
Denver 80223-9366

Front Range Community College
3645 West 112th Ave.
Westminster 80030

Mesa State College
P.O. Box 2647
Grand Junction 81502

Morgan Community College
17800 County Rd. 20
Fort Morgan 80701

Northeastern Junior College
100 College Dr.
Sterling 80751

Pikes Peak Community College
5675 South Academy Blvd.
Colorado Springs 80906-5498

Pueblo Community College
900 West Orman Ave.
Pueblo 81004

T H Pickens Technical Center
500 Airport Blvd.
Aurora 80011

Trinidad State Junior College
600 Prospect St.
Trinidad 81082

CONNECTICUT

Baran Institute of Technology
611 Day Hill Rd.
Windsor 06095

New England Technical Institute of
Connecticut, Inc.
200 John Downey Dr.
New Britain 06051

Porter and Chester Institute
138 Weymouth Rd.
Enfield 06082

Porter and Chester Institute
670 Lordship Blvd.
Stratford 06497

Porter and Chester Institute
125 Silas Deane Hwy.
Wethersfield 06109

DELAWARE

Delaware Technical and Community
College, Owens
Box 610
Georgetown 19947

FLORIDA

ATI Enterprises of Florida, Inc., ATI
Career Training Center
3501 Northwest Ninth Ave.
Oakland Park 33309

Atlantic Vocational Technical Center
4700 Coconut Creek Pkwy.
Coconut Creek 33063

Automotive Transmission School
453 East Okeechobee Rd.
Hialeah 33010

Central Florida Community College
3001 Southwest College Rd.
Ocala 34474

Daytona Beach Community College
1200 Volusia Ave.
Daytona Beach 32114

Florida Community College at
Jacksonville
501 West State St.
Jacksonville 32202

Lee County High Technical Center,
Central
3800 Michigan Ave.
Fort Myers 33916

Lively Technical Center
500 North Appleyard Dr.
Tallahassee 32304

Miami-Dade Community College
300 Northeast Second Ave.
Miami 33132

Miami Lakes Technical Education
Center
5780 Northwest 158th St.
Miami Lakes 33169

Pinellas Technical Education Center,
Clearwater
6100 154th Ave. N
Clearwater 34620

Robert Morgan Vocational Technical
Institute
18180 Southwest 122nd Ave.
Miami 33177

Saint Augustine Technical Center
2980 Collins Ave.
Saint Augustine 32095-1919

Santa Fe Community College
3000 Northwest 83rd St.
Gainesville 32606

Seminole Community College
100 Weldon Blvd.
Sanford 32773-6199

Sheridan Vocational Center
5400 Sheridan St.
Hollywood 33021

South Florida Community College
600 West College Dr.
Avon Park 33825

Suwannee-Hamilton Area Vocational
and Adult Center
415 Southwest Pinewood Dr.
Live Oak 32060

Washington-Holmes Technical Center
757 Hoyt St.
Chipley 32428

GEORGIA

Albany Technical Institute
1021 Lowe Rd.
Albany 31708

Athens Area Technical Institute
U.S. Hwy. 29 N
Athens 30610-0399

Atlanta Area Technical School
1560 Stewart Ave. SW
Atlanta 30310

Augusta Technical Institute
3116 Deans Bridge Rd.
Augusta 30906

Carroll Technical Institute
997 South Hwy. 16
Carrollton 30117

Chattahoochee Technical Institute
980 South Cobb Dr.
Marietta 30060-3398

Columbus Technical Institute
928 45th St.
Columbus 31904-6572

Coosa Valley Technical Institute
785 Cedar Ave.
Rome 30161

Dekalb Technical Institute
495 North Indian Creek Dr.
Clarkston 30021

Griffin Technical Institute
501 Varsity Rd.
Griffin 30223

Gwinnett Technical Institute
5150 Sugarloaf Pkwy.
Lawrenceville 30043

Heart of Georgia Technical Institute
560 Pinehill Rd.
Dublin 31021

Lanier Technical Institute
P.O. Box 58
Oakwood 30566

Moultrie Area Technical Institute
361 Industrial Dr.
Moultrie 31768

National Business Institute
243 West Ponce De Leon Ave.
Decatur 30030

North Georgia Technical Institute
Georgia Hwy. 197
P.O. Box 65
Clarkesville 30523

Okefenokee Technical Institute
1701 Carswell Ave.
Waycross 31501

Pickens Technical Institute
100 Pickens Tech Dr.
Jasper 30143

South Georgia Technical Institute
1583 Souther Field Rd.
Americus 31709

Valdosta Technical Institute
4089 Valtech Rd.
Valdosta 31602-9796

West Georgia Technical Institute
303 Fort Dr.
La Grange 30240

HAWAII

Employment Training Center, UH
Community Colleges
879 North King St.
Honolulu 96813

Hawaii Community College
200 West Kawili St.
Hilo 96720-4091

Honolulu Community College
874 Dillingham Blvd.
Honolulu 96817

Leeward Community College
96-045 Ala Ike
Pearl City 96782

Maui Community College
310 Kaahumanu Ave.
Kahului 96732

New York Technical Institute
1375 Dillingham Blvd.
Honolulu 96817

IDAHO

Boise State University
1910 University Dr.
Boise 83725

Idaho State University
741 South Seventh Ave.
Pocatello 83209

Lewis-Clark State College
500 Eighth Ave.
Lewiston 83501

North Idaho College
1000 West Garden Ave.
Coeur D'Alene 83814

ILLINOIS

Black Hawk College
6600 34th Ave.
Moline 61265

Carl Sandburg College
2232 South Lake Storey Rd.
Galesburg 61401

City Colleges of Chicago, Chicago City-
Wide College
226 West Jackson Blvd.
Chicago 60606-6997

City Colleges of Chicago, Harry S.
Truman College
1145 Wilson Ave.
Chicago 60640

College of Du Page
425 22nd St.
Glen Ellyn 60137-6599

College of Lake County
19351 West Washington St.
Grayslake 60030-1198

Coyne American Institute, Inc.
1235 West Fullerton Ave.
Chicago 60614

Elgin Community College
1700 Spartan Dr.
Elgin 60123

Highland Community College
2998 West Pearl City Rd.
Freeport 61032-9341

Illinois Central College
One College Dr.
East Peoria 61635-0001

Illinois Eastern Community Colleges,
Olney Central College
305 North West St.
Olney 62450

Illinois Valley Community College
815 North Orlando Smith Ave.
Oglesby 61348-9692

John A Logan College
700 Logan College Rd.
Carterville 62918

John Wood Community College
150 South 48th St.
Quincy 62301-9147

Joliet Junior College
1215 Houbolt Rd.
Joliet 60431

Kaskaskia College
27210 College Rd.
Centralia 62801

Kishwaukee College
21193 Malta Rd.
Malta 60150

Lake Land College
5001 Lake Land Blvd.
Mattoon 61938

Lewis and Clark Community College
5800 Godfrey Rd.
Godfrey 62035

Lincoln Land Community College
Shepherd Rd.
Springfield 62194-9256

Lincoln Technical Institute
7320 West Agatite Ave.
Norridge 60656

Lincoln Technical Institute
8920 South Cicero Ave.
Oak Lawn 60453

MacMurray College
East College Ave.
Jacksonville 62650

Prairie State College
202 Halsted St.
Chicago Heights 60411

Rend Lake College
468 North Ken Graz Pkwy.
Ina 62846

Rock Valley College
3301 North Mulford Rd.
Rockford 61114

Sauk Valley Community College
173 Illinois Rte. 2
Dixon 61021

Southeastern Illinois College
3575 College Rd.
Harrisburg 62946

Southern Illinois University,
Carbondale
Faner Hall 2179
Carbondale 62901

Spoon River College
23235 North Co 22
Canton 61520

Triton College
2000 Fifth Ave.
River Grove 60171

Universal Technical Institute, Inc.
601 Regency Dr.
Glendale Heights 60139

Washburne Trade School
3233 West 31st St.
Chicago 60623

Waubonsee Community College
Rte. 47 at Harter Rd.
Sugar Grove 60554-0901

INDIANA

ITT Technical Institute
4919 Coldwater Rd.
Fort Wayne 46825

Ivy Tech State College, Central Indiana
One West 26th St.
Indianapolis 46206-1763

Ivy Tech State College, East Central
4301 South Cowan Rd.
Box 3100
Muncie 47302

Ivy Tech State College, Lafayette
3101 South Creasy Ln.
P.O. Box 6299
Lafayette 47903

Ivy Tech State College, Northwest
1440 East 35th Ave.
Gary 46409

Ivy Tech State College, South Central
8204 Hwy. 311
Sellersburg 47172

Ivy Tech State College, Southeast
590 Ivy Tech Dr.
Madison 47250

Ivy Tech State College, Wabash Valley
7999 U.S. Hwy. 41
Terre Haute 47802-4898

Vincennes University
1002 North First St.
Vincennes 47591

IOWA

Des Moines Community College
2006 Ankeny Blvd.
Ankeny 50021

Eastern Iowa Community College
District
306 West River Dr.
Davenport 52801-1221

Hawkeye Community College
1501 East Orange Rd.
Waterloo 50704

Indian Hills Community College
525 Grandview
Ottumwa 52501

Iowa Lakes Community College
19 South Seventh St.
Estherville 51334

Iowa Western Community College
2700 College Rd.
Box 4C
Council Bluffs 51502

Kirkwood Community College
P.O. Box 2068
Cedar Rapids 52406

North Iowa Area Community College
500 College Dr.
Mason City 50401

Northeast Iowa Community College
Hwy. 150 S
P.O. Box 400
Calmar 52132-0400

Northwest Iowa Community College
603 West Park St.
Sheldon 51201

Southeastern Community College
1015 South Gear Ave.
Drawer F
West Burlington 52655-0605

Southwestern Community College
1501 Townline
Creston 50801

Western Iowa Tech Community College
4647 Stone Ave.
P.O. Box 5199
Sioux City 51102-5199

KANSAS

Flint Hills Technical College
3301 West 18th St.
Emporia 66801

Kansas City Area Vocational Technical
School
2220 North 59th St.
Kansas City 66104

KAW Area Technical School
5724 Huntoon
Topeka 66604

Manhattan Area Technical College
3136 Dickens Ave.
Manhattan 66503

North Central Kansas Technical College
Hwy. 24
Box 507
Beloit 67420

Northeast Kansas Area Vocational
Technical School
1501 West Riley St.
P.O. Box 277
Atchison 66002

Northwest Kansas Area Vocational
Technical School
P.O. Box 668
Goodland 67735

Pittsburg State University
1701 South Broadway
Pittsburg 66762

Salina Area Vocational Technical
School
2562 Scanlan Ave.
Salina 67401

Southeast Kansas Area Vocational
Technical School
600 Roosevelt
Coffeyville 67337

KENTUCKY

Kentucky Tech, Ashland Regional
Technology Center
4818 Roberts Dr.
Ashland 41102

Kentucky Tech, Bowling Green
Regional Technology Center
845 Loop Dr.
Bowling Green 42101-3601

Kentucky Tech, Hazard Regional
Technology Center
101 Vo-Tech Dr.
Hazard 41701

Kentucky Tech, Jefferson Regional
Technology Center
727 West Chestnut
Louisville 40203-2036

Kentucky Tech, Somerset Regional
Technology Center
230 Airport Rd.
Somerset 42501

Mayo State Regional Technology Center
Third St.
Paintsville 41240

Northern Kentucky State Vocational
Technical School
1025 Amsterdam Rd.
Covington 41011

LOUISIANA

Delgado Community College
501 City Pk Ave.
New Orleans 70119

Louisiana Technical College,
Alexandria Campus
4311 South MacArthur Dr.
Alexandria 71302-3137

Louisiana Technical College, Avoyelles
Campus
508 Choupique St.
Cottonport 71327

Louisiana Technical College, Baton
Rouge Campus
3250 North Acadian Hwy. E
Baton Rouge 70805

Louisiana Technical College, Florida
Parishes
P.O. Box 130
Greensburg 70441

Louisiana Technical College, Folkes
Campus
3337 Hwy. 10
Jackson 70748

Louisiana Technical College, Gulf Area
Campus
1115 Clover St.
Abbeville 70510

Louisiana Technical College, Jefferson
Campus
5200 Blair Dr.
Metairie 70001

Louisiana Technical College,
Jumonville Memorial Campus
P.O. Box 725
New Roads 70760

Louisiana Technical College, Lafayette
Campus
1101 Bertrand Dr.
Lafayette 70502-4909

Louisiana Technical College, Mansfield
Campus
943 Oxford Rd.
Mansfield 71052

Louisiana Technical College, Ruston
Campus
1010 James St.
Ruston 71273-1070

Louisiana Technical College, Sabine
Valley Campus
1255 Fischer Rd.
Many 71449

Louisiana Technical College,
Shreveport-Bossier Campus
2010 North Market St.
Shreveport 71137

Louisiana Technical College, Sidney N
Collier Campus
3727 Louisa St.
New Orleans 70126

Louisiana Technical College, Slidell
Campus
1000 Canulette Rd.
Slidell 70459

Louisiana Technical College, Sowela
Campus
3820 J Bennett Johnston Ave.
Lake Charles 70615

Louisiana Technical College, Sullivan
Campus
1710 Sullivan Dr.
Bogalusa 70427

Louisiana Technical College, T H Harris
Campus
337 East South St.
Opelousas 70570

Louisiana Technical College, West
Jefferson Campus
475 Manhattan Blvd.
Harvey 70058

Louisiana Technical College System,
Young Memorial
900 Youngs Rd.
Morgan City 70380

MAINE

Northern Maine Technical College
33 Edgemont Dr.
Presque Isle 04769

Southern Maine Technical College
Fort Rd.
South Portland 04106

MARYLAND

Allegany College of Maryland
12401 Willowbrook Rd. SE
Cumberland 21502

Catonsville Community College
800 South Rolling Rd.
Catonsville 21228

Harford Community College
401 Thomas Run Rd.
Bel Air 21015

Lincoln Technical Institute
9325 Snowden River Pky.
Columbia 21046

MASSACHUSETTS

Mount Wachusett Community College
444 Green St.
Gardner 01440

Tad Technical Institute
45 Spruce St.
Chelsea 02150

MICHIGAN

Alpena Community College
666 Johnson St.
Alpena 49707

Delta College
University Center 48710

Henry Ford Community College
5101 Evergreen Rd.
Dearborn 48128

Kirtland Community College
10775 North Saint Helen Rd.
Roscommon 48653

Macomb Community College
14500 Twelve Mile Rd.
Warren 48093-3896

Monroe County Community College
1555 South Raisinville Rd.
Monroe 48161

Mott Community College
1401 East Court St.
Flint 48503

Northern Michigan University
1401 Presque Isle
Marquette 49855

Oakland Community College
2480 Opdyke Rd.
Bloomfield Hills 48304-2266

Washtenaw Community College
P.O. Drawer 1
Ann Arbor 48106-1610

MINNESOTA

Dakota County Technical College
1300 East 145th St.
Rosemount 55068

Hennepin Technical College
9000 Brooklyn Blvd.
Brooklyn Park 55445

Lake Superior College
2101 Trinity Rd.
Duluth 55811

Minneapolis Community and Technical
College
1501 Hennepin Ave.
Minneapolis 55403-1779

Minnesota West Community and
Technical College
1011 First St. W
Canby 56220

Minnesota West Community and
Technical College
1593 11th Ave.
Granite Falls 56241

Minnesota West Community and
Technical College
401 West St.
Jackson 56143

Northland Community and Technical
College
Hwy. 1 E
Thief River Falls 56701

Northwest Technical College, Detroit
Lakes
900 Hwy. 34 E
Detroit Lakes 56501

Northwest Technical College, Moorhead
1900 28th Ave. S
Moorhead 56560

Red Wing-Winona Technical College,
Winona Campus
1250 Homer Rd.
P.O. Box 409
Winona 55987

Ridgewater College, A Community and
Technical College, Willmar
P.O. Box 1097
Willmar 56201

Riverland Community College
1900 Eighth Ave. NW
Austin 55912

Riverland Community College, Albert
Lea-Mankato
2200 Tech Dr.
Albert Lea 56007

Saint Cloud Technical College
1540 Northway Dr.
Saint Cloud 56303

Saint Paul Technical College
235 Marshall Ave.
Saint Paul 55102

MISSISSIPPI

Coahoma Community College
3240 Friars Point Rd.
Clarksdale 38614

East Central Community College
Decatur 39327

East Mississippi Community College
P.O. Box 158
Scooba 39358

Hinds Community College, Raymond
Campus
Raymond 39154

Holmes Community College
Hill St.
Goodman 39079

Itawamba Community College
602 West Hill St.
Fulton 38843

Mississippi Delta Community College
P.O. Box 668
Moorhead 38761

Mississippi Gulf Coast Community
College
Central Office
P.O. Box 67
Perkinston 39573

Northeast Mississippi Community
College
Cunningham Blvd.
Booneville 38829

Northwest Mississippi Community
College
510 North Panola Hwy. 51 N
Senatobia 38668

Pearl River Community College
Station A
Poplarville 39470

MISSOURI

Gibson Technical Center
P.O. Box 169
Reeds Spring 65737

Grand River Technical School
1200 Fair St.
Chillicothe 64601

Linn Technical College
One Technology Dr.
Linn 65051

Pike-Lincoln Technical Center
Rte. 1
P.O. Box 38
Eolia 63344

Ranken Technical College
4431 Finney Ave.
Saint Louis 63113

Rolla Technical Institute
1304 East Tenth St.
Rolla 65401

Saint Louis Community College, Forest
Park
5600 Oakland Ave.
Saint Louis 63110

Sikeston Area Vocational Technical
School
1002 Virginia St.
Sikeston 63801

Waynesville Technical Academy
810 Roosevelt
Waynesville 65583

MONTANA

Helena College of Technology of the
University of Montana
1115 North Roberts St.
Helena 59601

Montana State University, College of
Technology, Billings
3803 Central Ave.
Billings 59102

Montana State University, College of
Technology, Butte
25 Basin Creek Rd.
Butte 59701

NEBRASKA

Central Community College Area
P.O. Box 4903
Grand Island 68802

Metropolitan Community College Area
5300 North 30th St.
Omaha 68111

Mid Plains Community College
416 North Jeffers
North Platte 69101

Northeast Community College
801 East Benjamin
P.O. Box 469
Norfolk 68702-0469

Southeast Community College Area
1111 O St.
Ste. 111
Lincoln 68520

Universal Technical Institute, Inc.
902 Capitol Ave.
Omaha 68102

Western Nebraska Community College
1601 East 27th St. NE
Scottsbluff 69361-1899

NEW JERSEY

Lincoln Technical Institute
2299 Vauxhall Rd.
Union 07083

Pennco Tech
Erial Rd.
P.O. Box 1427
Blackwood 08012

Salem County Vocational Technical
Schools
RD 2
P.O. Box 350
Woodstown 08098

NEW MEXICO

Albuquerque Technical Vocational
Institute
525 Buena Vista SE
Albuquerque 87106

New Mexico Junior College
5317 Lovington Hwy.
Hobbs 88240

New Mexico State University, Dona Ana
P.O. Box 30001
Dept. 3DA
3400 South Espina
Las Cruces 88003-0105

San Juan College
4601 College Blvd.
Farmington 87402

NEW YORK

Apex Technical School
635 Ave. of the Americas
New York 10011

Berk Trade and Business School
312 West 36th St.
New York 10018-6402

Corning Community College
Spencer Hill
Corning 14830

CUNY Bronx Community College
West 181st St. & University Ave.
Bronx 10453

CUNY New York City Technical College
300 Jay St.
Brooklyn 11201

Erie Community College, North
Campus
Main St. and Youngs Rd.
Williamsville 14221

Hudson Valley Community College
80 Vandenburgh Ave.
Troy 12180

Monroe Community College
1000 East Henrietta Rd.
Rochester 14623

Onondaga Community College
4941 Onondaga Rd.
Syracuse 13215

Rockland Community College
145 College Rd.
Suffern 10901

SUNY College of Agriculture &
Technology at Morrisville
Morrisville 13408

SUNY College of Technology at Alfred
Alfred 14802

SUNY College of Technology at Canton
Cornell Drive
Canton 13617

SUNY College of Technology at Delhi
Delhi 13753

NORTH CAROLINA

Alamance Community College
P.O. Box 8000
Graham 27253

Blue Ridge Community College
College Dr.
Flat Rock 28731-9624

Caldwell Community College and
Technical Institute
Box 600
Lenoir 28645

Carteret Community College
3505 Arendell St.
Morehead City 28557

Central Carolina Community College
1105 Kelly Dr.
Sanford 27330

Central Piedmont Community College
P.O. Box 35009
Charlotte 28235-5009

Cleveland Community College
137 South Post Rd.
Shelby 28152

Coastal Carolina Community College
444 Western Blvd.
Jacksonville 28546-6877

Craven Community College
800 College Ct.
New Bern 28562

Davidson County Community College
297 Davidson Community College Rd.
Lexington 27292

Edgecombe Community College
2009 West Wilson St.
Tarboro 27886

Forsyth Technical Community College
2100 Silas Creek Pkwy.
Winston Salem 27103

Gaston College
201 Hwy. 321 S
Dallas 28034

Guilford Technical Community College
Box 309
Jamestown 27282

Halifax Community College
P.O. Drawer 809
Weldon 27890

Isothermal Community College
P.O. Box 804
Spindale 28160

Johnston Community College
P.O. Box 2350
Smithfield 27577-2350

McDowell Technical Community
College
Rte. 1
Box 170
Marion 28752

Montgomery Community College
P.O. Box 787
Troy 27371

Randolph Community College
629 Industrial Pk Ave.
Asheboro 27204

Sandhills Community College
2200 Airport Rd.
Pinehurst 28374

Stanly Community College
141 College Dr.
Albemarle 28001

Surry Community College
P.O. Box 304
Dobson 27017-0304

Tri-County Community College
2300 Hwy. 64 E
Murphy 28906

Wake Technical Community College
9101 Fayetteville Rd.
Raleigh 27603-5696

Wayne Community College
3000 Wayne Memorial Dr.
Goldsboro 27533-8002

Wilkes Community College
Collegiate Dr.
Wilkesboro 28697

NORTH DAKOTA

Bismarck State College
P.O. Box 5587
Bismarck 58506-5587

North Dakota State College of Science
800 North Sixth St.
Wahpeton 58076

United Tribes Technical College
3315 University Dr.
Bismarck 58501

OHIO

Choffin Career Center
200 East Wood St.
Youngstown 44503

Columbus Paraprofessional Institute
1900 East Grandville Rd.
Bldg. A
Ste. 210
Columbus 43229

Gallia Jackson Vinton JVSD
Box 157
Rio Grande 45674

Northwestern College
1441 North Cable Rd.
Lima 45805

Pickaway Ross Joint Vocational School
District
895 Crouse Chapel Rd.
Chillicothe 45601-9010

Portage Lakes Career Center
4401 Shriver Rd.
Greensburg 44232-0248

Tri-County Vocational School
15675 St. Rte. 691
Nelsonville 45764

Trumbull County Joint Vocational
School District
528 Educational Hwy.
Warren 44483

OKLAHOMA

Caddo-Kiowa Area Vocational Technical
School
P.O. Box 190
Fort Cobb 73038

Central Oklahoma Area Vocational
Technical School
Three Court Circle
Drumright 74030

Francis Tuttle Area Vocational
Technical Center
12777 North Rockwell Ave.
Oklahoma City 73142-2789

Great Plains Area Vocational Technical
School
4500 West Lee Blvd.
Lawton 73505

Kiamichi AVTS SD #7, Hugo
107 South 15th
Hugo 74743

Kiamichi AVTS SD #7, McCurtain
Rte. 3 & Hwy. 70 N
Box 177
Idabel 74745

Kiamichi AVTS SD #7, Poteau
1509 South McKenna
Poteau 74953

Metro Area Vocational Technical School
District 22
1900 Springlake Dr.
Oklahoma City 73111

Oklahoma Northwest Area Vocational
Technical School
1801 South 11th St.
Alva 73717

Oklahoma State University, Okmulgee
1801 East Fourth St.
Okmulgee 74447-3901

Platt College
309 South Ann Arbor
Oklahoma City 73128

Pontotoc Area Vocational Technical
School
601 West 33rd
Ada 74820

Southern Oklahoma Technology Center
2610 Sam Noble Pkwy.
Ardmore 73401

Tulsa County Area Vocational Technical
School District 18, Southeast
4600 South Olive
Broken Arrow 74011-1706

OREGON

Blue Mountain Community College
P.O. Box 100
Pendleton 97801

Clackamas Community College
19600 Molalla Ave.
Oregon City 97045

Lane Community College
4000 East 30th Ave.
Eugene 97405

Linn-Benton Community College
6500 Southwest Pacific Blvd.
Albany 97321

Portland Community College
P.O. Box 19000
Portland 97280-0990

PENNSYLVANIA

ICS-International Correspondence
Schools
Oak St. and Pawnee Ave.
Scranton 18515

Johnson Technical Institute
3427 North Main Ave.
Scranton 18508-1495

Mercer County Area Vocational
Technical School
776 Greenville Rd.
Mercer 16137-0152

New Castle School of Trades
Youngstown Rd. 1
Pulaski 16143

Pennco Tech
3815 Otter St.
Bristol 19007

Pennsylvania College of Technology
One College Ave.
Williamsport 17701

Remington Education Center, Vale
Campus
135 West Market St.
Blairsville 15717

Rosedale Technical Institute
4634 Browns Hill Rd.
Pittsburgh 15217

RHODE ISLAND

New England Institute of Technology
2500 Post Rd.
Warwick 02886

SOUTH CAROLINA

Greenville Technical College
Station B
P.O. Box 5616
Greenville 29606-5616

Midlands Technical College
P.O. Box 2408
Columbia 29202

Spartanburg Technical College
P.O. Box 4386
Spartanburg 29305

York Technical College
452 South Anderson Rd.
Rock Hill 29730

SOUTH DAKOTA

Lake Area Technical Institute
230 11th St. NE
Watertown 57201

Mitchell Technical Institute
821 North Capital St.
Mitchell 57301

Southeast Technical Institute
2301 Career Place
Sioux Falls 57107

Western Dakota Technical Institute
800 Mickelson Dr.
Rapid City 57701

TENNESSEE

Chattanooga State Technical
Community College
4501 Amnicola Hwy.
Chattanooga 37406

Nashville Auto Diesel College, Inc.
1524 Gallatin Rd.
Nashville 37206

State Technical Institute at Memphis
5983 Macon Cove
Memphis 38134

Tennessee Technology Center at Athens
1635 Vo Tech Dr.
P.O. Box 848
Athens 37371-0848

Tennessee Technology Center at
Crossville
P.O. Box 2959
Crossville 38557

Tennessee Technology Center at Crump
Hwy. 64 W
P.O. Box 89
Crump 38327

Tennessee Technology Center at
Elizabethton
1500 Arney St.
Elizabethton 37643

Tennessee Technology Center at
Harriman
P.O. Box 1109
Harriman 37748

Tennessee Technology Center at
Hohenwald
813 West Main
Hohenwald 38462-2201

Tennessee Technology Center at
Jackson
2468 Westover Rd.
Jackson 38301

Tennessee Technology Center at
Knoxville
1100 Liberty St.
Knoxville 37919

Tennessee Technology Center at
Livingston
740 High Tech Dr.
Livingston 38570

Tennessee Technology Center at
McKenzie
16940 Highland Dr.
P.O. Box 427
McKenzie 38201

Tennessee Technology Center at
McMinnville
241 Vo Tech Dr.
McMinnville 37110

Tennessee Technology Center at
Memphis
550 Alabama Ave.
Memphis 38105-3604

Tennessee Technology Center at
Morristown
821 West Louise Ave.
Morristown 37813

Tennessee Technology Center at
Murfreesboro
1303 Old Fort Pkwy.
Murfreesboro 37129

Tennessee Technology Center at
Nashville
100 White Bridge Rd.
Nashville 37209

Tennessee Technology Center at Pulaski
1233 East College St.
Pulaski 38478

Tennessee Technology Center at
Shelbyville
1405 Madison St.
Shelbyville 37160

Tennessee Technology Center at
Whiteville
P.O. Box 489
Whiteville 38075

TEXAS

Alvin Community College
3110 Mustang Rd.
Alvin 77511

Amarillo College
P.O. Box 447
Amarillo 79178

American Trades Institute
6627 Maple Ave.
Dallas 75235

Austin Community College
5930 Middle Fiskville Rd.
Austin 78752

Bee County College
3800 Charco Rd.
Beeville 78102

Brookhaven College
3939 Valley View Ln.
Farmers Branch 75244-4997

Cedar Valley College
3030 North Dallas Ave.
Lancaster 75134

Central Texas College
P.O. Box 1800
Killeen 76540-1800

Cisco Junior College
Rte. 3
Box 3
Cisco 76437

Del Mar College
101 Baldwin
Corpus Christi 78404-3897

Eastfield College
3737 Motley Dr.
Mesquite 75150

El Paso Community College
P.O. Box 20500
El Paso 79998

Grayson County College
6101 Grayson Dr.
Denison 75020

Hill College
P.O. Box 619
Hillsboro 76645

Houston Community College System
22 Waugh Dr.
P.O. Box 7849
Houston 77270-7849

Howard County Junior College District
1001 Birdwell Ln.
Big Spring 79720

Lamar University, Port Arthur
1500 Proctor St.
Port Arthur 77640

Lee College
200 Lee Dr.
Baytown 77520-4703

Lincoln Technical Institute
2501 East Arkansas Ln.
Grand Prairie 75052

North Harris Montgomery Community
College District
250 North Sam Houston Pkwy. E
Ste. 300
Houston 77060

Odessa College
201 West University
Odessa 79764

Ranger College
College Circle
Ranger 76470

Saint Philip's College
1801 Martin Luther King Dr.
San Antonio 78203

San Antonio Training Division
9350 South Presa
San Antonio 78223-4799

San Jacinto College, Central Campus
8060 Spencer Hwy.
Pasadena 77505

School of Automotive Machinists
1911 Antoine
Houston 77055

South Plains College
1401 College Ave.
Levelland 79336

Southwest Texas Junior College
2401 Garner Field Rd.
Uvalde 78801

Tarrant County Junior College
1500 Houston St.
Fort Worth 76102

Texarkana College
2500 North Robison Rd.
Texarkana 75599

Texas Southmost College
80 Fort Brown
Brownsville 78520

Texas State Technical College,
Harlingen
2424 Boxwood
Harlingen 78550-3697

Texas State Technical College,
Sweetwater
300 College Dr.
Sweetwater 79556

Texas State Technical College, Waco
3801 Campus Dr.
Waco 76705

Texas Vocational School, Inc.
1921 East Red River
Victoria 77901-5625

Trinity Valley Community College
500 South Prairieville
Athens 75751

Universal Technical Institute, Inc.
721 Lockhaven Dr.
Houston 77073

Western Technical Institute
1000 Texas St.
El Paso 79901

Wharton County Junior College
911 Boling Hwy.
Wharton 77488

UTAH

Bridgerland Applied Technology Center
1301 North, 600 West
Logan 84321

Davis Applied Technology Center
550 East, 300 South
Kaysville 84037

Dixie College
225 South, 700 East
Saint George 84770

Salt Lake Community College
P.O. Box 30808
Salt Lake City 84130

Salt Lake Community College, Skills
Center
South City Campus
1575 South State St.
Salt Lake City 84115

Sevier Valley Applied Technology
Center
800 South, 200 South
Richfield 84701

Utah Career College
1144 West 3300 S
Salt Lake City 84119-3330

Utah Valley State College
800 West, 1200 South
Orem 84058

Weber State University
3750 Harrison Blvd.
Ogden 84408

VIRGINIA

Advanced Technology Institute
5700 Southern Blvd.
Virginia Beach 23462

Southside Training Skill Center,
Nottoway County
P.O. Box 258
Crewe 23930

Wise Skills Center
515 Hurricane Rd. N
Wise 24293

WASHINGTON

Bates Technical College
1101 South Yakima Ave.
Tacoma 98405

Bellingham Technical College
3028 Lindbergh Ave.
Bellingham 98225

Big Bend Community College
7662 Chanute St.
Moses Lake 98837

Edmonds Community College
20000 68th Ave. W
Lynnwood 98036

Grays Harbor College
1620 Edward P Smith Dr.
Aberdeen 98520

Green River Community College
12401 Southeast 320th St.
Auburn 98092

Lake Washington Technical College
11605 132nd Ave. NE
Kirkland 98034

Lower Columbia College
P.O. Box 3010
Longview 98632

Perry Technical Institute
2011 West Washington Ave.
Yakima 98903

Seattle Community College, South
Campus
6000 16th Ave. SW
Seattle 98106

Shoreline Community College
16101 Greenwood Ave. N
Seattle 98133

Spokane Community College
North 1810 Greene Ave.
Spokane 99207

Walla Walla Community College
500 Tausick Way
Walla Walla 99362

WEST VIRGINIA

Cabell County Vocational Technical
Center
1035 Norway Ave.
Huntington 25705

WISCONSIN

Blackhawk Technical College
P.O. Box 5009
Janesville 53547

Chippewa Valley Technical College
620 West Clairemont Ave.
Eau Claire 54701

Fox Valley Technical College
1825 North Bluemound Dr.
Appleton 54913-2277

Gateway Technical College
3520 30th Ave.
Kenosha 53144-1690

Lakeshore Technical College
1290 North Ave.
Cleveland 53015

Madison Area Technical College
3550 Anderson St.
Madison 53704

Mid-State Technical College
500 32nd St. N
Wisconsin Rapids 54494

Milwaukee Area Technical College
700 West State St.
Milwaukee 53233-1443

Moraine Park Technical College
235 North National Ave.
Fond Du Lac 54936-1940

Northcentral Technical College
1000 Campus Dr.
Wausau 54401-1899

Northeast Wisconsin Technical College
2740 West Mason St.
P.O. Box 19042
Green Bay 54307-9042

Southwest Wisconsin Technical College
1800 Bronson Blvd.
Fennimore 53809

Waukesha County Technical College
800 Main St.
Pewaukee 53072

Western Wisconsin Technical College
304 North Sixth St.
P.O. Box 908
La Crosse 54602-0908

Wisconsin Indianhead Technical
College
505 Pine Ridge Dr.
P.O. Box 10B
Shell Lake 54871

WYOMING

Casper College
125 College Dr.
Casper 82601

Laramie County Community College
1400 East College Dr.
Cheyenne 82007

Automotive Technology

ALABAMA

Bessemer State Technical College
1100 Ninth Ave.
Bessemer 35021

ARIZONA

Eastern Arizona College
Church St.
Thatcher 85552-0769

CALIFORNIA

Butte College
3536 Butte Campus Dr.
Oroville 95965

Cerritos College
11110 Alondra Blvd.
Norwalk 90650

De Anza College
21250 Stevens Creek Blvd.
Cupertino 95014

Riverside Community College
4800 Magnolia Ave.
Riverside 92506-1299

Skyline College
3300 College Dr.
San Bruno 94066

COLORADO

Denver Institute of Technology
7350 North Broadway
Denver 80221

CONNECTICUT

Porter and Chester Institute
320 Sylvan Lake Rd.
Watertown 06779-1400

DELAWARE

Delaware Technical Community
College, Stanton-Wilmington
400 Stanton-Christiana Rd.
Newark 19702

IOWA

Des Moines Community College
2006 Ankeny Blvd.
Ankeny 50021

KANSAS

McPherson College
1600 East Euclid
P.O. Box 1402
McPherson 67460

KENTUCKY

Jefferson Community College
109 East Broadway
Louisville 40202

Kentucky Tech, Madisonville Regional
Technology Center
150 School Ave.
Madisonville 42431

MAINE

Central Maine Technical College
1250 Turner St.
Auburn 04210

MASSACHUSETTS

Franklin Institute of Boston
41 Berkeley St.
Boston 02116

Quinsigamond Community College
670 West Boylston St.
Worcester 01606

Springfield Technical Community
College
One Armory Square
Springfield 01105

MICHIGAN

Ferris State University
901 South State St.
Big Rapids 49307

Henry Ford Community College
5101 Evergreen Rd.
Dearborn 48128

Lansing Community College
419 North Capitol Ave.
Lansing 48901-7210

MINNESOTA

Alexandria Technical College
1601 Jefferson St.
Alexandria 56308

MISSOURI

ITT Technical Institute
13505 Lakefront Dr.
Earth City 63045

Jefferson College
1000 Viking Dr.
Hillsboro 63050

Longview Community College
500 Longview Rd.
Lees Summit 64081

Tad Technical Institute
7910 Troost Ave.
Kansas City 64131

MONTANA

Miles Community College
2715 Dickinson
Miles City 59301

NEW HAMPSHIRE

New Hampshire Community Technical
College, Manchester-Stratham
1066 Front St.
Manchester 03102

New Hampshire Community Technical
College, Nashua
505 Amherst St.
Nashua 03061-2052

NEW JERSEY

Brookdale Community College
765 Newman Springs Rd.
Lincroft 07738-1599

Camden County College
P.O. Box 200
Blackwood 08012

Gloucester County College
1400 Tanyard Rd.
Sewell 08080

NEW YORK

SUNY College of Technology at
Farmingdale
Melville Rd.
Farmingdale 11735-1021

OHIO

Cincinnati State Technical and
Community College
3520 Central Pkwy.
Cincinnati 45223

Owens Community College
39335 Oregon Rd.
Toledo 43699-1947

Sinclair Community College
444 West Third St.
Dayton 45402

Stark State College of Technology
6200 Frank Ave. NW
Canton 44720

University of Akron, Main Campus
302 Buchtel Common
Akron 44325-4702

Washington State Community College
710 Colegate Dr.
Marietta 45750

OKLAHOMA

Oklahoma State University, Okmulgee
1801 East Fourth St.
Okmulgee 74447-3901

OREGON

Mount Hood Community College
26000 Southeast Stark St.
Gresham 97030

Oregon Institute of Technology
3201 Campus Dr.
Klamath Falls 97601-8801

PENNSYLVANIA

Community College of Allegheny
County
800 Allegheny Ave.
Pittsburgh 15233-1895

Harrisburg Area Community College,
Harrisburg
One Hacc Dr.
Harrisburg 17110

Lehigh Carbon Community College
4525 Education Park Dr.
Schnecksville 18078-2598

Northampton County Area Community
College
3835 Green Pond Rd.
Bethlehem 18020-7599

Pennsylvania College of Technology
One College Ave.
Williamsport 17701

Reading Area Community College
P.O. Box 1706
Reading 19603-1706

Remington Education Center, Vale
Campus
135 West Market St.
Blairsville 15717

Thaddeus Stevens State School of
Technology
750 East King St.
Lancaster 17602

TENNESSEE

Tennessee Technology Center at
Dickson
740 Hwy. 46
Dickson 37055

TEXAS

Lamar University, Beaumont
4400 Mlk
P.O. Box 10001
Beaumont 77710

VERMONT

Vermont Technical College
P.O. Box 500
Randolph Center 05061

WISCONSIN

Madison Area Technical College
3550 Anderson St.
Madison 53704

Commercial Pilot Training

ALABAMA

Alabama Aviation and Technical
College
US Hwy. 231
Ozark 36360

Gold Dust Flying Service
Talladega Airport
P.O. Box 75
Eastaboga 36260

ALASKA

Alaska Flying Network, Inc.
403 North Willow
Ste. 1
Kenai 99611

Take Flight Alaska
1740 East Fifth Ave.
Anchorage 99501-2897

ARIZONA

North Aire
6500 MacCurdy Dr.
Ste. 7
Ernest A Love Field
Prescott 86301

CALIFORNIA

Aero Tech Academy
1745 Sessums Dr.
Redlands 92374

Benbow Aviation Flight School
3201 Airport Dr.
Torrance 90505

Long Beach City College
4901 East Carson St.
Long Beach 90808

Mount San Antonio College
1100 North Grand
Walnut 91789

Pacific States Aviation, Inc.
51 John Glenn Dr.
Concord 94520

Professional Pilot Training
3000 North Clybourn Ave.
Burbank 91505

Rolling Hills Aviation
3115 West Airport Dr.
Torrance 90505

San Diego Mesa College
7250 Mesa College Dr.
San Diego 92111-4998

COLORADO

Aims Community College
Box 69
Greeley 80632

Colorado Northwestern Community
College
500 Kennedy Dr.
Rangely 81648-3598

Durango Air Service, Inc.
1340 Airport Rd.
Durango 81301

Emery Aviation College
2315 East Pikes Peak Ave.
Colorado Springs 80909

FLORIDA

Broward Community College
225 East Las Olas Blvd.
Fort Lauderdale 33301

Embry-Riddle Aeronautical University
600 South Clyde Morris Blvd.
Daytona Beach 32114-3900

Flight Safety International
P.O. Box 2708
Vero Beach 32961-2708

Florida Institute of Technology
150 West University Blvd.
Melbourne 32901-6975

Miami-Dade Community College
300 Northeast Second Ave.
Miami 33132

GEORGIA

Epps Air Service
1 Aviation Way
Dekalb-Peachtree Airport
Atlanta 30341

Quality Aviation, Inc.
1951 Airport Rd.
Ste. 205
Atlanta 30341

ILLINOIS

Airgo, Inc.
2331 East Calumet St.
Centralia 62801-6577

American Flyers
3 North 40 Powis Rd.
West Chicago 60185

Decatur Aviation, Inc.
790 South Airport Rd.
Decatur 62521

Southern Illinois University,
Carbondale
Faner Hall 2179
Carbondale 62901-4512

University of Illinois at Urbana
601 East John St.
Champaign 61820

INDIANA

Vincennes University
1002 North First St.
Vincennes 47591

IOWA

Denison Aviation, Inc.
Municipal Airport
Denison 51442

KANSAS

Kansas State University
Anderson Hall
Manhattan 66506

MASSACHUSETTS

North Shore Community College
One Ferncroft Rd.
Danvers 01923

MICHIGAN

Lansing Community College
419 North Capitol Ave.
Lansing 48901-7210

Northern Air Flight Training
5500 44th St.
Grand Rapids 49512

Northwestern Michigan College
1701 East Front St.
Traverse City 49686

Oakland Community College
2480 Opdyke Rd.
Bloomfield Hills 48304-2266

NEVADA

Aerleon
2634 Airport Dr.
Ste. 101
North Las Vegas 89030

NEW HAMPSHIRE

Daniel Webster College
20 University Dr.
Nashua 03063-1300

NEW JERSEY

Mercer County Community College
1200 Old Trenton Rd.
Trenton 08690

Raritan Valley Flying School
Rte. 206
Princeton Airport
Princeton 08540

NEW YORK

Prior Aviation Service, Inc.
50 North Airport Dr.
Buffalo 14225-1490

NORTH CAROLINA

Guilford Technical Community College
Box 309
Jamestown 27282

Lenoir Community College
P.O. Box 188
Kinston 28502-0188

OREGON

Eagle Flight Center
Portland-Hillsboro Airport
Hillsboro 97124

Lane Community College
4000 East 30th Ave.
Eugene 97405

Mount Hood Community College
26000 Southeast Stark St.
Gresham 97030

PENNSYLVANIA

Community College of Allegheny
County
800 Allegheny Ave.
Pittsburgh 15233-1895

Community College of Beaver County
One Campus Dr.
Monaca 15061

Haski Aviation, Inc.
RD 2
P.O. Box 316
New Castle 16101

SOUTH CAROLINA

North American Institute of Aviation
Conway-Horry Co. Airport
P.O. Box 680
Conway 29528

TEXAS

Central Texas College
P.O. Box 1800
Killeen 76540-1800

Fletcher Aviation Group
9000 Randolph St.
Houston 77061

Mountain View College
4849 West Illinois
Dallas 75211

Qualiflight Training, Inc.
151 Meacham Airport
Bld 4n
Fort Worth 76106

San Jacinto College, Central Campus
8060 Spencer Hwy.
Pasadena 77505

Texas State Technical College, Waco
3801 Campus Dr.
Waco 76705

UTAH

Dixie College
225 South, 700 East
Saint George 84770

WASHINGTON

Crossings Aviation
1302 26th Ave. NW
Gig Harbor 98335

Galvin Flying Service, Inc.
7001 Perimeter Rd.
Seattle 98108

WISCONSIN

Gateway Technical College
3520 30th Ave.
Kenosha 53144-1690

Diesel Technology

ALABAMA

Douglas MacArthur State Technical
College
1708 North Main St.
Opp 36467

ALASKA

Alaska Vocational Technical Center
809 Second Ave.
Seward 99664

ARIZONA

Mesa Community College
1833 West Southern Ave.
Mesa 85202

Universal Technical Institute, Inc.
3121 West Weldon Ave.
Phoenix 85017

ARKANSAS

Black River Technical College
Hwy. 304
P.O. Box 468
Pocahontas 72455

Foothills Technical Institute
1800 East Moore St.
P.O. Box 909
Searcy 72143

Pulaski Technical College
3000 West Scenic Dr.
North Little Rock 72118

CALIFORNIA

College of the Redwoods
7351 Tompkins Hill Rd.
Eureka 95501-9302

Merced College
3600 M St.
Merced 95348-2898

Oxnard College
4000 South Rose Ave.
Oxnard 93033

Sequoia Institute
420 Whitney Place
Fremont 94539

COLORADO

Denver Automotive & Diesel College
460 South Lipan St.
Denver 80223-9366

CONNECTICUT

Baran Institute of Technology
611 Day Hill Rd.
Windsor 06095

FLORIDA

Saint Augustine Technical Center
2980 Collins Ave.
Saint Augustine 32095-1919

GEORGIA

Albany Technical Institute
1021 Lowe Rd.
Albany 31708

HAWAII

Hawaii Community College
200 West Kawili St.
Hilo 96720-4091

IDAHO

Boise State University
1910 University Dr.
Boise 83725

College of Southern Idaho
P.O. Box 1238
Twin Falls 83301

Idaho State University
741 South Seventh Ave.
Pocatello 83209

North Idaho College
1000 West Garden Ave.
Coeur D'Alene 83814

ILLINOIS

Illinois Valley Community College
815 North Orlando Smith Ave.
Oglesby 61348-9692

Lincoln Technical Institute
7320 West Agatite Ave.
Norridge 60656

Southeastern Illinois College
3575 College Rd.
Harrisburg 62946

Universal Technical Institute, Inc.
601 Regency Dr.
Glendale Heights 60139

Vatternot College
501 North Third St.
Quincy 62301

INDIANA

Oakland City College
143 North Lucretia St.
Oakland City 47660-1099

IOWA

Des Moines Community College
2006 Ankeny Blvd.
Ankeny 50021

Iowa Western Community College
2700 College Rd.
P.O. Box 4C
Council Bluffs 51502

KANSAS

KAW Area Technical School
5724 Huntoon
Topeka 66604

Northwest Kansas Area Vocational
Technical School
P.O. Box 668
Goodland 67735

Salina Area Vocational Technical
School
2562 Scanlan Ave.
Salina 67401

KENTUCKY

Kentucky Tech, Bowling Green
Regional Technical Center
1845 Loop Dr.
Bowling Green 42101-3601

Kentucky Technical, Madisonville
Regional Technical Center
150 School Ave.
Madisonville 42431

LOUISIANA

Louisiana Technical College, Gulf Area
Campus
1115 Clover St.
Abbeville 70510

Louisiana Technical College, Lamar
Salter Campus
15014 Lake Charles Hwy.
Leesville 71446

Louisiana Technical College, Sullivan
Campus
1710 Sullivan Dr.
Bogalusa 70427

Louisiana Technical College, Teche
Area Campus
609 Ember Rd.
New Iberia 70562-1057

Louisiana Technical College System,
Young Memorial
900 Youngs Rd.
Morgan City 70380

MARYLAND

Diesel Institute of America
Rte. 40
P.O. Box 69
Grantsville 21536

MASSACHUSETTS

Tad Technical Institute
45 Spruce St.
Chelsea 02150

MINNESOTA

Alexandria Technical College
1601 Jefferson St.
Alexandria 56308

Dakota County Technical College
1300 East 145th St.
Rosemount 55068

Lake Superior College
2101 Trinity Rd.
Duluth 55811

Minnesota West Community and
Technical College
1011 First St. W
Canby 56220

Northwest Technical College, East
Grand Forks
Hwy. 220 N
East Grand Forks 56721

Northwest Technical College, Moorhead
1900 28th Ave. S
Moorhead 56560

MISSOURI

Crowder College
601 Laclede
Neosho 64850

Ranken Technical College
4431 Finney Ave.
Saint Louis 63113

MONTANA

Montana State University, College of
Technology, Billings
3803 Central Ave.
Billings 59102

NEBRASKA

Central Community College Area
P.O. Box 4903
Grand Island 68802

Mid Plains Community College
416 North Jeffers
North Platte 69101

Northeast Community College
801 East Benjamin
P.O. Box 469
Norfolk 68702-0469

NEW JERSEY

Engine City Technical Institute
2365 Rte. 22 W
Union 07083

Lincoln Technical Institute
2299 Vauxhall Rd.
Union 07083

Pennco Tech
Erial Rd.
P.O. Box 1427
Blackwood 08012

NEW MEXICO

Albuquerque Technical Vocational
Institute
525 Buena Vista SE
Albuquerque 87106

Crownpoint Institute of Technology
P.O. Box 849
Crownpoint 87313

NEW YORK

SUNY College of Agriculture &
Technology at Cobleskill
Cobleskill 12043

SUNY College of Technology at Alfred
Alfred 14802

SUNY College of Technology at
Farmingdale
Melville Rd.
Farmingdale 11735-1021

NORTH CAROLINA

Coastal Carolina Community College
444 Western Blvd.
Jacksonville 28546-6877

NORTH DAKOTA

North Dakota State College of Science
800 North Sixth St.
Wahpeton 58076

University of North Dakota, Williston
1410 University Ave.
Williston 58801

OHIO

Northwestern College
1441 North Cable Rd.
Lima 45805

Owens Community College
30335 Oregon Rd.
Toledo 43699-1947

OKLAHOMA

Central Oklahoma Area Vocational
Technical School
Three Court Circle
Drumright 74030

Gordon Cooper Area Vocational
Technical School
1 John C Bruton Blvd.
Shawnee 74801

Kiamichi AVTS SD #7, Hugo
107 South 15th
P.O. Box 699
Hugo 74743

Oklahoma State University, Okmulgee
1801 East Fourth St.
Okmulgee 74447-3901

OREGON

Blue Mountain Community College
P.O. Box 100
Pendleton 97801

Portland Community College
P.O. Box 19000
Portland 97280-0990

PENNSYLVANIA

New Castle School of Trades
Youngstown Rd. 1
Pulaski 16143

Pennsylvania College of Technology
One College Ave.
Williamsport 17701

SOUTH CAROLINA

Greenville Technical College
Station B
P.O. Box 5616
Greenville 29606-5616

Trident Technical College
P.O. Box 118067
Charleston 29423-8067

York Technical College
452 South Anderson Rd.
Rock Hill 29730

SOUTH DAKOTA

Western Dakota Technical Institute
800 Mickelson Dr.
Rapid City 57701

TENNESSEE

Tennessee Technology Center at
Harriman
P.O. Box 1109
Harriman 37748

Tennessee Technology Center at
Memphis
550 Alabama Ave.
Memphis 38105-3604

Nashville Auto Diesel College, Inc.
1524 Gallatin Rd.
Nashville 37206

TEXAS

American Trades Institute
6627 Maple Ave.
Dallas 75235

Lee College
200 Lee Dr.
Baytown 77520-4703

Lincoln Technical Institute
2501 East Arkansas Ln.
Grand Prairie 75052

Texas State Technical College,
Harlingen
2424 Boxwood
Harlingen 78550-3697

Texas State Technical College,
Sweetwater
300 College Dr.
Sweetwater 79556

Universal Technical Institute, Inc.
721 Lockhaven Dr.
Houston 77073

UTAH

Salt Lake Community College
P.O. Box 30808
Salt Lake City 84130

Utah Valley State College
800 West, 1200 South
Orem 84058

VIRGINIA

Advanced Technology Insitute
5700 Southern Blvd.
Ste. 100
Virginia Beach 23462

Washington County Adult Skill Center
848 Thompson Dr.
Abingdon 24210

WASHINGTON

Bellingham Technical College
3028 Lindbergh Ave.
Bellingham 98225

Clark College
1800 East McLoughlin Blvd.
Vancouver 98663-3598

Lake Washington Technical College
11605 132nd Ave. NE
Kirkland 98034

Seattle Community College, South
Campus
6000 16th Ave. SW
Seattle 98106

Spokane Community College
North 1810 Greene Ave.
Spokane 99207

WISCONSIN

Chippewa Valley Technical College
620 West Clairemont Ave.
Eau Claire 54701

Fox Valley Technical College
1825 North Bluemound Dr.
Appleton 54913-2277

Madison Area Technical College
3550 Anderson St.
Madison 53704

Milwaukee Area Technical College
700 West State St.
Milwaukee 53233-1443

Northeast Wisconsin Technical College
2740 West Mason St.
P.O. Box 19042
Green Bay 54307-9042

Western Wisconsin Technical College
304 North Sixth St.
P.O. Box 908
La Crosse 54602-0908

WYOMING

Casper College
125 College Dr.
Casper 82601

Laramie County Community College
1400 East College Dr.
Cheyenne 82007

Sheridan College
3059 Coffeen Ave.
Sheridan 82801

Maritime Occupations

CALIFORNIA

Stone Boat Yard
2517 Blanding Ave.
Alameda 94501

FLORIDA

Florida Community College at
Jacksonville
501 West State St.
Jacksonville 32202

Manatee Vocational Technical Center
5603 34th St. W
Bradenton 34210

Sarasota County Technical Institute
4748 Beneva Rd.
Sarasota 34233-1798

Seminole Community College
100 Weldon Blvd.
Sanford 32773-6199

LOUISIANA

Louisiana Technical College, South
Louisiana Campus
201 St. Charles St.
P.O. Box 5033
Houma 70361-5033

Louisiana Tech College System, Young
Memorial
P.O. Box 2148
Morgan City 70381

MAINE

Southern Maine Technical College
Fort Rd.
South Portland 04106

MICHIGAN

Northwestern Michigan College
1701 East Front St.
Traverse City 49686

MINNESOTA

Northwest Technical College, Detroit
Lakes
900 Hwy. 34 E
Detroit Lakes 56501

OKLAHOMA

Metro Area Vocational Technical School
District 22
1900 Springlake Dr.
Oklahoma City 73111

OREGON

West Coast Training, Inc.
P.O. Box 22469
2525 Southeast Stubb St.
Milwaukie 97222

RHODE ISLAND

New England Institute of Technology
2500 Post Rd.
Warwick 02886

VIRGINIA

Marine Safety Consultants, Tidewater
School of Navigation
100 West Plume St.
Ste. 450
Norfolk 23510

Transportation and Public Utilities Technology

ALABAMA

Shoals Community College
800 George Wallace Blvd.
Muscle Shoals 35662

ALASKA

Mila Administrative Services
3330 Artic Blvd.
Ste. 201
Anchorage 99503

ARIZONA

Arizona Institute of Business and
Technology
925 South Gilbert Rd.
Ste. 201
Mesa 85204

Chaparral Career College
4585 East Speedway Blvd.
Ste. 204
Tucson 85712

Eastern Arizona College
Church St.
Thatcher 85552-0769

Lamson Junior College
1126 North Scottsdale Rd.
Ste. 17
Tempe 85281-1700

Pima Community College
2202 West Anklam Rd.
Tucson 85709-0001

CALIFORNIA

Career Development Center
255 East Bonita Ave.
Pomona 91767

Citrus College
1000 West Foothill Blvd.
Glendora 91741-1899

City College of San Francisco
50 Phelan Ave.
San Francisco 94112

College of Marin
835 College Ave.
Kentfield 94904

Computer Education Institute
24551 Raymond Way
Ste. 155
Lake Forest 92630

East Los Angeles Skill Center
3921 Selig Place
Los Angeles 90031

Fil-Am Employment and Training
Center
2940 16th St.
Ste. 319
San Francisco 94103

Merritt College
12500 Campus Dr.
Oakland 94619

Mount Diablo Vocational Services
490 Golf Club Rd.
Pleasant Hill 94523

Mount San Antonio College
1100 North Grand
Walnut 91789

Rancho Santiago Community College
District
1530 West 17th Street
Santa Ana 92706

San Joaquin Valley College
201 New Stine Rd.
Bakersfield 93309

Santa Barbara Business College
211 South Real Rd.
Bakersfield 93309

Santa Barbara Business College
4333 Hansen Ave.
Fremont 94536

Southwestern College
900 Otay Lakes Rd.
Chula Vista 91910

Vallecitos CET, Inc.
597 C St.
Hayward 94541

Watterson College
150 South Los Robles Blvd.
Ste. 100
Pasadena 91101

COLORADO

Mesa State College
P.O. Box 2647
Grand Junction 81502

Parks College
9065 Grant St.
Denver 80229

T H Pickens Technical Center
500 Airport Blvd.
Aurora 80011

CONNECTICUT

Huntington Institute, Inc.
193 Broadway
Norwich 06360

Stone Academy
1315 Dixwell Ave.
Hamden 06514

Tunxis Community-Technical College
Rtes. 6 and 177
Farmington 06032

DELAWARE

Goldey-Beacom College
4701 Limestone Rd.
Wilmington 19808

FLORIDA

Business Training Institute of Lakeland,
Inc.
4222 South Florida Ave.
Lakeland 33813

Lee County High Technical Center,
Central
3800 Michigan Ave.
Fort Myers 33916

National School of Technology, Inc.
16150 Northeast 17th Ave.
North Miami Beach 33162

Orlando College
5421 Diplomat Cir.
Orlando 32810

Politechnical Institute of Florida
500 West 29th St.
Hialeah 33012

Sheridan Vocational Center
5400 Sheridan St.
Hollywood 33021

Suwannee-Hamilton Area Vocational
and Adult Center
415 Southwest Pinewood Dr.
Live Oak 32060

GEORGIA

Meadows Junior College
1170 Brown Ave.
Columbus 31906

National Business Institute
243 West Ponce De Leon Ave.
Decatur 30030

HAWAII

Brigham Young University, Hawaii
Campus
55-220 Kulanui St.
Laie 96762

Employment Training Center, UH
Community Colleges
879 North King St.
Honolulu 96813

Hawaii Business College
33 South King St.
Fourth Fl.
Ste. 405
Honolulu 96817

Heald College School of Business and
Technology
1500 Kapiolani Blvd.
Honolulu 96816

Honolulu Community College
874 Dillingham Blvd.
Honolulu 96817

Maui Community College
310 Kaahumanu Ave.
Kahului 96732

ILLINOIS

College of Du Page
425 22nd St.
Glen Ellyn 60137-6599

The College of Office Technology
1520 West Division St.
Chicago 60622

Oakton Community College
1600 East Golf Rd.
Des Plaines 60016

Sanford-Brown College
3237 West Chain of Rocks Rd.
Granite 62040

William Rainey Harper College
1200 West Algonquin Rd.
Palatine 60067-7398

INDIANA

Indiana Business College
802 North Meridian St.
Indianapolis 46204

Indiana Business College
1809 North Walnut
Muncie 47303

Indiana University, Purdue University,
Fort Wayne
2101 Coliseum Blvd. E
Fort Wayne 46805

IOWA

Hamilton College
2300 Euclid
Des Moines 50310

Hamilton College, Mason City Branch
100 First St. NW
Mason City 50401

KANSAS

The Brown Mackie College
100 East Santa Fe
Ste. 300
Olathe 66061

Topeka Technical College
1620 Northwest Gage
Topeka 66618

KENTUCKY

Kentucky Technical, Daviess County
Vocational Technical School
1901 Southeastern Pkwy.
Owensboro 42303

Midway College
512 Stephens St.
Midway 40347-1120

Owensboro Junior College of Business
1515 East 18th St.
P.O. Box 1350
Owensboro 42302

LOUISIANA

Coastal College, Hammond
4304 Yokum Rd.
Hammond 70403

Nicholls State University
University Station
La Hwy. 1
Thibodaux 70310

Remington College
303 Rue Louis XIV
Lafayette 70508

MAINE

Beal College
629 Main St.
Bangor 04401

MASSACHUSETTS

Fisher College
118 Beacon St.
Boston 02116

Mount Wachusett Community College
444 Green St.
Gardner 01440

Newbury College, Inc.
129 Fisher Ave.
Brookline 02146

Northern Essex Community College
Elliott Way
Haverhill 01830-2399

Quinsigamond Community College
670 West Boylston St.
Worcester 01606

MICHIGAN

Baker College of Flint
G1050 West Bristol Rd.
Flint 48507

Davenport College, Lansing
220 East Kalamazoo
Lansing 48933

Delta College
University Center 48710

Dorsey Business Schools
30821 Barrington
Madison Heights 48071

Dorsey Business Schools
15755 Northline Rd.
Southgate 48195

Ferris State University
901 South State St.
Big Rapids 49307

Macomb Community College
14500 Twelve Mile Rd.
Warren 48093-3896

Muskegon Community College
221 South Quarterline Rd.
Muskegon 49442

Payne-Pulliam School of Trade and
   Commerce, Inc.
2345 Cass Ave.
Detroit 48201-3305

Suomi College
601 Quincy St.
Hancock 49930

MINNESOTA

Alexandria Technical College
1601 Jefferson St.
Alexandria 56308

Anoka-Ramsey Community College
11200 Mississippi Blvd.
Coon Rapids 55433-3470

Hennepin Technical College
900 Brooklyn Blvd.
Brooklyn Park 55445

Minnesota West Community and
   Technical College
1593 11th Ave.
Granite Falls 56241

Normandale Community College
9700 France Ave. S
Bloomington 55431

Opportunities Industrialization Center,
   East Metro
334 Chester St.
Saint Paul 55107

Rasmussen College, Mankato
501 Holly Ln.
Mankato 56001

Rasmussen College, Saint Cloud
245 North 37th Ave.
Saint Cloud 56303

MISSISSIPPI

Coahoma Community College
3240 Friars Point Rd.
Clarksdale 38614

MISSOURI

Saint Louis Community College, Forest
   Park
5600 Oakland Ave.
Saint Louis 63110

Sikeston Area Vocational Technical
   School
1002 Virginia St.
Sikeston 63801

Tri County Technical School
Second and Pine
Eldon 65026

MONTANA

University of Great Falls
1301 Twentieth St. S
Great Falls 59405-4996

NEBRASKA

Lincoln School of Commerce
1821 K St.
Lincoln 68501-2826

NEW HAMPSHIRE

Hesser College
Three Sundial Ave.
Manchester 03103

NEW JERSEY

Business Training Institute
Four Forest Ave.
Paramus 07652

Empire Technical School of New Jersey
576 Central Ave.
East Orange 07018

Ho-Ho-Kus School
50 South Franklin Tpk.
Ramsey 07446

Thomas A Edison State College
101 West State St.
Trenton 08608-1176

NEW MEXICO

International Business College
650 East Montana
Las Cruces 88001

NEW YORK

Bryant and Stratton Business Institute,
   Buffalo
1028 Main St.
Buffalo 14202

Bryant and Stratton Business Institute,
   Main Syracuse
953 James St.
Syracuse 13203-2502

Bryant and Stratton Business Institute,
   Rochester
82 Saint Paul St.
Rochester 14604

CUNY Bronx Community College
West 181st St. & University Ave.
Bronx 10453

CUNY College of Staten Island
2800 Victory Blvd.
Staten Island 10314

CUNY Hostos Community College
500 Grand Concourse
Bronx 10451

CUNY Kingsborough Community
   College
2001 Oriental Blvd.
Brooklyn 11235

CUNY La Guardia Community College
31-10 Thomson Ave.
Long Island City 11101

CUNY New York City Technical College
300 Jay St.
Brooklyn 11201

Elmira Business Institute
180 Clemens Center Pkwy.
Elmira 14901

Global Business Institute
1931 Mott Ave.
Far Rockaway 11691

Global Business Institute
209 West 125th St.
New York 10027

Hunter Business School
3601 Hempstead Tpke.
Levittown 11756

Mater Dei College
5428 St. Hwy. 37
Ogdensburg 13669

Paul Smith's College of Arts and Science
New York 12970

Professional Business Institute
125 Canal St.
New York 10002-5049

Saint John's University, New York
8000 Utopia Pkwy.
Jamaica 11439

Taylor Business Institute
120 West 30th St.
New York 10001

NORTH CAROLINA

Brookstone College
7815 National Service Rd.
Greensboro 27409

NORTH DAKOTA

Interstate Business College
2720 32nd Ave. SW
Fargo 58103

Minot State University
500 University Ave. W
Minot 58707

Valley City State University
101 Southwest College St.
Valley City 58072

OHIO

Ashtabula County Joint Vocational
   School
1565 State Rte. 167
Jefferson 44047

Boheckers Business College
326 East Main St.
Ravenna 44266

Bradford School
6170 Busch Blvd.
Columbus 43229

Coshocton County Joint Vocational
   School District
23640 County Rd. 202
Coshocton 43812

Davis College
4747 Monroe St.
Toledo 43623

ITT Technical Institute
1030 North Meridian Rd.
Youngstown 44501

Knox County Career Center
306 Martinsburg Rd.
Mount Vernon 43050

Lakeland Community College
7700 Clocktower Dr.
Kirtland 44094-5198

Lorain County Community College
1005 Abbe Rd. N
Elyria 44035

Ohio University, Eastern Campus
National Rd. W
Saint Clairsville 43950

Ohio University, Main Campus
Athens 45701

Ohio University, Southern Branch
1804 Liberty Ave.
Ironton 45638

Professional Skills Institute
20 Arco Dr.
Toledo 43607

Sinclair Community College
444 West Third St.
Dayton 45402

Stautzenberger College
1637 Tiffin
Findlay 45840

Stautzenberger College
5355 Southwyck Blvd.
Toledo 43614

Technology Education College
288 South Hamilton Rd.
Columbus 43213

University of Akron, Main Campus
302 Buchtel Common
Akron 44325-4702

University of Akron, Wayne College
1901 Smucker Rd.
Orrville 44667

Urbana University
College Way
Urbana 43078

U S Grant Joint Vocational School
3046 Rte. 125
Bethel 45106

Vocational Guidance Services
2239 East 55th St.
Cleveland 44103

Warren County Career Center
3525 North SR 48
Lebanon 45036-1099

Washington State Community College
710 Colegate Dr.
Marietta 45750

OKLAHOMA

Kiamichi AVTS SD #7, Hugo
107 South 15th
Hugo 74743

Platt College
3801 South Sheridan
Tulsa 74145

OREGON

Columbia College
8800 Southeast Sunnyside Rd.
Clackamas 97015

PENNSYLVANIA

Antonelli Medical and Professional
   Institute
1700 Industrial Hwy.
Pottstown 19464

Baptist Bible College and Seminary
538 Venard Rd.
Clarks Summit 18411

Churchman Business School
355 Spring Garden St.
Easton 18042

Computer Learning Network, Resident
   School
1110 Fernwood Ave.
Camp Hill 17011

Consolidated School of Business
2124 Ambassador Cir.
Lancaster 17603

Erie Business Center
246 West Ninth St.
Erie 16501

Laurel Business Institute
11-15 Penn St.
Uniontown 15401

Martin School of Business
2417 Welsh Rd.
Philadelphia 19114

Orleans Technical Institute
1330 Rhawn St.
Philadelphia 19111-2899

Philadelphia Elwyn Institute
4040 Market St.
Philadelphia 19104-3003

Sawyer School
717 Liberty Ave.
Pittsburgh 15222

Westmoreland County Community
College
Youngwood 15697-1895

SOUTH DAKOTA

National American University
321 Kansas City St.
Rapid City 57701

Nettleton Career College
100 South Spring Ave.
Sioux Falls 57104

TENNESSEE

Fugazzi College
5042 Linbar Dr.
Ste. 200
Nashville 37211

Tennessee Technology Center at Athens
1635 Vo Tech Dr.
P.O. Box 848
Athens 37371-0848

Tennessee Technology Center at
Crossville
P.O. Box 2959
Crossville 38557

Tennessee Technology Center at
Knoxville
1100 Liberty St.
Knoxville 37919

Tennessee Technology Center at
Murfreesboro
1303 Old Fort Pkwy.
Murfreesboro 37129

Tennessee Technology Center at
Nashville
100 White Bridge Rd.
Nashville 37209

Tennessee Technology Center at
Newbern
340 Washington St.
Newbern 38059

Tennessee Technology Center at
Shelbyville
1405 Madison St.
Shelbyville 37160

Tennessee Technology Center at
Whiteville
P.O. Box 489
Whiteville 38075

TEXAS

Amari Institute, Inc.
4111 Directors Row
Ste. 110
Houston 77092

Bradford School of Business
4669 Southwest Fwy.
Ste. 300
Houston 77027

Central Texas Commercial College
P.O. Box 1324
Brownwood 76801

Hallmark Institute of Technology
8901 Wetmore Rd.
San Antonio 78216

South Texas Vocational Technical
Institute, McAllen Branch
2901 North 23rd St.
McAllen 78501

Southern Careers Institute, South Texas
1414 North Jackson Rd.
Pharr 78577

UTAH

Bridgerland Applied Technology Center
1301 North, 600 West
Logan 84321

Snow College
150 East College Ave.
Ephraim 84627

Weber State University
3750 Harrison Blvd.
Ogden 84408

VERMONT

Champlain College
163 South Willard St.
Burlington 05401

VIRGINIA

ECPI College of Technology
5555 Greenwich Rd.
Ste. 300
Virginia Beach 23462

ECPI Technical College
800 Moorefield Park Dr.
Richmond 23230

ECPI Technical College
5234 Airport Rd.
Roanoke 24012

J Sargeant Reynolds Community
College
P.O. Box 85622
Richmond 23285-5622

New River Community College
Drawer 1127
Dublin 24084-1127

Thomas Nelson Community College
P.O. Box 9407
Hampton 23670

WASHINGTON

Lake Washington Technical College
11605 132nd Ave. NE
Kirkland 98034

Spokane Falls Community College
West 3410 Fort George Wright Dr.
Spokane 99224

WEST VIRGINIA

Huntington Junior College
900 Fifth Ave.
Huntington 25701

Mercer County Technical Educational
Center
1397 Stafford Dr.
Princeton 24740

WISCONSIN

Lakeshore Technical College
1290 North Ave.
Cleveland 53015

MBTI Business Training Institute
606 West Wisconsin Ave.
Milwaukee 53203

Northeast Wisconsin Technical College
2740 West Mason St.
P.O. Box 19042
Green Bay 54307-9042

WYOMING

Central Wyoming College
2660 Peck Ave.
Riverton 82501

Truck Driver Training

ALABAMA

Bevill State Community College
100 State St.
Sumiton 35148

Reid State Technical College
I65 and Hwy. 83
Evergreen 36401

ARIZONA

American Institute of Technology
440 South 54th Ave.
Phoenix 85043

Western Truck School
3201 East Broadway
Phoenix 85006

ARKANSAS

Cossatot Technical College
183 Hwy. 399
De Queen 71832

Cotton Boll Technical Institute
I55 And Hwy. 148
Burdette 72321

Crowley's Ridge Technical School
I40 Crowley's Ridge Rd.
Forrest City 72336-0925

Northwest Technical Institute
709 South Old Missouri Rd.
Springdale 72764

Ozarka Technical College
218 South Dr.
P.O. Box 10
Melbourne 72556-0010

Pulaski Technical College
3000 West Scenic Dr.
North Little Rock 72118

Quapaw Technical Institute
200 Mid America Blvd.
Hot Springs 71913

Southeast Arkansas Technical College
1900 Hazel
Pine Bluff 71603

University of Arkansas Community
College, Batesville
P.O. Box 3350
Batesville 72503

CALIFORNIA

California Career School
1100 Technology Cir.
Anaheim 92805

College of the Redwoods
7351 Tompkins Hill Rd.
Eureka 95501-9302

Falcon Truck School
2402 Sacramento St.
Vallejo 94590

Imperial Truck Driving School
6101 Wilmington Ave.
Los Angeles 90001

Marin Regional Occupational Program
P.O. Box 4925
San Rafael 94913

Precision Truck School, Inc.
7700 Edgewater Dr.
Ste. 836
Oakland 94621

Transportation Guidance and
Assistance Truck Driving
2332 South Peck Rd.
Ste. 191
Whittier 90601

Truck Driving Academy
2757 South Golden State Blvd.
Fresno 93725

Truck Driving Academy
5711 Florin Perkins
Ste. A
Sacramento 95828

Western Truck School
5800 State Rd.
Bakersfield 93308

Western Truck School
6996 Mission Gorge Rd.
San Diego 92120

Western Truck School
3101 Whipple Rd.
Ste. 24
Union City 94587

Western Truck School
4519 West Capitol Ave.
West Sacramento 95691

COLORADO

Community College of Denver
P.O. Box 173363
Denver 80217

MTA School
5300 Colorado Blvd.
Commerce City 80022

United States Truck Driving School, Inc.
8150 West 48th Ave.
Wheat Ridge 80033

CONNECTICUT

Allstate Commercial Drivers Training
School
11 Constitution Blvd. S.
Shelton 06484

New England Tractor Trailer Training of
Connecticut
32 Field Rd.
Somers 06071

DELAWARE

Delaware Technical and Community
College, Owens
P.O. Box 610
Georgetown 19947

FLORIDA

Diesel Institute of America
4710 East Broadway Ave.
Tampa 33605

Miami Lakes Technical Education
Center
5780 Northwest 158th St.
Miami Lakes 33169

MTA Schools
6000 Cinderlane Pkwy.
Orlando 32810

Pinellas Technical Education Center
901 34th St. S
Saint Petersburg 33711

Washington-Holmes Technical Center
757 Hoyt St.
Chipley 32428

William T McFatter Vocational
Technical Center
6500 Nova Dr.
Davie 33317

GEORGIA

Alliance Tractor Trailer Training Center
333 Industrial Blvd.
McDonough 30253

Carroll Technical Institute
997 South Hwy. 16
Carrollton 30117

National Business Institute
243 West Ponce De Leon Ave.
Decatur 30030

Savannah Technical Institute
5717 White Bluff Rd.
Savannah 31405-5594

South Georgia Technical Institute
1583 Souther Field Rd.
Americus 31709

Valdosta Technical Institute
4089 Valtech Rd.
Valdosta 31602-9796

Walker Technical Institute
265 Bicentennial Trail
Rock Spring 30739

INDIANA

C-1 Professional Training Center
6555 East 30th St.
Indianapolis 46219

Vincennes University
1002 North First St.
Vincennes 47591

IOWA

Eastern Iowa Community College
District
306 West River Dr.
Davenport 52801-1221

Kirkwood Community College
P.O. Box 2068
Cedar Rapids 52406

Northwest Iowa Community College
603 West Park St.
Sheldon 51201

Southwestern Community College
1501 Townline
Creston 50801

Western Iowa Tech Community College
4647 Stone Ave.
P.O. Box 5199
Sioux City 51102-5199

KANSAS

Fort Scott Community College
2108 South Horton
Fort Scott 66701

Wichita Area Technical College
201 North Water
Wichita 67202-1292

LOUISIANA

Coastal College, Hammond
4304 Yokum Rd.
Hammond 70403

Delta-Ouachita Regional Technical
Institute
609 Vocational Pkwy.
West Monroe 71291

Diesel Driving Academy
8136 Airline Hwy.
Baton Rouge 70815

Diesel Driving Academy
P.O. Box 36949
Shreveport 71133

MARYLAND

All-State Career School
201 South Arlington Ave.
Baltimore 21223

Diesel Institute of America
Rte. 40
P.O. Box 69
Grantsville 21536

MASSACHUSETTS

New England Tractor Trailer Training
School
1093 North Montello St.
Brockton 24011-0642

MICHIGAN

American Truck Driving of Michigan
150 South Michigan Ave.
Coldwater 49036

Professional Drivers Institute
18266 West US 12 W
P.O. Box 276
New Buffalo 49117

MINNESOTA

Alexandria Technical College
1601 Jefferson St.
Alexandria 56308

Century Community and Technical
College
3300 Century Ave. N
White Bear Lake 55110

Dakota County Technical College
1300 East 145th St.
Rosemount 55068

Minnesota West Community and
Technical College
P.O. Box 250
Pipestone 56164

Northwest Technical College, East
Grand Forks
Hwy. 220 N
East Grand Forks 56721

Pine Technical College
1000 Fourth St.
Pine City 55063

Red Wing-Winona Technical College,
Winona
1250 Homer Rd.
P.O. Box 409
Winona 55987

Riverland Community College
1900 Eighth Ave. NW
Austin 55912

MISSISSIPPI

Copiah-Lincoln Junior College
P.O. Box 457
Wesson 39191

East Mississippi Community College
P.O. Box 158
Scooba 39358

Itawamba Community College
602 West Hill St.
Fulton 38843

Mississippi Gulf Coast Community
College
Central Office
P.O. Box 67
Perkinston 39573

MISSOURI

Columbia Area Vocational Technical
School
4203 South Providence Rd.
Columbia 65203

Crowder College
601 Laclede
Neosho 64850

NEBRASKA

Central Community College Area
P.O. Box 4903
Grand Island 68802

Custom Diesel Drivers Training, Inc.
9915 South 148th St.
Omaha 68138

Southeast Community College Area
1111 O St.
Ste 111
Lincoln 68520

NEVADA

A-1 Truck Driving Training
1105 Industrial Rd.
Boulder City 89005

All Rite Trade School
93 West Lake Mead Dr.
Henderson 89015

Nevada Training Corporation
2215C Renaissance Dr.
Las Vegas 89119

NEW HAMPSHIRE

Northeast Career Schools
749 East Industrial Park Dr.
Manchester 03109

NEW JERSEY

Jersey Tractor Trailer Training
178 Manor Rd.
East Rutheford 07073

NEW MEXICO

Albuquerque Technical Vocational
Institute
525 Buena Vista SE
Albuquerque 87106

NEW YORK

All Star Driving School
17 Cortland Dr.
Loudonville 12211

Chauffeurs Training School
12 Railroad Ave.
Albany 12205

Commercial Driver Training
600 Patton Ave.
West Babylon 11704

National Tractor Trailer School
175 Katherine St.
Buffalo 14210

National Tractor Trailer School, Inc.
4650 Buckley Rd.
P.O. Box 208
Liverpool 13088-0208

NORTH CAROLINA

Alliance Tractor Trailer Center
Hwy. 25 S
Arden 28704

Alliance Tractor Trailer Training
Centers
P.O. Box 579
Benson 27504

Charlotte Truck Driver Training School
500 North Hoskins Rd.
Charlotte 28216

Johnston Community College
P.O. Box 2350
Smithfield 27577-2350

NORTH DAKOTA

Dickinson State University
Third St. and Eighth Ave. W
Dickinson 58601

OHIO

Columbus Paraprofessional Institute
1900 East Grandville Rd.
Bldg. A
Ste. 210
Columbus 43229

Hamric Truck Driving School
1156 Medina Rd.
Medina 44256

OKLAHOMA

Central Oklahoma Area Vocational
Technical School
Three Court Circle
Drumright 74030

OREGON

International Institute of
Transportation Resources
15828 Southeast 114th St.
Clackamas 97015

PENNSYLVANIA

All-State Career School
501 Seminole St.
Lester 19029

MTA Schools
1180 Zeager Rd.
Elizabethtown 17022

RHODE ISLAND

Nationwide Tractor Trailer Driving
School
Washington Hwy.
P.O. Box 174
Lincoln 02865

New England Tractor Trailer Training
School
10 Dunnell Ln.
Pawtucket 02860

SOUTH CAROLINA

Greenville Technical College
Station B
P.O. Box 5616
Greenville 29606-5616

Nielsen Electronics Institute
1600 Meeting St.
Charleston 29405

TENNESSEE

Chattanooga State Technical
Community College
4501 Amnicola Hwy.
Chattanooga 37406

Tennessee Technology Center at Crump
Hwy. 64 W
P.O. Box 89
Crump 38327

Tennessee Technology Center at
Knoxville
1100 Liberty St.
Knoxville 37919

Tennessee Technology Center at
Memphis
550 Alabama Ave.
Memphis 38105-3604

Tennessee Technology Center at
Morristown
821 West Louise Ave.
Morristown 37813

Tennessee Technology Center at
Nashville
100 White Bridge Rd.
Nashville 37209

TEXAS

Action Career Training
273 Cr 287
Merkel 79536

Lee College
200 Lee Dr.
Baytown 77520-4703

Tri State Semi Driver Training, Inc.
3001 North I-45
Palmer 75152

UTAH

Bridgerland Applied Technology Center
1301 North, 600 West
Logan 84321

Utah Valley State College
800 West, 1200 South
Orem 84058

VIRGINIA

Advanced Technology Institute
5700 Southern Blvd.
Ste. 100
Virginia Beach 23462

Alliance Tractor Trailer Training Center
100 Nye Rd.
Martinsville 24112

WASHINGTON

Bates Technical College
1101 South Yakima Ave.
Tacoma 98405

Directory—Institutions Offering Career Training   **171**

Seattle Community College, South
Campus
6000 16th Ave. SW
Seattle 98106

Skagit Valley College
2405 College Way
Mount Vernon 98273

Chippewa Valley Technical College
620 West Clairemont Ave.
Eau Claire 54701

Diesel Truck Drivers Training School
Hwy. 151 and Elder Ln.
Sun Prairie 53590

Fox Valley Technical College at
Appleton
1825 North Bluemound Dr.
Appleton 54913-2277

Index

All jobs mentioned in this volume are listed and cross-referenced in the index. Entries that appear in all capital letters have occupational profiles. For example, AIR TRAFFIC CONTROLLER, AIRLINE PILOT, and BICYCLE MECHANIC so on are profiles in this volume. Entries that are not capitalized refer to jobs that do not have a separate profile but for which information is given.

Under some capitalized entries there is a section titled "Profile includes." This lists jobs that are mentioned in the profile. For example, in the case of DOCKWORKER, jobs that are described in the profile are Checker, Gear repairer, and Winch operator.

Some entries are followed by a job title in parentheses after the page number on which it can be found. This job title is the occupational profile in which the entry is discussed. For instance, the Blacksmith entry is followed by the profile title (Railroad maintenance worker).

Affirmative action, 18

Agricultural pilot, 116 (Airline pilot)

AIR TRAFFIC CONTROLLER, 113–115 (Profile)

Air transport industry: snapshot, 4; summer jobs in, 6; trade/professional journals, 26

AIRCRAFT DISPATCHER, 84–85 (Profile)

AIRCRAFT MECHANIC, 86–87 (Profile includes: Line maintenance crew)

Airframe mechanic. See AIRCRAFT MECHANIC

AIRLINE BAGGAGE/FREIGHT HANDLER, 27–28 (Profile)

AIRLINE FLIGHT ATTENDANT, 88–89 (Profile)

Airline industry, 7

AIRLINE PILOT, 115–118 (Profile includes: Agricultural pilot, Business pilot, Captain, Check pilot, Copilot, Helicopter pilot, Test pilot)

AIRLINE RESERVATIONS AGENT, 28–29 (Profile)

AIRLINE TICKET AGENT, 30–31 (Profile)

AIRPORT MANAGER, 118–120 (Profile)

AIRPORT UTILITY WORKER, 31–32 (Profile)

American Counseling Association, 12

Amtrak, 9

Application form, 23–25

Auto body painter, 33 (Auto body repairer)

AUTO BODY REPAIRER, 32–34 (Profile includes: Auto body painter)

AUTOMOBILE DRIVING INSTRUCTOR, 90–91 (Profile)

Automobile industry: history in U.S., 2–3; overview of, 3–5; parts/dealerships, 5

AUTOMOTIVE EXHAUST EMISSIONS TECHNICIAN, 92–93 (Profile)

AUTOMOTIVE MECHANIC, 93–95 (Profile)

Automotive trade/professional journals, 26

Aviation inspector, 109 (Transportation inspector)

Aviation/air transport trade/professional journals, 26

AVIONICS TECHNICIAN, 95–96 (Profile)

Baker, 101 (Merchant marine steward/cook)

BICYCLE MECHANIC, 34–35 (Profile)

Big Three, 3–4

Blacksmith, 62 (Railroad maintenance worker)

Blind ad, 15

Boilermaker, 62 (Railroad maintenance worker)

BRIDGE/LOCK TENDER, 35–36 (Profile)

Bus dispatcher. See TRUCK/BUS DISPATCHER

Bus driver, 45 (Local transit operator). See also INTERCITY BUS DRIVER; SCHOOL BUS DRIVER; SPECIAL SERVICE BUS DRIVER

Bus transport trade/professional journals, 26

Business pilot, 116 (Airline pilot)

Captain, 115 (Airline pilot); 127 (Merchant marine captain)

CAR RENTAL/LEASING AGENT, 96–98 (Profile includes: Customer service representative, Station manager)

Car repairer, 62 (Railroad maintenance worker)

CAR WASH WORKER, 37–38 (Profile includes: Cashier, Manager)

Career counseling, 12

Career planning, 11–12

CareerBuilder, 14

Cashier, 37 (Car wash worker). See also GAS STATION CASHIER; PARKING CASHIER

Check pilot, 116 (Airline pilot)

Checker, 38–39 (Dockworker)

Chief cook, 101 (Merchant marine steward/cook)

Chief engineer, 129 (Merchant marine engineer)

Chief steward, 101 (Merchant marine steward/cook)

Chronological resume, 21

Civil service, 17

Classified advertising, 15–16

Contracts, 19

Cook. See MERCHANT MARINE STEWARD/COOK

Copilot, 115 (Airline pilot)

Cover letter, 21–23

Crop duster. See AIRLINE PILOT

Customer service representative, 96 (Car rental/leasing agent)

Dealerships, auto industry, 5

Deckhand. See SAILOR

DIESEL MECHANIC, 98–100 (Profile includes: Diesel truck mechanic, Heavy equipment diesel mechanic)

Diesel truck mechanic, 99 (Diesel mechanic)

Discrimination, job, 18–19

Dispatcher, 60 (Railroad clerk). *See also* AIRCRAFT DISPATCHER; TAXI DISPATCHER; TOW TRUCK DISPATCHER; TRUCK/BUS DISPATCHER

DOCKWORKER, 38–40 (Profile includes: Checker, Gear repairer, Winch operator)

Educational background, 21

Electrical worker, 62 (Railroad maintenance worker)

Employee rights, 18–19, 25

Employment, temporary, 17

Employment services, 16–17

Engineer. *See* FLIGHT ENGINEER; MERCHANT MARINE ENGINEER; RAILROAD ENGINEER; TRAFFIC ENGINEER; TRANSPORTATION ENGINEER

Fair Labor Standards Act, 19

Firer, 129 (Merchant marine engineer)

Firing, 19

First assistant engineer, 129 (Merchant marine engineer)

First mate, 127 (Merchant marine captain)

First officer. *See* AIRLINE PILOT

FLEET MANAGER, 120–121 (Profile)

Flight attendant. *See* AIRLINE FLIGHT ATTENDANT

FLIGHT ENGINEER, 121–123 (Profile)

FLIGHT INSTRUCTOR, 123–125 (Profile)

Flight superintendent. *See* AIRCRAFT DISPATCHER

Ford, Henry, 2

Forklift operator. *See* INDUSTRIAL TRUCK OPERATOR

Freight handler. *See* AIRLINE BAGGAGE/FREIGHT HANDLER

Fulton, Robert, 2

Future: of rail freight industry, 9; of transportation employment, 7; of trucking industry, 6–7

GAS STATION CASHIER, 40–41 (Profile)

Gear repairer, 39 (Dockworker)

Heavy equipment diesel mechanic, 99 (Diesel mechanic)

Helicopter pilot, 116 (Airline pilot)

Help-wanted ads, 15

History, transportation industry, 1–3

INDUSTRIAL TRAFFIC MANAGER, 125–126 (Profile)

INDUSTRIAL TRUCK OPERATOR, 41–43 (Profile)

INTERCITY BUS DRIVER, 43–44 (Profile)

Intermodal freight, 9

Internet, 14–15, 16

Interviews, job, 23, 25–26

Job databases, online, 14–15

Job discrimination, 18–19

Job finder's checklist, 13

Job-hunting techniques, 13–17

Jobs: projected in transportation, 7; summer jobs in transportation, 6; top-paying in transportation, 8

Jobs, getting: career planning, 11–12; evaluation of jobs, 12; interview, 25–26; job opportunities, finding, 12–17; marketing yourself, 17–25; trade/professional journals, 26

Letter campaigns, 13–14

Line maintenance crew, 86 (Aircraft mechanic)

LOCAL TRANSIT OPERATOR, 45–46 (Profile includes: Bus driver, Subway conductor, Subway driver, Trolley driver)

LOCAL TRUCK DRIVER, 47–48 (Profile)

Locomotive engineer. *See* RAILROAD ENGINEER

LONG-HAUL TRUCK DRIVER, 48–50 (Profile includes: Moving van driver)

Longshoreman. *See* DOCKWORKER

Machinist, 62 (Railroad maintenance worker)

Manager, 37 (Car wash worker). *See also* AIRPORT MANAGER; FLEET MANAGER; INDUSTRIAL TRAFFIC MANAGER; Station manager; TRUCK TERMINAL MANAGER

MARINE TECHNICIAN, 51–52 (Profile)

Marine transportation trade/professional journals, 26

Marketing, self, 17–25

Mass transit industry, overview of, 9; snapshot, 4

Mechanic. *See* AIRCRAFT MECHANIC; AUTOMOTIVE MECHANIC; DIESEL MECHANIC; MOTORBOAT MECHANIC; MOTORCYCLE MECHANIC

MERCHANT MARINE CAPTAIN, 127–128 (Profile includes: Captain, First mate, Second mate, Third mate)

MERCHANT MARINE ENGINEER, 129–130 (Profile includes: Chief engineer, Firer, First assistant engineer, Oiler, Second assistant engineer, Third assistant engineer, Water tender, Wiper)

MERCHANT MARINE PURSER, 130–131 (Profile)

MERCHANT MARINE RADIO OFFICER, 132–133 (Profile)

MERCHANT MARINE STEWARD/COOK, 101–102 (Profile includes: Baker, Chief cook, Chief steward, Mess attendant, Second cook, Third cook, Utility hand)

Mess attendant, 101 (Merchant marine steward/cook)

Monster Board, 14

Motor vehicle industry snapshot, 4

MOTORBOAT MECHANIC, 52–53 (Profile)

MOTORCYCLE MECHANIC, 54–55 (Profile)

MOVER, 56–57 (Profile)

Moving van driver, 49 (Long-haul truck driver)

Networking, 16

North American Free Trade Agreement (NAFTA), 2

Occupational Safety and Health Act, 19

Occupational Safety and Health Administration (OSHA), 19

Oiler, 129 (Merchant marine engineer)

Online job databases, 14–15

OSHA (Occupational Safety and Health Administration), 19

PARKING ANALYST, 102–103 (Profile)

PARKING ATTENDANT, 57–59 (Profile)

PARKING CASHIER, 59–60 (Profile)

Parts, automotive, 5

Phone campaign, 13

Pilot. *See* AIRLINE PILOT

Placement services, 16

Planning, career, 11–12

Power plant mechanic. *See* AIRCRAFT MECHANIC

Private employment agencies, 17

Professional/trade journals, 12, 26

Public transportation inspector, 109 (Transportation inspector)

Rail freight industry, 8–9

RAILROAD CLERK, 60–62 (Profile includes: Dispatcher)

RAILROAD CONDUCTOR, 104–106 (Profile includes: Road service conductor, Yard conductor)

RAILROAD ENGINEER, 106–108 (Profile)

Railroad engineer, 135 (Transportation engineer)

Railroad industry: history of in U.S., 2; snapshot, 4; trade/professional journals, 26

Railroad inspector, 109 (Transportation inspector)

RAILROAD MAINTENANCE WORKER, 62–63 (Profile includes: Blacksmith, Boilermaker, Car repairer, Electrical worker, Machinist, Sheet metal worker)

RAILROAD SIGNAL/SWITCH OPERATOR, 63–65 (Profile)

RAILROAD TRACK WORKER, 65–66 (Profile)

References, 21

Resume, 18–23

Retail driver, 67 (Route delivery driver)

Rights, employee, 18–19, 25

Road service conductor, 104 (Railroad conductor)

ROUTE DELIVERY DRIVER, 67–68 (Profile includes: Retail driver, Wholesale driver)

SAILOR, 68–70 (Profile)

SCHOOL BUS DRIVER, 70–71 (Profile)

Sea transport summer jobs, 6

Seaman. See SAILOR

Second assistant engineer, 129 (Merchant marine engineer)

Second cook, 101 (Merchant marine steward/cook)

Second mate, 127 (Merchant marine captain)

Second officer. See FLIGHT ENGINEER

Self-evaluation, 11

Self-inventory chart, 11, 19

SERVICE STATION ATTENDANT, 71–73 (Profile)

Sheet metal worker, 62 (Railroad maintenance worker)

Shipping industry snapshot, 4

Situation-wanted ads, 15–16

Skills, special, 21

SPECIAL SERVICE BUS DRIVER, 73–75 (Profile)

Special skills, 21

Staffing services, 17

State employment services, 16–17

Station manager, 96 (Car rental/leasing agent)

Steward. See MERCHANT MARINE STEWARD/COOK

Subway conductor, 45 (Local transit operator)

Subway driver, 45 (Local transit operator)

TAXI DISPATCHER, 75–76 (Profile)

TAXI DRIVER, 76–78 (Profile)

Technology: in airline industry, 7; in auto industry, 4–5

Temporary employment, 17

Test pilot, 116 (Airline pilot)

Third assistant engineer, 129 (Merchant marine engineer)

Third cook, 101 (Merchant marine steward/cook)

Third mate, 127 (Merchant marine captain)

TIRE CHANGER/REPAIRER, 78–79 (Profile)

TOW TRUCK DISPATCHER, 79–80 (Profile)

TOW TRUCK OPERATOR, 80–82 (Profile)

Trade/professional journals, 12, 26

TRAFFIC ENGINEER, 133–135 (Profile)

Traffic engineer, 135 (Transportation engineer)

Traffic manager. See INDUSTRIAL TRAFFIC MANAGER

TRAFFIC TECHNICIAN, 108–109 (Profile)

TRANSPORTATION ENGINEER, 135–137 (Profile includes: Railroad engineer, Traffic engineer)

Transportation industry: airline industry, 7; auto industry, 3–5; history of, 1–3; mass transit, 9; overview of, 1; rail freight industry, 8–9; trade/professional journals, 26; trucking industry, 5–7; water transportation industry, 7–8

TRANSPORTATION INSPECTOR, 109–110 (Profile includes: Aviation inspector, Public transportation inspector, Railroad inspector)

Trolley driver, 45 (Local transit operator)

Truck driver. See INDUSTRIAL TRUCK OPERATOR; LOCAL TRUCK DRIVER; LONG-HAUL TRUCK DRIVER; ROUTE DELIVERY DRIVER; TOW TRUCK OPERATOR

TRUCK TERMINAL MANAGER, 111–112 (Profile)

TRUCK/BUS DISPATCHER, 82–83 (Profile)

Trucking industry: future of, 6–7; overview of, 5–6; snapshot, 4; trade/professional journals, 26

Unemployment compensation, 19

Unions, 17

Utility hand, 101 (Merchant marine steward/cook)

Water tender, 129 (Merchant marine engineer)

Water transportation industry, 7–8

Web site resources, 14–15, 16

Wholesale driver, 67 (Route delivery driver)

Winch operator, 39 (Dockworker)

Wiper, 129 (Merchant marine engineer)

Work characteristics checklist, 11–12

Work experience, 21

Workplace evaluation, 11–12

Wright, Orville, 3

Wright, Wilbur, 3

Yard conductor, 104 (Railroad conductor)